Under a Yellow Sky

Under a Yellow Sky

A tale of the sea and a coming of age

Simon J. Hall

Whittles Publishing

Published by
Whittles Publishing Ltd.,
Dunbeath,
Caithness, KW6 6EG,
Scotland, UK

www.whittlespublishing.com

ISBN 978-184995-094-7

Printed by
4edge Limited, UK

Contents

Age 16

I went to sea one day in the early 1970s, several weeks after I turned 16. My life was never the same again. Everything I have written is true. No, that's not quite right: everything I have written is intended to be true. It is a bit blurred at the edges because I am looking back through a long lens; my memory is not infallible and this will have distorted the order of occurrences and muddled the characters.

I have taken liberties with some technical details, although the direction is correct, even if some of the specifics are not: I am aware of this and make my apologies to those of you who are sticklers for accuracy. Similarly, those of you who were there with me at the time may remember some things differently: I'll be glad to debate these with you over a quiet ale one day.

Last, I admit to a bit of deliberate shuffling of events in the interest of continuity, as well as some tinkering with the names to prevent embarrassment – but I know who you all are…

1

Seeds

I sometimes puzzle why I went to sea, because with me, there was no underlying drive that sent me to strange parts across the other side of the world. There was no family history of maritime adventure and my parents had no expectation of me in this area. One minute I was a schoolboy – average, skinny, callow, under-confident – the next I was in a cheap hotel in Hamburg, sandwiched among a string of bars off the *Reeperbahn*, waiting for my ship to dock, living with a mixed bag of characters who were beyond my imagination and understanding. I had flown the nest now and my game was on. I couldn't return home – there were too many barriers: pride; curiosity; expectations of others; shame if I turned back; the things I had to prove to myself, to family. My quest. My test.

When I turned 15 I had no earthly idea what I was going to do in life. I vaguely mulled over the future, but only in a schoolboy context, in which my horizon was the weekend, or possibly to the end of term. Otherwise it was couched in juvenile fantasy: war hero, football hero, superhero, long-lost relative of a gazillionaire and so forth.

My father was a pilot – an RAF officer with a war pedigree. He was a real hero, a big man with an RAF moustache, who I never got close to. He had a huge presence, was loud and confident and commanding. I always did what he said. He was of a generation that had no time for lads with long hair, women in high places, popular music, fashion, homosexuals, cowards, liars, shirkers or teetotallers. He disliked people who failed to do their duty or who were flash or crooked or unpatriotic. He loathed people who had made big and lorded it over the rest. Strangely, he wasn't a racist. He came from Fulham, went to war when the recruiters believed he was old enough, learnt to fly, got a commission then had a 'good war', bombing bits of Europe.

I remember we would look at maps together and I was always impressed when he would point to some obscure part of the Balkans and say: "Bombed there… and there. Flew up from Alex overnight. Oh look… bombed there too," pointing to somewhere else. I envied his going to war and I told him this. He would look back at me with his steady brown eyes and say: "I don't blame you, son. They were the best times of my life. Every day was a thrill. We were either bored so we had a party in the mess or we flew out to get shot at by the Germans and bomb people." Not very politically correct, my father. No lecture on man's inhumanity to man; just: "The best times of my life."

I wanted best times of my life too; I wanted to do all the things that my father had done, but I couldn't make myself join the RAF, because in my mind, everything that made it the place to be was gone. There were no more Spitfires or Hurricanes or Lancaster Bombers; there was no war. I would never drink ice-cold in Alex or horseplay in the mess or run for an air-raid shelter or use blackouts or crouch behind sandbags on a desert airfield perimeter while German bullets whanged overhead, or scramble; scramble across a field in Kent, or be in a crowd in a city in a blackout where everyone wore uniform.

I didn't want to be in the new air force. My father flew Wellington Bombers at 19, then evolved into a Hurricane fighter pilot, duelling with Germans flying *Messerschmitts* in the skies over Europe when he was 21. My uncle was a Spitfire pilot who straffed Rommel's staff car; how could I ever join the RAF and live up to that? My father took me flying in Chipmunks a couple of times, and once in a Jet Provost: I probably disappointed him by never showing any real interest in joining up. I never explained to him how I felt and he never asked.

Then, one day, he gave me a magazine article and said: "Read this." I did. The article was about going to sea as a deck cadet officer in the Merchant Navy. It was full of pictures of men in smart uniforms and gold braid, all sun-tans and rugged faces against a backdrop of exotica. I don't remember being captivated, I just remember thinking: 'Yes, I'll go to sea.' That was a development within the family: my father and his two brothers had joined the RAF, while the men on my mother's side had joined the Army. There was no one in the extended family tree who had ever gone to sea. I became a family curiosity.

Throughout my childhood we moved every three years or so, around the country or around the world whenever my father was posted to a new RAF squadron. I was 15 and we moved from Singapore to Berkshire – a long step. I had to go for an interview at the new school and I remember the headmaster asking me: "Well then Simon, do you want to stay for sixth form and then go on to university?"

"No. I'm leaving at 16 and going to sea." I was matter-of-fact. My father looked at me, amused.

My mother tried to rescue the situation: "That's what he's thinking at the moment, but it's a bit early yet, ha, ha."

The head and I looked at each other. We knew where we stood.

And so it took shape. I went to the new school, which I didn't like. At 15, friends are harder to make than at 11. My classmates had all been together since they started school and I was on the fringe. The groups and gangs were formed and I soon realised that I ran the danger of ending up with the sad and the bullied, so I reacted by painting myself as a mysterious loner who was biding time before setting off around the globe.

My schoolmates in Berkshire didn't quite know how to treat me; most were starting to form their own plans: the dull were leaving as soon as they could, destined for local labour fodder, the others were staying for sixth form. All the science buffs wanted to work in nearby Harwell, the rest had half-formed ideas of working in various businesses, mostly local, many with their families. A few had university plans. My mysterious loner persona placed me as being tolerated on the edge of school society and mostly left alone. I began to put myself in a position I couldn't retreat from.

Before the O-level exams at the end of the summer term, I went to London for an interview with a shipping company, to apply for a place as a deck cadet with their oil tanker fleet. They sent me a travel warrant and I found my way to the Hotel Europa, off the Cromwell Road near Earls Court.

It was a funny, quirky place, a tall dirty-white terraced building in a row of tall dirty-white white terraced buildings, silent as a crypt inside, with a hunchback porter and a creaking old-fashioned cage lift that went so slowly it barely seemed to move. I felt as if I were cast in an old black-and-white film.

In the evening I went down for dinner and was placed on a table with a pock-marked youth a year my senior called Dave. He was going for the same interview the next day. Dave was 17 and made himself out as a man of the world. He announced we would go to Soho after dinner and 'get some girls'. My experience of getting some girls was brief sporadic groping on a few odd occasions but I hammed that I was up for this and off we went: me in my grey school suit, Dave in a cool brown corduroy jacket.

The evening was disastrous because the pubs wouldn't serve me and the club we went to wouldn't let me in. I was humiliated, unable to carry off my image: in my boyish daydreams I might have been a sophisticated, nightclubbing girl-magnet, but my dreams crashed to earth in the cold reality of West End London on a Tuesday evening. I couldn't pretend it wasn't happening though, not when I was drinking coke in a garish pub off Leicester Square while Dave downed his manly pint. He sighed. We went back to the Hotel Europa early.

The next day was another move forward, another step, another piece of progress towards the point of no return. Seven of us sat on hard chairs in a cream-painted room in a big slab block building overlooking the Thames. Mr.Harman was a tough looking man, a senior second engineer officer who told us that he was on secondment ashore, doing a tour in recruitment. He lectured us for an hour.

Mr.Harman pulled no punches. He was there to scare out the weak and the timid and the ones that wouldn't fit. He told us that we would have to work six days a week at sea and study on the seventh. When the ship was in port we would have to work seven days. We would work eight hours a day minimum, usually nearer 12, sometimes more. He told us the engine room was so hot it hurt to breathe and the engineers became so filthy that they never got the oil and grease out of their skin. The deck officers worked until they dropped, and in port got as filthy as the engineers – but they had to change into best uniform several times a day, and so had to scrub themselves clean continually in water that was usually cold.

As cadets we would be contracted for three-and-a-half years, be poorly paid and have to do all the ghastly jobs that even the lowest crew-member would refuse to do. We would be constantly reminded that we had no rights and were the lowest form of marine life and everyone would shout at us and abuse us. The officers would think we were their slaves, whereas the crew would hate us and bully us because one day we would be in charge of them. We would hardly ever get off the ship, and when we did, it would be for a few dangerous hours in some dreadful dockland miles from town where we stood a good chance of getting robbed and beaten. We would live two to a cabin, nine feet by six feet, and sleep in hard narrow bunks. The cabin would have no toilet but would have a sink, although we had better not piss in it or there would be trouble. It would be baking hot in the tropics and freezing cold in the winter, because we would start off by being shipped off in the old wrecks that either had no air-conditioning and heating, or which had machinery that only worked when it felt like working.

We would live the sandwich principle of college, sea, college, sea. When at sea, we would be on a ship for between six and nine months and be given five days paid leave for every month at sea. College would be the School of Navigation in Plymouth. At the end of the three-and-a-half years, we would go back to the School of Navigation for another six months and then take our professional examinations. This would be a solid week, in which we would sit a series of three-hour examinations in mathematics, physics, law, naval architecture, engineering, meteorology, electronics, navigation and half a dozen other subjects I forgot. We would have to get 65% minimum in every single subject, otherwise we would fail the whole lot, without compromise.

In the summing up, we were told that if we got through that – which not many people did – we would be wise, tough, resourceful and respected, and would be set for a rewarding well-paid and adventurous life. Some of us nodded at Mr. Harman in agreement, to show that we were in fact already wise.

I met Dave four years later, up the Hooghly River near Calcutta. By that time I was third mate of a white oil tanker, and we tied up alongside a sister ship in the fleet. Dave was onboard, still a cadet – a very old one too, having taken another 12 months before deciding to go to sea.

I came across Mr. Harman too, a year after that in a bar on Anson Road in Singapore, and he told me he had been dismissed from recruitment for being too graphic in his descriptions and had been sent back to sea. I never saw any of the others who attended that interview day; they must have thought they were steering towards hell and fled to sanity before it was too late.

The train continued to roll. I explained to my family and whoever else would listen what a time I was going to have and how exciting it was all going to be, my every sentence and boast was another barrier to me staying ashore. On an August morning the post arrived, giving me notice that I had passed the requisite O-levels to be accepted. I shouted upstairs to my father. He told me to write to the shipping company and tell them. I wrote a rather solemn, unpractised letter, enclosing my examination pass papers. A week later I received a contract to be signed by my father and I, an appointment for a medical examination, a uniform and kit list, and sundry instructions. The September intake at the School of Navigation was full, so they were going to send me straight to sea first for three months or so. If all went according to plan, I would ship out in early October. My life was at ten to midnight.

My medical examination was held at the shipping company offices, where I was probed and studied and tested and given intensive eyesight and colour sight examinations. They gave me a hearing test, which involved me putting on a set of headphones and confirming when I could no longer hear a diminishing beeping noise. This was largely guesswork, helpfully aided by the doctor who grinned and bobbed his head when the noise was still in existence and started to look sad and shake his head from side to side when it was disappearing. One of the doctors told me that I had a wandering pacemaker which made me nod, because I didn't know what else to do; I didn't know if it was serious. He discussed the matter sagely with another doctor and then told me it was fine, although I should check up on it from time to time. Check up on what? I wouldn't know a wandering pacemaker from a wandering albatross. Once they decided that I was fighting fit, I was inoculated for cholera, tetanus, TABT and yellow fever and pronounced A1 OK to go. That night I read carefully through the contract with my parents, we signed, and I walked down the road in the quiet dark suburban English night to drop it in the post box. Five to midnight.

The next week I went with my father to Miller Rayners, the naval tailor in Fenchurch Street, clutching my kit list. I was attended by a stooped scraggy man in a black jacket with a measure around his neck, who looked exactly like I felt a tailor should look. He measured me and discussed the problems of growing lads with my father, as if I wasn't there. I was kitted out in doeskin best blues with gleaming brass buttons, four sets of tropicals, battledress, raincoat, uniform shirts and ties, two caps, oilskins, work clothes, sea-boots, jumpers and sundries, which included a wood-handled Green River knife – of which I was particularly proud. I tried on all the kit. When I got home I had to put on everything all over again, swanking around the sitting room to the delight of my mother. I looked the part: my father was proud, I was proud I made him proud, my mother wept slightly in happy proud misery at her baby boy leaving home. One minute to midnight; no going back.

My seaman's ID card and discharge book arrived, so did my orders: fly to Hamburg to join the SS *Valvata*, westward-bound for New York and Venezuela. The clock struck: donnnngggggg!

2

Cold Shower in Hamburg

So I flew to Hamburg, with another first-tripper called Starling. Between us, we had precious little idea of what was going on, how we were supposed to act and what we were supposed to do – but we were desperate not to appear as fools, which of course made us look ever more foolish.

I believed I looked more the part of the world traveller; Starling was short and pale and looked younger than he was. He carried an expression of utter bewilderment. I was taller, I had worked hard on my world-weary expression and I smoked; I probably looked far more ridiculous than Starling.

We had met at Heathrow Airport in the late morning, holding our identical joining instructions, which told us to make rendezvous with the radio officer at the BEA information desk. He was an ancient man with white hair and a gnarled face. He laughed when he saw us, which made us feel even more uncomfortable. He checked our papers, took us through baggage check-in and passport control, pointed out the way to the departure gate, gave us instructions to meet him there in an hour-and-a-half, then abandoned us to go to the bar.

Shortly before boarding, we assembled with the rest of the *Valvata's* joining party at the departure gate with the radio officer, who everyone called 'Sparks'. He checked us all from a manifest. There were a couple of sailors missing: Sparks called out their names several times, had an animated discussion with the others about where they might be, and then crossed them off the list. The party comprised me and Starling, two senior cadets (lads of about 19 who ignored us completely), the second officer and his wife, the third officer and his wife, Sparks himself, and a rough-looking crowd of about ten people who I took to be crew-members, headed up by a hatchet-faced man who was the bosun.

Virtually everyone was drunk: the exceptions were me, Starling and the second officer's wife, who looked as bewildered as Starling.

On the plane, everyone proceeded to get even drunker while me and Starling kept a low profile and talked about where the ship was bound.

"I was told it was heading for Curacao then Venezuela," he informed me.

"I was told New York and Venezuela, but I heard Sparks tell the second officer that we were going to Rouen," I said, then added that my father had telephoned the shipping company yesterday and they told him France then either New York or possibly Italy.

In short, no one had any idea: not us, not the officers and apparently not the shipping company itself.

When we landed at Hamburg in the early evening, the remainder of the journey was eye-opening, embarrassing and unnerving. The joining party were all far more drunk now, having been drinking on the plane as furiously as the stewardess would allow; even the second officer's wife looked loosened up as she stood with a soppy smile on her face, watching the world around her. We were the noisiest group at the baggage carousel by a long way. As the luggage started to arrive, one of the crew vomited on his feet and everyone in our group groaned and cheered and hooted. We all got our bags and set off at a charge for the airport bar, where everyone was refilled and Starling and I were given a glass of German lager each.

In the coach from the airport, two of the crew started fighting at the back until the bosun walked down the aisle and banged their heads together, literally. I had been hearing that expression since I was a child – when my brother Peter and I squabbled my mother would announce: "I'll bang your heads together if you don't stop!", but I had never seen it as a reality. One moment the two crew-members were sitting side-by-side, ineffectively trying to punch each other; the next the bosun had strode down the coach, grabbed the hair on the back of each head, yanked them apart then smashed their foreheads together with a crack like breaking wood. They melted onto the seat.

"Now shut up and behave!" he shouted at the two slumped bodies. Someone gave a half-hearted cheer; the bosun glared at him and he went quiet.

We pulled up at a grubby dilapidated-looking hotel at the end of a row of warehouses. I rose to get off. Sparks waved at me to sit down: "This is for the crew, not the officers. Ours is next."

"Why aren't we staying at the same hotel?" I asked.

"Don't ask stupid questions. We're not staying with that lot. Try and keep your mouth shut and you'll learn more."

But I was too stupid to keep my mouth shut: "Do I get treated as an officer then? I'm just a cadet."

Sparks gave me a withering look: "You're a cadet officer, which means you're learning to be an officer. The real officers are going to treat you like a dog and the crew are going to laugh at you and ignore anything you say, but you still have officer status, which means you get to stay in a decent hotel, while that shower get to stay in a dump, so sit down and be grateful."

The crew disembarked noisily and then argued with the driver until all their bags were sorted out. The second officer got off to ensure the crew only took their own gear.

"Wait 'til tomorrow when we get picked up," said Sparks. "The driver will pick up the crew first then come to get us. They'll all start bitching when they see our hotel is better than theirs. That'll get the trip off to a good start."

We arrived at our hotel ten minutes later. It was grim-looking, even if it was supposed to be better than the crews'. The officer's hotel was right on the pavement in a busy street of bars, clubs and restaurants, positioned between a noisy garish bar and a night-club. The bar had huge windows and you could see all the patrons clustered around tables or hunched at the bar, clutching their drinks in the thick smog. It looked as if it never closed. The night club contrasted the openness of the bar with a shuttered secretive appearance and just a small blue sign which said 'Nite-Club.' It looked seedy.

From the outside, the hotel itself was a grubbier version of the place I stayed at in Earls Court when I went for my interview, although inside it was much brighter and noisier. Sparks had the hotel vouchers and he sorted out the rooms. Everyone was desperate to check-in so they could get out on the town. The general banter was to quickly dump the bags in the rooms and then meet in the bar next door, which seemed as good a starting place as any. The two senior cadets were going to go to the nearby *Reeperbahn* – the Hamburg red light district – whereas the second and third officers and their wives, together with Sparks, were going to have a few drinks then get a meal afterwards. They all agreed to meet in the bar to have a few warm-up drinks and make plans. Starling and I were not invited; we had to share a room. Sparks gave us a voucher to have a meal at the hotel.

We went down to the basement restaurant after depositing our bags. We only seemed to be allowed the set meal of the day, which was a large lump of pork knuckle with lumpy potatoes and grey cabbage. We both ate our knuckle and left the rest. After dinner we took a stroll to see the sights and bright lights, peering through the big windows of the bar next door as we passed. They were all in there – second and third officer, radio officer, senior cadets, the two wives – gathered at the bar in an animated clump, drinks in hands, more drinks on the bar top.

The next morning the bus arrived to take us to the ship, with the crew sneering at us as Sparks had predicted. The officer party was very subdued and sat in silence for the trip to the docks.

The *Valvata* loomed above us as we disembarked from the bus: black hull, green decks, two white-painted accommodation islands, one in the middle of the ship and one at the stern. Two masts rose up off either deck, backed by thick wire supporting stays. The West German flag flew at the truck (the highest point of the highest mast); the Red Ensign flew at the stern. A red danger flag was also hoisted. She was harnessed to the dock by eight-inch polypropylene ropes.

The *Valvata* was a 32,000-ton deadweight black-oil tanker, built in the previous decade at the Furness Shipbuilding Company on Teeside. Black oils are the third breakdown from crude oil. When oil is taken from the ground it is in its raw state: crude oil. The big crude oil carriers, the largest of all tankers, take this to the refineries, where it gets cooked. The first items to separate out in the cooking process are the high-grade gases, methane and propane. Next comes the distillation of the different grades of white oil: jet fuel, naptha, white spirit, high-octane petrol, medium-grade motor fuel, paraffin, kerosene etc. Then come the black oils: motor oil, diesel, engine oils, lubricants, burning oil. After all that has been taken out, it is only the sludge that is left behind: the bitumen and tar and plastics. You can get a lot out of a barrel of crude oil.

I learnt all this as time went by, although when we arrived at the dock and the *Valvata* came into view, all I knew was that I was about to board an old, rusty, dirty ship. A thick industrial smell hung in the air, a smell that punched you in the throat.

My heart and hopes sank like stones thrown into a dark pool as I climbed the gangway. She was a hulk, rusting and aged. All my dreams of a smart sleek ship peopled by smart sleek people fled; the brochures had lied to me. The hull plating was scarred by dents and scrapes, curdled with rust and grime; the lower sections were encrusted with slime and barnacles. As I stepped onto the deck, the plating crunched underfoot; sections were hunched with rust – great slabs of it were flaking off, as if riven by some terrible disease. The white paintwork had long weeping tears of brown rust stains running down to the deck. The handrails were scabbed with grime. Big black rubber hoses were connected to manifolds on the main-deck with sludgy puddles of black oil underneath. The smell of oil pervaded everything.

Everywhere was cluttered; stores were being swung aboard by a small derrick, forming piles of boxes and crates and drums. Machinery in bits littered the place, worked on by grubby men in greasy overalls. More men stood around in groups; everyone looked filthy. Everywhere I looked there were ropes and nets and rails and ladders and gangways and alleyways, joining and crossing and connecting; a journey across the decks seemed perilous in itself.

The third officer chivvied me and Starling along to the island of accommodation at the centre of the ship – 'the midships' as he called it. A predatory-looking man in his mid-thirties with dark receding hair and eyebrows that grew together, leant hunched on the midships rails and watched us as we approached, staggering with our big suitcases. He wore battledress uniform, three gold stripes on his epaulettes.

The third officer went up to him and introduced himself: "I'm the new third mate, Clive Ballam, and this is my wife Claire. These are the two new deck apes," gesturing at us. "That's the new second mate and his wife coming along the flying bridge, with the new sparks. There's two senior apes somewhere."

The mean-looking man looked at him. He didn't introduce himself. "The third mate's on deck: you better get down there and relieve him; he wants to go home. He's been on here nine months; he was told he would only be away for four. His fiancé's left him, poor bugger." He turned to the third officer's wife: "Hello Claire, I'm John, the chief officer." He gave her a short smile. She gave a quick nervous grin back.

The third officer went to say something, then changed his mind and walked into the accommodation block, Claire trailing behind. The chief officer turned on us, black eyes boring into me, pinning me down.

"First-trippers?" No smile. He was unnerving. I'd never had a full-grown hard man turn his will on me before. I didn't know how to react. Starling was the same. We just goggled back at him. "Deaf?"

We remained mute.

"Are you both deaf and dumb? Answer me for God's sake! Christ, what have I done to deserve dim-witted first trip deck apes?"

'Why are we apes?' I thought. "I'm Hall, sir," I said, in what I believed to be a brave voice.

"I'm Starling," squeaked Starling.

"Go in and find your cabins and get changed into your white boiler suits, then come back out here. Go on, get a move on." He turned away from us. We scuttled off.

A rough looking steward in a dirty white jacket showed us our cabins, each a six-foot-by-nine-foot box with a bunk, a sink and a locker. Light came in though a single brass-framed porthole. At least we had a cabin each; we were expecting to share. The steward sniggered as he showed us where we would be living.

"It's 'orrible 'ere," he said, gesturing to my cabin. "The last cadet had TB."

"Why are they calling us 'apes'?" I said.

"'Coz up until a couple of years ago, you were called deck apprentices, known as 'deck apes'. Now you're deck cadets, but all the old-timers will still call you apes. But you're lower than apes. I quite liked 'deck apes', but I can't stand deck cadets: you're all bloody useless. Cadets are the lowest form of marine life, everyone knows that. Apes were better than cadets."

He stood back and smirked, pleased with the progress he was making on guiding us towards misery. He carried on: "This is an 'orrible ship and you're goin' to 'ave an 'orrible time, I can guarantee it. The foods crap, the Old Man's mad and the mate hates apes. It doesn't get any worse. You'll hate it and want to go home in a few days, but you can't. You're stuck here! Ha!"

He went off, snorting happily to himself at our impending suffering. I changed into my brand-new starch-white boiler suit, met Starling at his cabin door and we went out on deck.

The third mate (officer) met us on deck. He had changed into a clean but stained boiler suit. It was a sort of creamy white with blotches, which made our stiff, gleaming, snow-white suits stand out – an advert that shouted: 'Look at me in all my newness!' We followed him down the ladder onto the deck, where he found the third mate he was relieving, sitting astride a large pipe. They had a conversation that was mostly unintelligible to me: it was a technical handover of sorts with talk of ullages, manifolds and stripping pumps, then moving on to sea-watches and lifeboats. They then talked about the food (awful), the crew (lazy and violent), the beer (German and good), the Old Man (captain – mad as a hatter), the mate (chief officer – nasty), the chief engineer (queer), the trip (Petite Couron, New York then Venezuela).

The departing third mate went off to get changed and go home, while Clive Ballam collared the duty AB (able seaman), discussed which tanks were being pumped out, and then told him to teach us how to take ullages. Off we went with the AB, a sniggering man

The SS Valvata picking up a pilot (www.fotoflite.com).

called Stamp, who taught us to lower a tape measure through an opening in the deck called the ullage pipe. The tape had a wooden float on the end, the wooden float would rest on the surface of the oil and we would read off the depth of the oil in the tank. We mastered this and had to take ullages every half hour and write them in chalk on a board outside the chief mate's office. Starling was told he would have to work the afternoon-watch and was sent off to get changed and be back to take over from me at noon.

I followed the third mate around for the rest of the morning and he gave me a running induction in shipboard basics. He taught me port from starboard, bow from stern, deck from deckhead, fore from aft; he explained a wall was a bulkhead and told me that only fools, fireman and first-trippers sat on ships rails. I surreptitiously smeared my gleaming white boiler suit with oil from the ullage pipes and manifolds, to try and disguise its glossy new appearance.

While we were standing under the flying-bridge – the raised walkway that ran from the accommodation block at the centre of the ship, midships, to the accommodation block at the stern, I heard a terrible screaming, interspersed with whimpering. It went something like this:

"What the bloody hell are you playing at?"

"Whuhh..."

"What do you mean, 'Whuhhh'? Are you deaf? Are you deaf? Are you bloody deaf, you half-wit?"

"Whuhh..uh..uhhh..."

"Arrgggghhhhhh!! Answer me!"

"Uhh."

"God help me! I've got a moron onboard! What have I done to deserve this?"

"I'm suh, suh, sorry."

"You are going to be sorry! Do you think this is your daddy's yacht?"

"No."

"Arrgghhh! No, what?"

"No, sir."

"So it's not your daddy's yacht?"

"No, sir."

"So it's not your daddy's yacht?"

"No, sir!"

"No?"

"No, sir!"

"Then why are you dressed like that?"

"L-l-l-l-l-like what, sir?"

"Like that! Like that! You idiot! In that poncey blazer and those stupid brown trousers! Brown trousers? Why are you wearing brown trousers? Have you shit yourself?"

"No, sir."

There was a silence for several seconds. I looked up. Starling was standing on the flying bridge, next to the chief mate. Starling looked petrified with fear. The chief mate looked vicious enough to kill him.

The chief mate spoke again, a lower grating voice: "Listen, Starling. Never, ever, ever let me see you on this ship in your shore-gear again unless you are going ashore. This is a ship and onboard ship you wear your uniform. You have a brand new uniform your daddy has bought you, so wear it. When you are on deck, wear your white boiler suit; when you are off deck, wear your uniform. Understand?"

"Yes, sir! I'm sorry, sir."

"Bugger off and get changed."

"Yes, sir!"

"Bugger off!"

Starling scurried back to his new bolt-hole.

I looked at the third mate. He grinned at me and we walked aft to check the ullages. Stamp walked behind us, chortling. I was in a different world.

Starling took over from me at midday. He looked chastened. His starch white suit contrasted with my freshly seasoned one. The second officer took over from the third officer. Another sailor took over from Stamp. The third officer told me to 'hand over' to Starling, which baffled me.

I gaped at the two officers, waiting for a clue. They looked at me in amusement and said nothing. I said: "It's all yours," which caused the two mates and Stamp and his relief to laugh out loud. They then looked at me expectantly, waiting for me to provide them with more laughs. I looked at the third mate appealingly, desperately. He told me to show Starling the ullage board and that would do. I did, and then went off to get cleaned up and changed.

☆   ☆   ☆

I sat on the edge of my bunk in my new blues uniform, wondering what to do and where to go. I didn't want to go on the flying bridge and get flayed alive by the chief mate, but I couldn't just sit on my bunk. I was hungry. I looked out the door. The third mate and his wife Claire walked by. "Come on," he said, without breaking step. I followed dutifully.

We went to the officers' bar, which was in the aft accommodation block. On the walk down, the third mate told me that we would all be signing on in the afternoon and I should go up to the captain's cabin at four o'clock, with my discharge book, seaman's card and passport.

There were about a dozen people in the bar of the *Valvata*, including the chief mate, Sparks and the two senior cadets. The bar room was a large corner cabin, a fairly light place by ship standards due to having portholes on two sides. It was smoky and noisy, a small wood bar and four stools had been built in at one end and there were several armchairs and tables scattered about. Four men were playing cards around a green baize card table. Behind the bar was a fridge of beer, spirit optics fixed to the bulkhead, a sink, and a glass-fronted locker full of glasses. A variety of notices and posters were fixed to the bulkhead. Sitting at the end of the bar, smoking a pipe, was a fat man of about 50, with medal ribbons on his uniform and four gold stripes on his sleeves. He was the captain, the 'Old Man' as he was called by everyone – although not to his face. The Old Man was in discussion with another man of the same age, also with four gold stripes. I thought there were two captains for a minute. Then I noticed the second man had purple edges to his stripes, which made him the chief engineer. Earlier, the third mate had said that the chief engineer was queer; I didn't know if this was true or if it was a joke that was going over my head. He looked pretty normal to me, although to my inexperienced eye, normal meant he wasn't wearing a dress, carrying a handbag or flapping his wrist around. The captain appeared to ignore everyone except the chief engineer and the chief mate. I tried to keep out of the line of sight of the chief mate but his black eye flickered over me as I entered the bar and I felt a chill of fear.

The third mate bought me a beer and then called over the two senior cadets, who he introduced. "Look after him," he said, then walked over to join Sparks.

The senior cadets inspected me. They were old lads, probably 19 or more. One was called Paul, the other Rolo. Paul was square-shaped and friendly looking with direct eyes and greyish hair, Rolo was lanky with long blonde hair, prematurely balding. I liked Paul; he looked as if he knew what was going on. I wanted to be him. Rolo looked cruel, he looked the sort of person who would mock. He was.

"First-tripper, eh?" said Rolo.

"Yes," I replied.

"What's your name?"

"Hall. Simon Hall."

"How old are you, Simon?"

"Sixteen… and three months."

"Ooh, and three months, Paul."

Paul smiled: "You're going to hate it at sea, Simon," he said. I didn't know what to say, so I just smiled back. "No, I mean it. It's going to be horrible. Give it up as soon as you can. It's too late for Rolo and me, but you can still get out."

"Why are you saying that?" I asked. "If it was that bad, you would have left."

"We're doomed, Simon. We're stuck. We can't get out now. We're too old. But you can still make it. If you're quick."

Paul said this to me on most days from then on. He seemed to feel it was his duty to encourage me to leave the sea as soon as possible, although after this short daily speech, he helped me and guided me in finding out all the little things that made life at sea fit together.

Rolo was a different proposition. He liked to humiliate, to draw attention to every foolish move I made. He preferred to play to an audience of ABs, who equally enjoyed the sport of baiting the first-tripper. Rolo also liked to boast of all the women he had been with and would grill me in a loud voice about my sexual experience, which was none. He said he was going to take me ashore with him, get me drunk and then get me an ugly whore and I would wake up with a dose of VD and a tattoo… and then I would be a man. I vowed never, ever, ever to go ashore with Rolo.

Someone tapped me on the shoulder. I turned round. It was the chief mate: "You sixteen, Hall?"

"Yes, sir."

"Beer only, no spirits."

"Right, sir." He turned to the others. "How old are you two?"

"Nineteen, sir," said Paul.

"Eighteen, sir," said Rolo.

"Beer and spirits, but behave."

"Yes, sir."

"Yes, sir."

The mate went off.

"He's a tosser," said Rolo. "Everybody hates him."

"Why doesn't he like people?" I asked.

"Because he thinks he should be Old Man by now," said Paul, "but he's stuck as mate. He's a bitter bastard and he takes it out on everyone else, especially deck apes."

"Especially first-trippers," added Rolo.

"Why is he stuck as mate?" I asked.

"Because he's a tosser," Rolo replied.

We went through to the dining saloon to eat.

The saloon had a long table at one end, where I sat with the other juniors, and two other smaller tables. There were 11 of us altogether on the juniors' table; four deck cadets, four engineer cadets and three fifth engineers – known as 'fivers', although we were rarely all together because some were always on duty. Paul was the oldest cadet and the most senior, with only three months left before he finished his training and went back to college in preparation for his final examinations. His position was *de facto* fourth officer and he would share the four-to-eight watch with the mate, doing most things for him. The rest of us cadets were in various stages from 16-year-old first-trippers like me and Starling to second-and-third-trippers like Rolo and the engineer cadets. The fivers were juniors who had served their apprenticeships in shore-based engineering, mostly shipyards, and who had come to sea knowing about basic engineering but knowing little of shipboard life. They acted as juniors to the main watch-keeping engineer officers. These fivers felt themselves superior to cadets because they had already done their training, although cadets, particularly senior cadets like Paul, looked down on them as novices at sea. Fivers could be quite ancient; one of ours was 26.

The second table had the mid-ranking officers: the second and third mates, the third and fourth engineers, Sparks and the chief steward. The wives sat with their husbands, understandably.

The four senior officers sat on the square top-table, which was nearest the serving hatch. The captain sat imperiously under the light of the porthole, flanked by the chief engineer on his right and the chief mate on his left. Opposite him sat the second engineer. Two stewards in white coats ferried the food to us from the hatch. The second steward served the top-table exclusively while the other two tables were served by the rough and unpleasant man who I had encountered earlier. He made a point of banging down my plate with an exasperated sigh, to show his displeasure at serving me. We had a three-course lunch and ate with silver cutlery off crested china. The table cloth was of crisp white linen, as were the napkins, which were rolled within heavy silver napkin rings. The place had an antiquarian feel of faded splendour that was accepted by everyone without comment and which seemed at odds with the profanity and the suggestion of violence that hung in the air and pervaded the world outside.

After lunch, I went back to my cabin. I saw Starling down on the deck as I walked along the flying bridge. He was following the second officer. He had smeared his snow-white boiler suit with black hand prints.

I unpacked my possessions, stowing everything away as best I could in the functional lockers and drawers, then sat on my bunk and wondered what to do. At one time I went out for a walk around the ship, but I didn't know where to go – or more worryingly, where not to go – so it ended as a half-hearted stroll around the midships accommodation block and back to my cabin. The lower part of the midships block had the cadets down the starboard (right)-hand side and the three deck officers along the forward (front) part. Along the port (left) side were the showers and toilets, as well as the hospital and the chief steward's cabin. I was told later that this port side was known as 'bog alley'.

I was looking in the hospital door when the chief steward came along and introduced himself. He was a balding, dumpy man with thick glasses, a high voice and a strange accent. I didn't think he was English. Later I discovered he was from Sicily. People referred to him as 'The Wop', although not to his face. The Wop had a lot of power over the officers: power to make sure they were kept supplied with beer and cigarettes, or not; power to ensure their cabin was properly cleaned by the stewards, or not; power to make certain no one in the galley flobbed on their food. His power over me was taken for granted, even though I had no one to clean my cabin or serve me drinks and cigarettes.

He explained that the hospital had the only bath on the ship. I noticed that it had two steel-framed beds rather than wooden bunks built into the cabins and asked him why that was. The Wop said that the most common use for the hospital was to subdue drink-crazed sailors; they were handcuffed to the railings of the bed and left to scream and spew over themselves until they sobered up. I didn't know whether or not to believe him. He told me that an AB called McAllister was the worst of the worst onboard when he was drunk. The previous month, Mc-Allister had been cuffed to the bed and he had gnashed the pillow to pieces in his rage at being subdued, then smashed his head repeatedly against the bedpost, breaking his nose and knocking out several teeth, before vomiting all over the place. The Wop told me how hilarious it was to see him lying there groaning, covered in spew and blood and feathers. The chief mate was so revolted that he had a couple of buckets of water thrown over McAllister, to clean him up.

On the deck above us were the captain's suite and a guest cabin. Above that, on the top deck, was the bridge, and aft (behind) the bridge was Sparks' cabin. The Wop told me I had to go up and see the captain with my passport, seaman's card and discharge book at 4 o'clock to sign on. I went back to my cabin and sat there by myself, wondering whether to sign on and be at the mercy of the lunatics who lived in this bizarre world, or run.

I signed, joining the back of the queue at 4 o'clock. The captain didn't favour me by looking up from his desk: "Name?"

"Hall, sir."

"Passport." I gave it to him. "Seaman's card." I gave it to him. "Discharge book." I gave it to him. Pause… "First-tripper?"

"Yes, sir."

"Hmmph… Sign here," pointing to a place in the big register.

I signed. I left. I was a crew-member now, with Starling, with the frightening mate, the mad captain, the queer chief engineer, the rough steward, the violent bosun, the bullying Rolo, the sniggering Stamp, the crazed McAllister.

At eight o'clock that night I was back on duty, doing the same thing as before only in the dark, falling over pipes and protuberances and skidding on patches of oil. Several crew-members went clattering down the gangway, whooping, swearing, heading for the hedons of Hamburg as I skulked under the flying bridge with Stamp, taking ullages in the yellow glow of his safety torch. Later, we went to the foc'sle head (the raised deck at the fore end of the ship) and slackened off the mooring ropes, which had become tight due to the ship rising in the water as the oil was pumped out. We then went down the aft-end to the poop deck and did the same. We lowered the gangway every hour as the ship rose.

Towards the end of the watch, the third mate climbed down a swinging swaying rope ladder – a 'monkey ladder' – that we tied to the rails near the stern of the ship, so he could read the draft marks and see how high out of the water the *Valvata* was. The ladder swung wickedly under the stern in the sharp cold wind, while he hung on with one hand and used the other to shine a light at the waterline, using a torch that hung from a lanyard round his neck. It looked perilous; I prayed he would not ask me to do it – I felt sure I would drop into the icy oily water and die. Throughout the four-hour watch we did many other things I barely understood. I had never worked so hard in my life.

I showered in cold water at midnight, unable to get the oil out of my skin, giving up and falling into my narrow little bunk – dirty-tired, dog-tired, dead-tired, so tired my limbs weighed two tons each.

Hands shook me: "Get up."

"What? What? What?" I was baffled and lost.

"Get up. Get dressed." It was Paul the senior cadet.

"Why, what's happening?"

"We're sailing, that's what's happening."

"What time is it?"

"Four o'clock. Lovely time to go. We'll be stood down for breakfast and then you'll just have time for a shower before your watch at eight o'clock."

I swung my heavy legs onto the deck.

"Urrghhh, did you wash before you got into your bunk?" said Paul. "You're all manky."

I looked at my grimy hands. "I couldn't get the oil off," I explained weakly.

"Dirty swine. Next time use Savlon. Or if you can't find any, use kerosene. If you can't find any kerosene, go and sleep in the deck store, don't just climb into your bunk."

"Sorry, Paul."

"Filthy animal."

"Where do I go?"

"Go forward with the third mate."

"What do I wear?"

"Wear your manky boiler suit."

I went forward. People milled around. The third mate shouted into a voice-box that was bolted onto a platform. The voice-box squawked orders back at him, he shouted at the bosun who shouted at the sailors. I was told to stand out of the way while the sailors pulled in the ropes, wrapping them round the drums of the big clunking windlass, which reeled them in, sodden and dripping. Then they pulled up the fire wire and I was told to help coil down the ropes with Rolo. He laughed when I started to coil anti-clockwise, telling me I was a stupid first-tripper because everyone knows you coil ropes clockwise.

When that was all done, we all leaned on the rails as the big ship slid away from the dock, watching the lights of the docks as we moved out into the river. After a while, the box squawked: "Stand down except for anchor." The third mate dismissed everyone except the bosun and me and the three of us stayed for another half and hour as the *Valvata* moved down river, on call in case something went wrong and we had to let go the anchor in a hurry. It was bone cold as we glided down the ink-black channel out of Hamburg, between the clanking, blinking red and green buoys, into the early morning.

Finally, we were all stood down. It was six o'clock. I went and had another cold shower.

The next three months changed me, formed me – changed me from a schoolboy with foolish thoughts to a wary pack member, firmly rooted at the tail-end of the pack, keeping my distance, trying to keep up, always speaking to the top dogs with caution and deference. I was, along with Starling, as we had been told, the lowest form of marine life.

The sailors loved to have cadets onboard because the cadets would be given all the grim and ghastly jobs that the sailors would otherwise have to do. The deck officers loved to have cadets onboard because they could finally get the low jobs done without the AB's sullen mutterings and resentment and such bad grace that the job never got done properly anyway. Cadets could simply be ordered to do things. The senior cadets loved to have junior cadets onboard because it meant that they escaped all the rotten tasks that were given to those at the bottom of the heap. The captain and chief officer loved to have cadets onboard because it made the whole ship run in a smoother manner and it raised them to even greater heights: there was a huge gulf between top and bottom. The stewards resented the cadets onboard because they had to serve them in the saloon. Although they were quite happy to serve the officers, because that was their job after all, they found it demeaning to have to serve boys fresh out of school with no status or position whatsoever. Senior cadets were just about acceptable, but serving a first-tripper was mortifying for any steward, so they served first-trippers in an unpleasant manner, striving to make them as uncomfortable as possible. All the officers liked to have cadets onboard because the common tasks affecting everyone – such as who was going to run the projector on film night, who was going to restock the bar fridge, who was going to fetch this or deal with that – could now all be settled onto the cadets.

It was satisfactory all round, except for the cadets.

I had come away to sea with visions of being on the bridge in my smart uniform when the ship was at sea; learning to navigate, scanning the horizon with binoculars; steering the ship, using a sextant and doing a host of similar important roles. No such luck. I could look forward to the luxury of being on the bridge on Sunday mornings after the ship inspection. Otherwise I would mostly need to wait until my third year at sea. Right now I had a different set of tasks.

My first job at sea was to scrape all the greasy oil residue off the deck by the manifolds, using a long-handled scraper, before kneeling down on the swaying steel deck and finish off with a hand scraper. When that was done, I had to scrub the whole area with a stiff-bristled hand-brush using hot kerosene, and finally scrub it again with detergent. When I finished, my skin, nails, hair, ears, every part of me was engrained and encrusted with oil.

The bosun ambled by as I was clearing up and told me that anyone who used hot kerosene without rubber gloves was a fool because they were going to get raging dermatitis. At that moment I couldn't have cared less if I was set to catch raging syphilis. I had never before carried out such a filthy task... until my second job.

My second job was to connect a fire hose to the main water ring and hose out the shore toilet, which had become blocked up by huge Germans dockers crapping and then stuffing too much paper down the bowl. It was foul, I felt my throat thrunge as I opened the door and a nauseous wave of German arse gas blasted out. The bowl was overflowing, turds on the floor in heaps. I signalled to Starling to turn on the water. It came out with a rush, blasting shit and paper everywhere, mostly over me. I couldn't control the hose and it bucked up and down with me on the end, being flung around like a marionette before ending up in the side-scuppers, soaked through and covered with lumps of turd and scraps of soggy paper. The sailors working nearby screamed with laughter, as did the third mate and the lookout, who were watching from the bridge. People were called out to see the spectacle and I was aware of a gathering crowd, rocking with laughter as I sat miserably in the scuppers, picking bits of German shit off me.

My third job was to take temperatures of the 21 oil tanks that remained full, to make sure the right settings were applied to the internal heating coils, to keep the oil at the right temperature for its particular viscosity. This was explained to me before lunch and looked quite straightforward, being a case of simply lowering a brass-framed thermometer down into the tank to mid-depth, leaving it there for two minutes then pulling it up to take the reading.

Starling and I emerged after lunch to start. "Christ," said Starling. "Look at it."

I looked. I couldn't think what to say. So I said, "Christ!" The North Sea wind was up, the ship was rolling from side to side and on every third or fourth roll, the waves would break over the side and crash across the deck in a torrent. It looked deathly.

"Well, what are you two waiting for?" The chief mate had come up behind us. "Get changed and get out there. I want to see those temperatures before I lie down for the afternoon. It shouldn't take you long. Get on with it."

We changed into our boiler suits. I had a gleaming new one on after the toilet incident. We looked at each other and went down the ladder from the flying bridge. The first wave to hit me was knee-high, but I was squatting down to read the thermometer so the water came halfway up my back. The second knocked me flying and I was washed across the deck.

"Don't you break that bloody thermometer," the mate shouted down from the flying bridge.

I saw Starling go barrelling under the big fore and aft pipes on the crest of a wave, looking terrified. Another wave, a large one, washed right over me while I held onto the ullage pipe. I could feel the drag of the water pulling at me, but I held on tight until it passed.

We came off the deck after half an hour, soaked and bruised and shocked.

"Now, who could say that wasn't fun?" asked the mate. He even smiled. "Write up the temperature book and knock off for the afternoon, lads." He went off for his afternoon snooze. We went to our cabins to dry.

On the third day I was given the task of holystoning the wooden decks outside the captain's cabin, where he perambulated in the afternoon. Holystoning involved covering the deck with sand, soaking it with water, and then pushing a heavy cement block in a frame attached to a pole backwards and forwards, so as to clean and scrape the wooden decking. It was backbreakingly hard work and I was mulling over whether I would in fact rather be hosing out the toilets when someone spoke behind me.

"Rotten job, isn't it just?" A soft voice, a Scottish voice. Not a clipped bark from the city, something altogether more lilting and pleasant. I turned round and saw a tanned man of about 30 with a pleasant looking face.

"Yes," I said. "It's horrible."

"Holystoning is one of the worst things… I'm glad you boys are here. It makes our life so much nicer." He smiled. "Let me give you a tip, though. Use plenty of water, that's the trick. The water provides the lubrication and makes it easier to push the block. You've got too much sand and not enough water. Let me show you."

He filled my bucket and sloshed it over the area I was working, sprinkled a handful of sand, then wiped the cement block smoothly over the surface. I tried it. It was much easier.

"Thanks," I said to him. "That's very helpful. Who are you?"

"My name's Mac."

"Thanks Mac."

"That's OK, laddie." Mac smiled and wandered off.

The bosun walked up to me: "I see you've met McAllister."

I was shocked. "That's McAllister?" I asked.

"Aye. Nice isn't he? Wait till he gets drink in him. You'll see another side then."

I was to see McAllister with drink in him later in the voyage.

Each day was a shock: each day I encountered something that was so new and alien that I didn't know how to act. Starling and I were a source of huge amusement to the officers and crew, who never tired of finding new ways to make us look ridiculous. Over the first few days we took equal amounts of humiliation, although after that, to my dismay, I found myself being singled out as the prime target. Starling re-enforced his position of second-from-bottom by cunningly toadying to the officers and playing round-eyed admiring pupil to the ABs. I became wound up with rage: I saw him as a crawler although could do nothing as I helplessly watched him swim upstream, leaving me firmly marooned on the bottom rung of life on SS *Valvata*, as the lowest person in the lowest position; the lowest form of marine life.

After several weeks, when most of the well-worn jokes had been exhausted and I had learned the fundamentals – one end of the ship from the other; who did what; how the day at sea was put together – things eased off and I began to be accepted as a cadet, rather than a cadet who was also an imbecile. But those first four weeks – they were truly awful.

The nadir took place on the second Sunday, in the middle of the afternoon. I was lying on my bunk, reading, when Rolo banged on the door and barged in.

"Go and see the second mate on the bridge and ask him for a long-stand."

I set off, well used to being ordered to do things that held no meaning for me. The second mate looked at me, scratched his chin, went into the chart room for ten minutes then came out and said: "See the third engineer."

I went down into the bowels of the blast-hot engine room and found the third working on one of the pumps. He looked up, listened, then went back to his work. I waited for a quarter of an hour until he finished. He said: "The chief steward might have it."

So off I went again.

The chief steward sent me to Sparks, who sent me to the chief mate, who sent me to the bosun, who sent me to the carpenter, who sent me to various ABs, to the cook – and so it went on. Everyone listened, nodded, then when back to what they were doing while I stood there for a while. It didn't even begin to dawn on me that there was something wrong.

Finally I arrived at the chief engineer's office. He looked at me for several minutes – he seemed to be leering but perhaps it was my imagination. He told me to wait outside. I stood there for 45 minutes.

He came out: "OK, son: I think you've had your long stand. You've certainly been standing there long enough, off you go." I stood there for a moment, gawking at him. "You've been had, laddie. It's all part of the fun. You've had a long stand. Everyone's kept you standing."

I slunk away, crushed by the shame of my dawning gullibility. How they all laughed. Even Starling had a good snigger at my expense; he had been in on the plot along with the rest of the ship. I railed in silent fury at his treachery.

The evening meal was paralysing for me as the jibes and laughter flew thick and fast. The embarrassment was so acute it was physically painful.

Although no one missed a chance to remind me of my stupidity for the rest of the trip, I gained face for taking it well (they should have seen my inner mind, where I was taking it very badly) and things started to slowly take a turn for the better.

I didn't get seasick, ever. That was a plus-point for me. When we moved out of the Channel into the Atlantic on our way to New York, the *Valvata* settled into a long drawn-out roll, leaning into the western swell, heeling right over, pausing, then flopping back the other way with accelerating momentum. After the first few hours, people started to be affected. Several of the junior engineers missed meals, our grim steward slunk around silently with a doughy white face, the second mate's snooty wife stayed in her cabin. Seasickness had nothing to do with length of time at sea – it was whether your inner balance, through the inner ear apparently, was in harmony. If not, you were doomed to queasiness when things got rough. The longer someone was at sea, the better they adapted, although in essence you were either someone who got seasick or someone who didn't.

I didn't, Starling did. I thought: 'Oh, sweet revenge. Oh, thank you, Lord. Long stand, eh? How about a long vomit?' I delighted in Starling's misery over the three days of heavy rolling. The rougher the sea became, the merrier I was. There is nothing more calculated to make a sea-sick person feel worse than the exaggerated gaiety of a companion who feels fine.

We had stopped over in Petite Couron in France to discharge more tanks before setting off for New York; the *Valvata* was now only half-full of cargo and the morning tank temperatures took us less than an hour. That then gave the chief mate ample time in the day to ensure we had plenty of revolting tasks to fulfil: the more revolting the better as far as I was concerned.

Cleaning out and tidying up the paint store was a particularly foul choice for someone in Starling's state. The poorly-ventilated place was thick with the fumes of lead paint and kerosene; assorted oily messes slopped about in half-full paint tins. I rearranged the 20-litre drums of deck paint, stacking them in front of the doorway while I cleaned out behind the shelves, raking out clods of greasy gunk and slopping the mess on the deck in front of Starling, who was sitting there groaning. After a while, he dived towards the doorway, couldn't get past my wall of paint drums, turned in panic and heaved all over the paint brush shelf.

I tut-tutted: "You better clean that spew off those brushes before the storekeeper sees them," I said. "Otherwise, he won't be happy."

Starling groaned: "I hate this. I'm dying. I want to be off here." His voice was weak and pitiful, dry and croaking.

I laughed, then hawked and spat on the deck. He retched again.

✮   ✮   ✮

We steamed into New York harbour at midnight and had to anchor in the bay to wait for a pilot. While we were at anchor, I had my first pleasure of US hospitality: a small herd of blank-faced customs and immigration officials came onboard and interviewed everybody one-by-one. When my turn came, the interviewer stared at me, then stared at the photograph in my discharge book, then at me, then back at the book, then back at me. It was two in the morning and I had been roused from my bunk and told to report to the ship's office, where I was awaited. The chief steward was there as a witness, along with a junior customs and immigration official, learning the protocol of how to greet the USA's guests, no doubt.

"What's your name?" I stared at him. He had my name in the book in front of him. He had called me over by my name. "What's your name?"

"Simon Hall."

"Why are you visiting the USA?"

I stared at him, perplexed. "I'm on a ship."

"Why are you visiting the USA?"

"I'm serving on a ship and the ship is visiting the USA."

"What do you intend to do in the USA?"

"I don't intend to do anything. Perhaps go shopping."

"Do you realise you cannot stay in the USA?"

"I do now."

"Didn't you realise this before?"

"I didn't think about it."

"Are you a Communist?"

"No."

"Are you a Socialist?"

"No. I'm not any political type."

"Have you ever been a member of the Nazi Party?"

"No."

"Did you serve in the German armed forces during the war?"

I looked at him in disbelief. "I was born years after the war ended."

"So the answer is 'No'?"

"No."

"So the answer is 'Yes'?"

"The answer is 'No'; I did not serve in the German armed forces in the war."

"Do you take drugs?"

"No."

"Have you ever taken drugs?"

"No."

"Do you intend taking drugs in the future?"

"No."

"Have you ever been convicted of a criminal offence?"

"No."

"Any criminal offence of any type?"

"No."

"However small?"

"No."

"Do you realise that non-disclosure could mean you will be forbidden to land and immediately deported if you do so?"

"I have never done anything criminal."

"If you miss your ship you will be an illegal alien. Do you realise this?"

"Why would I want to miss my ship?"

"If you miss your ship you will be an illegal alien. Do you realise this?"

"I realise this. I promise not to stay in the USA."

"If you miss your ship you will be an illegal alien and you will be found and put in jail until you are deported. Do you understand this?"

"I understand."

And so it went on, and on, and on. Twenty minutes of the most crackpot questions imaginable, put to me with performance-art rudeness. I thought: 'Welcome to America.'

I didn't get ashore, apart from a walk along the quay, so at least I could say: "I've been to America."

New York in general – and the place we were berthed in Lower Manhattan in particular – was so dangerous at the time that we were not allowed off the ship unless in groups of three. This made it difficult because if I was not on deck working, then Starling was, otherwise we were so exhausted we were sleeping, which meant we couldn't even form a group of two. Even if we could, no one else would go ashore with us to be the third man; we were too low down the maritime chain to be seen with.

My impression of New York on my first visit was a cold, dirty, grim docklands populated by cold, grim, dangerous-looking people; the most unfriendly I had ever seen. From the customs and immigration officials to the dockers who connected the pipes to the ship, to the wharf men who took the ships ropes, to the security guards on the gangway, everyone: everyone was unrepentantly miserable, hostile and unpleasant. Why would I ever want to miss my ship here? I couldn't envisage the circumstances.

New York came and went. We had sat at anchor for two days and were then were in port for a day-and-a-half, discharging our black oil cargo.

From New York we sailed south to Lake Maracaibo in Venezuela. The weather turned warmer as we went south at a steady 15 knots. When we reached the Florida coast, the order came round at breakfast that 'whites' would be the uniform of the day. Starling and I ventured into the officers' bar that evening in our white shirts with gleaming cadet epaulettes rigid on our shoulders, our skinny white legs sticking out from our baggy white shorts and long white socks pulled up to the knee, with spotless white canvas shoes on our feet.

We took in the custom fit of the rest of the officers gathered at the bar: shirts hanging outside shorts that were shorter than ours, short white socks, casual shoes. We felt new and oafish. We stood out. Rolo laughed: "Look at this pair for Christ's sake."

Sparks said: "Easy does it lads. Put those whites through a double wash and get the starch out. I'm surprised you can walk." He gave us a Becks beer each.

"Clowns," said Rolo.

The day-work on the deck became more pleasant as the weather warmed. Everyone wore work shorts and went shirtless. The sun took the stark white shock off my skin, first pink then red then a pleasing light tan.

When the sun was strong and there was little chance of rain, the whole deck crew was turned out to start chipping the rust and old paint off the decks with little hammers. I found it absorbing work, squatting like a chimp among the sailors, all of us with goggles on, chipping away, making little patterns – lines, swirls, pictures – then chipping them all off: chipping, chipping, chipping, each of us lost in a world of our own design. Most people enjoyed chipping.

Spread out on the wings from the hand chippers were the air chippers: this was a coveted job for the more experienced. A pneumatic chipping-hammer was connected to the air-line that ran along under the flying bridge and was handled by a sailor who squatted on the deck, running the hammer along the rust and paintwork. An air-hammer could do five times as much as someone with an ordinary chipping hammer. I longed for the day I would be trusted with one. The racket on the deck from so many hammers striking steel was enormous; an unholy deafening din that had to be heard to be believed.

After the chippers came the brushers, scrubbing the freshly chipped metal bare with stiff wire brushes until it gleamed. I was less keen on wire-brushing; it was unsatisfying and harder on the arms, with less room for dreaming.

After the brushers came the painters, slopping red lead paint over everything, using big deck rollers, loading up from long paint trays set on the deck beside them.

The day started with everyone chipping – a phalanx of hand chippers working its way along the deck, flanked by four air chipping-hammers, two on either side. After lunch, the bosun dismissed two of the air hammers and moved a quarter of the hand chippers over to wire brushing. Following the mid-afternoon Smoko, half the remaining chippers were also moved onto brushing, with a few starting to roll the paint. The brushers gradually caught up with the remaining chippers and then the painters caught up with the brushers. When we all caught up with each other, the chippers stopped and stowed away the gear while the brushers and painters finished up. If the bosun judged it right, which he always did, the last drop of paint would be applied as it was time to knock off. The whole process was very satisfying. I became browner.

Maracaibo, in Venezuela, was disappointing. I had been hoping to go ashore and see some exotic stretch of South America, full of Latins dancing and playing guitars, but Maracaibo was just a jetty sticking out from a refinery, which was on the edge of a jungle. We weren't allowed past the end of the jetty. We were there for three days, picking up a full cargo of black oil products for Europe.

Everyone was nervous because a cadet on a Dutch ship had been shot the previous month by the army guards who always stayed onboard for security while any ship was in port. The cadet had apparently been pulling down the Venezuelan courtesy flag at sunset in a strong

*Looking forward:
steaming into a calm sea*

wind and he stood on it to stop it blowing away. The fiery lieutenant of the guard screamed at him in Spanish not to step on the national flag, but the cadet did not understand; the wind blew harder, the flag flapped around his legs, so he stamped on it to hold it down. The lieutenant saw this as a calculated mortal insult to the country, so he pulled out his pistol and shot the hapless cadet in the leg. It threatened to be a big incident but was quietened down by the oil company. The cadet was flown to the USA for expensive private treatment. The lieutenant was exiled to stand guard in a remote jungle village, forever, apparently. While we were there, great care was taken whenever any flag was hoisted or lowered. The process was undertaken by an AB and a cadet and was supervised by the duty officer. While this was happening, the guards made a point of looking anywhere else but at the flags, until the operation was completed.

The memorable incident while we were tied up at Maracaibo concerned McAllister. I was standing on the flying bridge by the midships accommodation block at midday with Stamp, waiting for Starling to arrive so I could hand over the watch, when McAllister came swaying up from aft, falling from one side to the other, bouncing off the rails.

"Oh, Christ," said Stamp. "'Ere's trouble. Look at 'im. 'E's loaded."

We watched McAllister approach.

"You're a bastard, Stamp!" roared McAllister. Stamp turned on his heel and ran down the ladder into the centre castle (the storage space under the midships accommodation). "That's right: run! Run! You cowardly bastard!"

He came up to me.

"Hello Mac," I said.

"You bastard!" He breathed a rotten beery gas into my face. "I hate bastard officers!" I stepped back.

"I'm not an officer, Mac. I'm a cadet. Lowest of the low, remember?"

His eyes were reamed with blood and hooded with suspicion. He hunched forward and stared at me. McAllister was built like a bull. "Cadets are officers – you're all the same: bastards."

"Hey, not me, Mac. I'll be promoted to bastard one day but now I'm just the lad who gets to do the jobs that are too shitty for you to do."

We looked at each other. A less hostile light came into McAllister's eyes and he smiled and put his grimy arm around my neck and pulled me towards him. He smelt like a farmyard animal.

"Yeah, you're right. You're all right, Simon. You're all right. You're not like the other bastards. You're not like a real officer. Not like that snotty little shit, the other first-tripper, he's a real officer. What's his name? He thinks he's cock of the walk. Where is the little bastard? I'll put him in his place."

He was referring to Starling, who I saw looking fearfully around the doorway of the ship's office. Although I couldn't suppress a smile at Starling's predicament, I was a little wounded to find that McAllister did not judge me to be real officer material.

McAllister saw him too: "You little bastard!" He screamed. "C'mere!"

Starling's head disappeared inside the office. McAllister turned to me. "Where's the mate? I'm going to smash his bloody head in, the bastard!"

I shrugged in a 'don't know' manner, as best I could, being restricted by McAllister's grip.

The chief mate appeared at the office doorway: "McAllister, get aft to your cabin! That's an order!" he shouted.

Mac let go of me and I stood up and rubbed my neck. "You can bugger off, you bastard!" he roared back at the mate.

"Get aft!"

"Bugger off!"

"Hall," the chief mate yelled at me: "get the bosun, now!" I paused. "Now!"

I went, running aft down the flying bridge.

A few minutes later I returned with the bosun and three ABs. I had wanted to see the chief mate fight McAllister. I wasn't sure who I would bet on. McAllister was stronger, but drunk, and the chief mate was far nastier. Probably the chief mate. I hoped I hadn't missed it.

I had. McAllister was face-down, the chief mate kneeling on his back holding Mac's arms up behind his head. The second mate sat on Mac's legs. McAllister thrashed and screamed and arched his back. All three men had blood on their faces.

"Bosun, get the handcuffs!" yelled the mate. "They're in the locker above my daybed." He turned to the three ABs: " Hurry! You lot, get over here and help!"

We manhandled McAllister to his feet, men holding onto each leg and arm, the chief mate held him by the hair. McAllister screamed at the top of his voice – he thrashed like a landed fish and we could barely control him. One of the ABs punched him in the stomach to slow him down then butted him in the face. McAllister's nose burst open: he spat blood on the AB's shirt. The AB butted him again. It took all our combined strength to restrain him.

The bosun returned with the cuffs and eventually McAllister was handcuffed to the rails on the flying bridge, where he screeched and frothed and kicked out.

"Hose him down," said the mate. "That'll cool him off."

A big canvas fire hose was run out and water ordered from the engine room. Stamp took delight in taking the lead hose position.

"You need a good wash, Mac, you smelly bastard," Stamp sniggered.

"I'll bloody kill you, Stamp!"

"Arrgh, shut up!"

The water came on and McAllister was blasted to the planks of the flying bridge. Stamp and party hosed him down for about a minute, until he was sodden and muted and flattened. The mate and the second mate walked back into the midships block to clean themselves up. The bosun went over and booted MacAllister in the kidneys as soon as they disappeared.

"You're nothin' but bloody trouble, Mac."

The army guards cheered.

McAllister was left there for the rest of the day, slumped on the deck, handcuffed to the rails in the heat of the afternoon, glowering at the world. At dinner-time, the midships officers went down the ladder and along the deck, rather than try and pass McAllister, who might lash out.

When I returned from dinner at seven in the evening, McAllister was leaning against the rail, chatting to the bosun, looking quite chipper. He looked at me as I approached warily.

"Hello, Simon," he said, in his quiet lilting voice. "You got roped into tying me down, I hear. I hope I didn't hurt you?"

"No, I'm fine, Mac," I replied.

"Good, good."

The chief officer arrived. McAllister hung his head. "You're a stupid bastard, Mac," he said.

"I know, sir. I'm really sorry."

"Look at my face. You've spilt my lip. It's swollen like a bloody balloon."

"I'm sorry, sir. It must have been a lucky punch."

"You're up before the Old Man in the morning. You're going in the log book."

"Yes, sir. I deserve to be punished." Mac looked doleful and defeated.

"Take him aft, bosun, and search his cabin for grog." The chief officer passed over the keys for the handcuffs and went into the midships accommodation block, shaking his head. I watched McAllister being led away.

We filled up at Maracaibo and headed northeast, across the Atlantic for Europe. It was a slow voyage and we were very low in the water, right down to the load-line marks. We were buffeted by bad weather the whole way. I had hoped to be home for Christmas but the prospect looked bleak.

Every morning, Starling and I went out on deck to take the tank temperatures – 30 tanks in all, three abreast from fore to aft. The laden ship had a slow roll and the low freeboard meant that the gunnels dipped into the water at every other roll, bringing a cascade of ocean rushing along the deck.

We learned to run like monkeys between the rolls, whipping off the ullage caps while the ship was rolling away from the water, dropping the thermometer on a string down into the oil, tying it off, cramming the cap back on, then leaping up on the pipework to avoid the torrent of water as the ship lurched back again. If we were too slow we were drenched and washed along, banged and bruised against the metalwork, dragged dangerously near the scuppers by the pull of the retreating water. When the water ran off the deck, we would jump down, knock off the ullage cap, pull up the thermometer, read it, cap back, run for the pipes. It made us very quick, very alert and very, very aware of the power and unpredictability of the sea. We cheered at each other whenever there was a near miss. Reading temperatures on a deep-laden tanker in the choppy Atlantic was a blast of fun for every young man who ever tried it; I never knew anyone who didn't find it exciting. It held a blend of challenge, speed, timing, danger and a huge burn of exhilaration as you made the jump to safety each time. It was fabulous.

We had Christmas near the Western Approaches to the English Channel. It was a bizarre experience, very different from the staid family affairs I was used to. The chief mate gave me and Starling the day off after we completed the morning temperature run. To make the job easier and because it was Christmas, Rolo stood on the flying bridge as we went round the tanks, writing down the temperatures as we shouted them up to him. This saved us memorising several at a time and periodically running up to the office to put them in the book.

Afterwards, we got showered and changed and went along to the bar. It was 10.30 a.m., and crowded; in full swing. I was given a beer and we all wished each other 'Happy Christmas'. The Wop was there, looking unhappy. I asked him what was wrong.

"The bloody crew. They came in and flooded the bar last night." He indicated the carpet that was still wet.

"What did they do?" I asked.

"Managed to get in somehow, blocked up the sink and turned the tap on. The place was awash when the steward came in to clean it this morning."

"Why would they do that?" I queried him.

The Wop looked at me, as if I were simple. "Why? Because they're crew and we're officers and they hate us: that's why. Why do you think?"

"I don't know. It just seems…" I struggled for words: "I don't know… so pointless."

"It's not pointless. They've annoyed us and they've put one over on us. No one got caught and it makes a great Christmas present for them to sit and laugh about it down in the crew mess. It's not pointless."

It seemed pointless to me.

Everyone drank a lot. The second officer, his wife, and the third engineer had to go and eat at 11.30 a.m., before the midday watch started. The rest of us stayed and drank more. I was getting the hang of drinking now.

The chief engineer gathered us cadets together before we went in to eat and told us that we had to do a Christmas sketch in the dining saloon before the Christmas meal. He talked in a low voice in a very conspiratorial way, putting his arms around us as he talked and leaning in close, his big lower lip shining as he hung his face close to mine. He told us that he wanted at least two good acts. When he went away, Rolo said: "Queer as a nine-bob note."

One of the engineer cadets said: "You should see him down below in the pit. He tries to look down the front of everyone's boiler suit."

"Filthy bastard! He ought to be castrated," Rolo responded.

The Christmas sketch sounded ominous and I wondered if I was about to encounter a major humiliation. I asked Paul what we were supposed to do.

"It's nothing," he said. "We'll all stand up and sing a song. Anything will do, they'll all be so pissed that they'll cheer whatever noise we make. Just follow my lead and don't worry about it."

"OK," I said, with misgivings.

I needn't have had any misgivings. It was just as Paul said.

We went through to the dining saloon to eat at 12.30 p.m.: everyone was in good spirits. We all stood with our heads bowed while the captain said a fairly witty grace, after which he shouted: "Merry Christmas, everyone!"

"Merry Christmas!" we all shouted back.

There were bottles of wine on the tables and the stewards pulled the corks and filled the glasses. The chief engineer stood up and announced that the cadets would now entertain the officers, as was traditional. The officers hooted and pounded the tables.

The eight of stood up and Paul led us to the area in front of the serving hatch, where we gathered in a clump. He and Rolo conferred with the engineer cadets and then turned to the front and started belting out an expletive-laden song to the tune of *Bye-bye, Blackbird*. The first verse started: 'Pack my bags and pack my grip, I'm not coming back next trip. Bye-bye, blackbird!" The song went on for about eight verses – Paul, Rolo and one of the engineer cadets knew the words while the rest of us enthusiastically joined in the chorus line, 'Bye-bye, blackbird!'

The officers cheered and banged the table-tops and demanded more. The finale was a wheelbarrow race, twice round the saloon. The third mate stood on a chair as barker and took bets from the tables and off we charged. Starling was my barrow. He put his hands on the deck and I held his legs. He set off at a furious pace, his arms pounding along. I was impressed and thought we were going to win, but an engineer pair came alongside and barged Starling into the bulkhead, his hands collapsed and we went down. We finished last. It was a good effort all round and we had a mighty applause from the officers.

The meal was colossal: eight courses, two hours. I drunk too much and went out to be sick over the side between the fillet mignon and the turkey. Starling drunk too much and sloped off to his bed halfway through. Rolo was outraged when he discovered this and went to his cabin and dragged him back in again. Poor Starling sat for the rest of the meal in grim misery, pretending to eat, under threat and order from Rolo to stay there until the end.

After the meal, I was in no state to join the others for cards in the bar for games, and weaved my way along the flying bridge to midships, chaperoned by the third mate and his wife, where I fell into my cabin and slipped into a comatose state.

I left the tanker SS *Valvata* in Rotterdam just before New Year, late in the day. We had called at Antwerp then Rotterdam. The ship was due to sail back to Hamburg after Rotterdam and I had been told that I might pay-off there with Starling. It was going to be touch-and-go as to whether we would be back in time for the start of term at the School of Navigation in Plymouth.

I was in the bar in the evening after we arrived in Rotterdam, an hour before my eight-to-midnight watch, playing cards with Sparks and two of the fivers, when the chief mate came in and said: "You and Starling are leaving in an hour, Hall. Get up to the Old Man's cabin and sign off." I looked at him in disbelief. "Come on! Snap to it! You've got to catch the night ferry to Harwich."

I said: "Who's going to do my watch?"

He looked at me for a bit. "Don't worry about that. We managed before you arrived and we'll cope after you leave. Off you go." His voice was almost kindly. Almost.

My best memory of the *Valvata*: walking down the gangway and seeing Rolo taking the ullages with Stamp. He was the lowest of the low now. I waved. He glowered at me.

The ship's agent put us on the night ferry to Harwich, each with a train warrant to get home from there. It was an uneventful crossing. We didn't have a cabin so we slumped into torpor in the forward lounge.

I telephoned my mother from Harwich railway station the next morning and said I would be home later in the day. My father was off flying somewhere and my mother couldn't drive so I finished the journey by walking the last mile from the bus station to home, alternately carrying and dragging my heavy sea kit.

I would have five days at home before starting college in early January. I came home three months older, I felt three years wiser. That evening I sat in the front room of my parent's house in front of the fire, the trappings of Christmas strung around me, eating crumpets and watching television and filtering the things I felt I could tell them. I often caught my parents and my brother Peter watching me. I felt… as if I now belonged somewhere else.

3

School for Tramps

January: bleak and grim on an early Sunday morning at Reading station. I stood among small groups of people, mostly twos and threes, with my suitcase and kitbag, watching the revolving letters on the black-and-white train-board tell me that my train to Plymouth would leave in 20 minutes. My father had driven me to the station from where we lived near Oxford and we stood around awkwardly at the station entrance. Peter had come too, to watch his little brother go. We made awkward conversation for a while: there didn't seem much to say, so I said goodbye to both of them. They said 'Good luck', and I hefted my kitbag and my Globetrotter suitcase and walked into the concourse.

The train had the old-fashioned carriages; compartments that seated 12 – two rows of six facing each other – with wood panels inside and badly-sprung seats under green check covers. I sat looking backwards during the journey, next to the window in a carriage of quiet, disparate people, watching the stations slide by like sad dreams in the weak winter sun: Didcot, Chippenham, Bath, Bristol, Taunton, Exeter St Davids, Dawlish. I remembered our family holiday in a caravan in Dawlish in the summer, where I met Debbie: Debbie from Dawlish, the first girl I ever properly asked out. I took her to the funfair and I learnt how to kiss, properly. She smelled of toffee. I also learnt how to be two-timed, when I was walking back through the caravan site with my mother one afternoon and found Debbie glued mouth-to-mouth with another young blood from three caravans up. I thought: 'The sneaky bastard; the two-timing bitch.' I was wounded and humiliated to the core. We walked past them; they were oblivious to us, like a couple of dogs locked together. We pretended not to notice. Back at the caravan, my mother mumbled sympathy. I tried to look as if I wasn't bothered.

Hey: if Debbie from Dawlish could see me now – back from Venezuela, back from the western ocean; a boy no more: a man who worked 16-hour days, burnt from the Caribbean sun, blasted by the Atlantic freeze. I saw myself walking past her without a backward glance, like Anna in the closing scene of *The Third Man*, leaving her in my dust with her spotty, snotty choice of boy. I squeezed satisfaction from the thought as the train crept out of Dawlish and hurried west towards Plymouth.

The train arrived in Plymouth in the early afternoon. Outside the station, I asked the way to Queen Anne Terrace, to the cadet hostel where I would live for the next six months. It was about half a mile away so I hefted my gear and walked.

Queen Anne Terrace was a large, red-bricked, five-story Victorian town house on the busy North Road, ten minutes walk from the city centre. Outside was a brass plaque, which read: 'Plymouth School of Navigation.'

Schooling in navigation and associated arts has a long history in Plymouth. The first School of Navigation was founded in 1862 for the purpose of teaching Merchant Navy officers and potential officers to obtain their certificates of competency. It survived as a separate college in its own right until Edwardian times, when it was absorbed as a separate department of the then Plymouth Technical College, where it continued as the department of navigation. At some point more recently, it had become the Plymouth School of Navigation.

Books on the history of maritime education in Plymouth tend to dwell on the School of Navigation, while ignoring that less-celebrated maritime training establishment, the Mount Edgcumbe Training Ship, which operated from 1877 until 1920. This ancient square rigger, a decommissioned Royal Navy warship, was where boys aged from 12 to 15 could sent by a magistrate if they were found to be homeless, destitute, begging, or in the company of thieves. Mount Edgcumbe was a brutal place where discipline was maintained by the birch and by a regime that kept the boys meaningfully engaged from when they were roused from their hammocks at 5.00 a.m., until they were stood down at 8.00 p.m. The ship held 250 inmates, who were ruled by a commander and three retired navy men. They were schooled in all manner of nautical knowledge. Even though by then boys were no longer being shipped off as powder monkeys in Royal Navy warships, these training ships still provided valuable sailors for Britain's huge fleets of the day. The number of inmates who died by drowning or in accidents was high; the place must have been a small piece of hell to those boys who were sent there.

I walked up the stone steps to Queen Anne Terrace with my kit and rang the bell. It was answered by a short, stocky lad of my age, wearing blues uniform. He had ginger hair and was heavily freckled. He looked at me expectantly.

"I'm Simon Hall. I'm starting at the school tomorrow and I've been told to report here today."

He smiled. "Oi'm Tom," he said, in a broad Irish accent. He held out his hand and we shook.

"Hello, Tom."

"Noice to meet you, Simon. Come on in."

The black and white tiled foyer was long and wide with a desk at one end.

"Should I be in uniform?" I asked.

"No, I'm duty cadet," Tom replied, pointing to the desk. "I sign people in and out, answer the door, answer the phone, do fire rounds and dat sort of ting. Duty cadet has to wear uniform. You'll get yous turn about every tree weeks." He consulted a list. "You're in cabin number six."

I followed him towards the back of the building and into a large room with six double bunks.

"Most of the cabins have four bunks or two, but you're one of a dozen in this pen. Oi'm in here too."

So was Starling, leaning over one of the lower bunks, unpacking his kit. He nodded at me and I nodded back: we hadn't particularly liked each other on the *Valvata* and I would have preferred to share with someone else. I expect he felt the same. There was also a lanky, gormless looking lad with goggle eyes. His name was Bell: he grinned inanely at me. Bell's habit was either to grin inanely or leave his mouth open, hanging on its hinges as if he had forgotten how to close it. The third person in the room introduced himself as Billy. Billy was well-bred, well-spoken and serious. He shook my hand solemnly and asked about my journey with careful concern.

Half of the occupants of number six had been there the previous term and they all had top bunks. The newcomers – me, Starling and Bell – slept below. I made up my bunk Board-of-Trade style – nothing tucked in, sheet and counterpane folded under – and then unpacked my possessions into my locker. Tom showed me to the store room where I stowed my suitcase. He told me that there would be a muster in the lounge at six o'clock, where a welcome speech would be given by the warden, Chiefy Rozer. He smiled.

Chiefy Rozer made me feel I was back on the poop deck of the *Valvata* among the blaspheming deckhands. He was a rough, unsmiling man for the college to choose to train cadets. Rough unsmiling men of fiction generally had a heart of gold, but not Chiefy. He had a cold heart of ship's brass, or perhaps a black heart, or maybe no heart at all. He hated most people, particularly cadets. He swore continuously and viciously, he humiliated us whenever he could, singling out and holding hapless cadets to ridicule, inviting everyone to join in the debasement.

Chiefy was an ex-RN chief petty officer, retired some 20 years back. Since then he had been warden of Queen Anne Terrace, in charge of cadet discipline for the School of Navigation, and lecturer for close-to-the-salt knowledge such as practical seamanship and survival training. I disliked him: most people did; some hated him. It was not until years later that it dawned on me that this was what he wanted; a bonded group of cadets, bonded by their common dislike of him. We had to call him 'Chief'; never 'Chiefy', never 'sir'. "Sir" was for officers', he told us, and all officers were queers, cowards and lazy bastards. He was a 'Chief Petty Officer' and it was the CPOs who ran the Navy.

Chiefy's six o'clock muster speech left us all in no doubt that he was running this ship. He stood in front of the fireplace, buttoned up in full uniform, grey and grizzled, built like a barrel, mean-faced, ragged-voiced, each word a stake in the heart. He made sure we knew what an awful time we were going to have and what an utterly worthless shower we were.

We would be woken at 05.45 to wash, dress and turn to for our morning cleaning duties. All cadets in Queen Anne Terrace, except the senior cadet, would have morning cleaning duties. There would be an inspection by the senior cadet at 06.30 every morning and anyone who failed would miss breakfast while they carried out their cleaning again. There would be a full inspection by Chiefy himself on Saturday morning, and woe betide anyone who wasn't up to scratch: the unfortunate would receive a weekend of labour and no shore-leave. At 07.00 every weekday we would all be turned out in the courtyard of the college, with the cadets from the three other hostels, to do an hour's drill, marching up and down to the entertainment of passers by. Breakfast was at 08.00 and lessons at the college started at 09.00. We would have an hour for lunch, and then back to college until 17.00. We would eat at 17.30 and then have evening classes from 18.30 until 19.30. After that, we had to come back to Queen Anne Terrace and were expected to do whatever evening work had been set. Then we could change out of uniform and go out for the rest of the night, provided we were back in the hostel for lights out at 22.30.

On Friday and Saturday we could stay out until midnight. On Saturday morning, after the big inspection, we had to walk to the Boat Centre, which was about a mile away, where we had sailing practice until 14.00, followed by two hours of practical seamanship. We then had the rest of the weekend off, with the exception of any extra studies or punishment that had been awarded for our slackness. Everyone would get one weekend pass to go home in the first term and two in the second term.

Chiefy predicted that a quarter of us would run back home within the month. It was obvious to him that most of us were useless rich-kid girlies who would not be able to cut it, and by the look of us, a large number were also disgusting homos that he was going to drive out because he hated homos more than he hated officers. He would make it his mission to ensure that all homos were thrown out so they could get back to their hairdressing salons.

Then came the finale of his speech – Chiefy screamed: "And I hate skivers! Worse than anything I hate skivers! If I catch any of you skiving you'll be scrubbing skid marks off the bog-bowl with your toothbrush – that'll bloody teach you!"

You could have heard a feather drop at the end of his speech. I resolved never to skive.

Queen Anne Terrace – the cadet hostel where the author stayed in Plymouth which is now student accomodation for the University of Plymouth.

The next morning at 05.45, the duty cadet for the day came in, put the lights on and shouted at us to get up. We all rolled out of our bunks. Tom had posted a duty roster on the wall; I was cleaning the lower stairs, which sounded easy.

I went to the communal bathroom and lined up for a sink. It was freezing cold. People were scratching and farting. No one spoke much. I had a wash in tepid water, cleaned my teeth and then set off to clean the stairs.

Cleaning the stairs turned out to be a ghastly and soul-destroying job. They were edged in white rubber and the job was to clean all the black shoe marks off with white dubbing polish. Every step was scarred almost black by the end of each day and had to be coated and scrubbed, coated and scrubbed, each morning. Whenever I turned my back, someone would walk down and leave fresh black smears. The only way to achieve a good result was to clean all steps as best as possible, and then, just before the inspection, quickly wipe them all again with fresh white polish to remove the latest marks.

The senior cadet in Queen Anne Terrace was a second-year engineer. Generally speaking, the deck cadets got on well enough with the engineer cadets, although there was a status rivalry between the two. The engineers thought their studies were more demanding and they were therefore brighter, whereas the deck cadets had an inbuilt superiority in the knowledge that they were the more senior stream of officer; only a deck cadet could become captain.

Sometimes the senior cadet was a Phase 3 deck cadet, who had done the initial college spell, been to sea for 18 months and then returned for a second stint at college. These Phase 3 men were older and meaner than the rest. They were the kings of the college. Rolo was back in college on Phase 3, having left the *Valvata* at Antwerp and with one day's leave – although he was not staying in Queen Anne Terrace, thankfully.

Our senior cadet was loud and merciless; two other second-year engineer sidekicks trailed beside him. He had a room to himself at the top of the building and was sometimes invited for tea with Chiefy and Mrs. Chiefy.

On this first inspection day, he walked into room six, followed by his acolytes and the duty cadet with his pen and notebook. The senior cadet wore white gloves. He walked around the room grabbing the corner of the bedding on the three bottom bunks as he went past, ripping them all to the floor. He then pushed one of the lockers away from the wall, bent down and ran a finger along the skirting board. He held up his hand; the finger of the white glove had a dark smear on it.

He stood in front of Tom: "None of these new boys knows how to make a Board-of-Trade bed and the place is a sty. Get it cleaned properly and get the bunks made up as they should be."

He left. We all turned to our wrecked room. I felt a heat rise in my chest, I wanted to go out and kick the senior cadet up the arse.

Tom exclaimed: "Don't stand around. Dis will happen every day until you make your bunks better. Get out and stand by your duty station. We'll clean up here afterwards."

I moved off to my lower stairs, to watch the senior cadet and his troop stamp up each bright white step, leaving a black smear on each. At the top he turned round and shouted: "And clean those white edges properly!"

Someone told me the senior cadet particularly disliked the latest Phase 1 intake because we had some actual sea experience, which made us different from the standard.

The morning drill was another new experience. I had no idea how to march and nor did any of the other Phase 1 cadets. We tried, Chiefy screamed, we tried harder, we failed, Chiefy screamed more. It rained, it was cold, we marched badly, we didn't get any better. There were not many passers by at that time of the morning but those with time on their hands stopped to watch the show. It must have been amusing for them.

Chiefy had pet hates, or more accurately, several people whom he hated even more than he hated the rest of us. One of them was a thick-necked lad with big lips and a receding chin. He was a second-termer who was known as Dong. Dong looked stupid and he certainly wasn't bright. Chiefy didn't care about that though: he hated Dong because Dong was uncoordinated to the point of disability.

When most people walk, they put their left leg forward and at the same time their left arm swings back; the natural gait of the *homo sapien*. Dong's natural gait was in reverse; his left arm would swing forward at the same time as his left leg went forward, making him move forward with a strange robotic motor, which drove Chiefy wild with rage. He would stand with his face two inches from Dong's and screech abuse at him, spraying poor Dong with a blanket of spittle. Chiefy would then turn to the ranks of cadets and screech: "Look at 'im! Look at 'im! He's got two left legs! He's a bloody cripple! March, Dong! Go on! March!" And Dong would set off, shambling jerkily like a badly-built machine. "Look at 'im! Look at 'im! You left-legged cripple!" Chiefy shrieked.

We smirked at Dong's predicament; thankful it was him and not us. Apart from looking glum, Dong seemed quite impervious to this daily assault, which enraged Chiefy even further.

We breakfasted at another hostel where we would have all our meals; it was next to the main college. There were about a hundred cadets in the dining hall and we sat where we could find space on the dark, shiny refectory benches. Chiefy and the other wardens, together with several lecturers and senior cadets, sat on the long top-table, which was placed crossways at the head of the room on a raised podium so they could look down on us. We lined up to take our food from the serving hatch; the top-table were served by three cadets. We took turns at being a server: a duty that came round every few weeks. We were all ravenous when we arrived for breakfast, having been up for hours cleaning and doing drill. I usually ate a mammoth pile of scrambled eggs, bacon, sausages and beans, washed down with sweet tea.

The main college accommodation block itself was 12 stories of slab concrete and plate window; a product of the architectural wave that ushered in the tower-block estate and the re-enforced concrete shopping precinct, and which caused the bulldozing of historic town centres. The bulldozing of the historic centre in Plymouth was actually carried out by Herman Goering in the 1940s, which the city council believed offered an excuse for the hideous replacement buildings. The inside of the block was not yet finished, with the upper four floors still being fitted out. Two hundred cadets lived in the completed part of the block with another hundred staying in the outside hostels. There were two intakes a year and I was in class P1 23, which stood for Phase One 23, being the 23rd intake since the late 1950s. There were 25 of us in P1 23 at the start and we had all done a stint at sea, the first intake to ever go to sea before first attending college.

The wardens and lecturers regarded us with faint suspicion because we were less intimidated than the usual intake that arrived direct from school. Chief Rozer was fearsome, but most of us had been conditioned by chief officers and bosuns who were equally fierce, so while we didn't enjoy it when Chiefy started screaming, we had already learnt to roll with the punches and we were not going to fall apart. Significantly, everyone from P1 23 went through to the end of the course, defying Chiefy's predictions that a lot would fall by the wayside to go back to our hairdressing salons. Tom told me that four of his intake, P1 22, had left within four weeks.

We took all our lessons together, although at night were scattered over the four hostels. About one-third of P1 23 were in Queen Anne Terrace, along with P1 22 cadets and engineers. We got to know each other during the first fortnight, and formed our various groups and alliances. The majority of us were contracted to the big tanker fleets, although there were a few who were with cargo liner companies, and tramps.

From the second day, I regretted not having joined a general cargo tramp company and kicked myself for signing with a tanker firm. Plymouth was a school for tramps. The ethos of the college was firmly general cargo tramp ships. A 'tramp' was a cargo vessel that wandered round the world, picking up cargos where it could, with no regular line, no ploughing to and from the same ports. All the lecturers were ex-tramp officers; all master mariners. Between and during classes, they would regale us with tales of taking copra from the south seas to Singapore then general goods to San Francisco, then south to Chile to load phosphates for Europe, east again with wine and cars… and so on. We tramped on tankers but real tramping needed real cargos. I vowed to go into general cargo tramping as soon as I finished my time, nearly three-and-a-half years into the future.

✳   ✳   ✳

I found common cause with two groups. The first was with some of my companions in room six: Bell, Starling and Billy, together with a lad called Phil from the next cabin. We explored the system together and learnt the diverse geography of our new world. Although Starling and I never hit it off on the *Valvata*, we were cordial and supported each other where need be. I found Bell to be an oaf and he was an irritant a lot of the time, although I still liked him and found his forced gormlessness amusing. Phil was from Lincoln and seemed a strange fit. He was pallid and unhealthy looking, a vegetarian in a time when such a person was an oddity; he was also very clever, probably the brightest in the class. Then there was Billy, a term ahead of us in P1 22. At first I found Billy good company but I grew to dislike him as the weeks past. Billy had a poisonous streak and was an unstable character. He could change in a snap from being charmingly funny to vicious and spiteful, ripping into someone for little reason, and then back again. I became increasingly distant from Billy as time went by, especially after 'the great knife attack'.

The Queen Anne Terrace knife incident made me an overnight hero, mostly within the narrow confines of Queen Anne Terrace, although spreading further within the college to some extent. The story grew and became more and more embellished and I admit to doing nothing to stop the spread in my favour. The whole event was all due to young men having too much to drink, to natural aggression, to stupidity, to pride and, I say so without blush, to some bravery on my part.

Billy was the catalyst. Five of us were out one Friday night: me, Phil, Bell, Starling and Billy, drifting around the several pubs that sold drinks to 16 and 17-year-olds drinking too much. Bell became particularly stupid when drunk: talking nonsense, knocking things over, falling down, embarrassing us all. Billy had taken a dislike to Bell and started beseeching the rest of us to leave him behind somewhere. We were drinking in the Unity – a dark noisy pub, a grim survivor of the wartime blitzing of Plymouth, an old building among modern blocks. Phil and Starling decided to go back early, refusing to take Bell with them, leaving him with Billy and me; Bell was rubber-limbed and near incoherent by that time.

Billy turned on Bell and berated him, slapping him, poking him, trying to provoke him. Bell sat swaying on his chair with a bovine expression on his face. I told Billy to leave him alone. Billy sulked, Bell swayed and grinned. I went to the toilets. When I returned, Bell was gone. Billy was still there waiting for me.

"Where's Bell?" I asked.

"He's gone," said Billy. "Come on, let's go down Union Street."

I was reluctant without knowing more. "Where did he go, Billy? He's in a bad state. We can't just leave him."

"Oh, for Christ's sake, he's just gone. He's big enough to look after himself. Gone back to the hostel, I expect. Come on, let's go."

We went. We wandered down to The Good Companions, another regular cadet pub that served the under-age, then to Union Street, the seedy part of town west of the centre. We had several more drinks. Billy was good company that evening, good fun. I didn't think anything else about Bell.

Later, when we were walking back, after about two hours I suppose, Billy suddenly gave an explosive laugh. "That Bell. What an idiot!"

"What do you mean?" I asked.

"When you were in the bogs at the Unity, I sent him up to the bar to get another three pints. Imagine his stupid face when he got back and we were gone."

I was shocked.

"That's bad form Billy. Why did you do that?"

"Look, Simon: I wasn't going to put up with that tosser all night. He's a pain in the arse. Anyway, he'll have had three pints of beer to keep him company."

I was annoyed and walked back to Queen Anne Terrace without speaking, ignoring Billy. When we arrived I went into the TV lounge and sat smoking with a couple of others. Billy went off to room six. Five minutes later, Tom burst into the lounge: "Simon, get in here, dere's trouble in our pen. Yous better help sort it out." I ran behind Tom to room six. What a spectacle it was. Bell stood there wearing only a pair of psychedelic-coloured underpants, arms hanging by his sides, head dropped forward on his chest. Billy, a good eight inches shorter, was stood up close, shouting abuse into Bell's face, telling him how much everyone hated him.

"You're a tosser, Bell!" He yelled. He shoved Bell, who stumbled back. Bell said nothing. "Everybody hates you! Everybody!" Billy shoved him again. Bell said nothing.

"I can't stand you and nor can anyone in this hostel! Why can't you get the hint and just bugger off?" He shoved him again. Bell fell against the wall. Bell whimpered.

"Leave him be Billy," shouted Tom.

"You stay out of it Tom, this is between me and Bell!" Billy shouted and pushed Bell again.

"Billy, leave him," I said. "He's too pissed to know what's going on."

"Bollocks," said Billy. He punched Bell in the mouth. Bell went down and rolled over on his stomach. His underpants came half off and his boney backside stuck up in the air. "Look at him," hooted Billy, and kicked Bell's backside. "You're hopeless," he shouted. "No wonder no one likes you." Tom and I dragged pulled Billy away. He was puffed up and strutting. He shook us off. "All right, all right, leave me alone," he said.

"Jesus," said Tom.

I turned around. Bell stood there swaying, his Green River knife out in front of him, his garish underpants hanging down. He looked ridiculous, he looked crazed, he looked dangerous. "I've had enough of you, Billy," he said. Billy went white and fell back against his bunk. Bell moved towards him. "I've had enough of you." He lurched towards Billy, waving his knife, Billy ducked and whimpered. Bell stood there in his psychedelic underpants, jaw hanging open. Billy backed up until his head banged against the wall and then stuck there as if paralysed.

I shouted, "No, Bell!"

Bell turned towards me, as if drawn by a lead towards the sound of my shout. His eyes were crazed, but they were wandering. He drooled. I thought: 'He's not dangerous, he doesn't know what's going on.' I hit him: a bad punch that glanced off his head, but he was on rubbery legs and he fell back and bounced off the door. I hit him again. He bounced again. I grabbed at the knife. He pulled his arm back and the blade sliced through my hand. It turned red instantly; we both looked at the blood welling out, my arm was crimson to the elbow. Bell looked shocked. He went white. He dropped the knife. I hit him with my bloody hand and he went down with a red imprint on his face.

Then a lot seemed to happen quickly. Someone wrapped a towel around my hand. Bell sat on his bunk in wretched shock. The senior cadet was called and in turn he called Chiefy. Chiefy looked at my hand and decided it was nothing, despite the blood coursing out. Someone got some butterfly plasters out of the first aid box and pseudo-stitched the cut together, then wrapped a huge tight plaster around the whole weeping mess. Chiefy rounded on Bell, took hold of him by the hair and dragged him to the front door, where he threw him into the street.

"I'm not having a nutter in this hostel while I'm warden. You can bugger off now! Go on, bugger off! Go home!"

Bell lived in Southampton, a hundred and fifty miles away.

Chiefy slammed the door. The senior cadet told him the story. Chiefy looked at me: "So, Bell was going to carve up the little fella here," indicating Billy, "and you stepped in and stopped it. That right?"

"It wasn't quite like that, Chief." I replied.

"It probably wasn't, but is that near enough?"

"I can't remember. It happened too quickly."

Chiefy stared at me for a moment. "Oh, well: show's over, lights out." He went back to his apartment at the rear of the building and slammed the door.

The foyer was crowded with cadets. We stood around looking at each other. We looked out the window of the TV lounge and saw Bell standing outside in his underpants, looking doleful. It started raining. A few cadets laughed and banged on the window; Bell looked in with spaniel eyes. It rained harder in big drops that bounced off his skinny shoulders, he hunched forward. I thought we had better let him in and said so. The others thought I was crazy.

"For God's sake, Simon: he might have kilt you and Billy wit dat knife," said Tom.

"He was pissed. He wouldn't have done anything."

"He did do something. Look at your hand." Blood was seeping through the plasters and dripping onto the floor. A few agreed with me. We all stood and looked out at Bell, who was now squatting down beside the dustbins, trying to keep out of the rain. A couple went by under an umbrella and looked at him with nervous caution.

Chiefy came back out of his apartment at the back of the hall and opened the front door.

"Come in here you cowardly bastard," he shouted. Bell scuttled in. Chiefy poked him in the chest. "If you ever cause trouble in this place again I'll beat the living hell out of you myself. Understand?" Bell nodded. Chiefy pushed him towards room six. Bell slunk inside and climbed into his bunk.

I was a hero the next day, which I basked in to some extent, as anyone would. Cadets who I had never met slapped me on the back. The Phase 3 seniors made approving noises. Rolo, my old shipmate from the *Valvata* who had done nothing but mock me for three months, came and took partial ownership of my heroics, appointing himself as my mentor. Even Chiefy seemed to take a liking to me.

Bell became a disgraced laughing stock for several weeks, derided by everyone. People clucked and sniggered and sneered when he came into the room. Chiefy gave him two weeks internment as duty cadet plus a week's toilet cleaning. I thought: 'Not bad for attempted murder.' Bell apologised to me abjectly, which I accepted, but it didn't stop him walking around looking as if his world had collapsed. I made no mention of the incident in my weekly telephone call home: slashed in a drunken knife fight in the hostel? I was supposed to be training to be an officer and gentleman. My mother would have had a seizure.

As the term went on, I developed another group of friends and pulled away from the room-six crowd. None of this second group lived in Queen Anne Terrace: they were split between the other hostels. John was one of life's charmers: he charmed me, he charmed the other cadets, he charmed every girl he met. John was from Watford. John was also tough, street-wise and handsome. I tried to be like John, in style, but I couldn't carry it off. John liked to fight; he had his hair cropped in the skinhead style of the early 1970s. Sometimes he shaved his head completely. Some people thought he was a bully and picked on people whom he would be able to beat, goading them to lashing out, so he could hit them. But he wasn't like that; he just liked to fight. I liked John. He liked me and held me in some respect, undue I always thought.

Barry was a pale youth, slightly older than me, who was aggressive in the way only smaller people can be. He was supremely confident of himself and would not back down before anyone. He had a temper like a wildcat and the ability to unnerve. Barry didn't need anyone and didn't like many people although he admired John and tolerated me. We grew to like each other. I don't know why I liked Barry. I expect it was because he was one of those people who, when you were with him, made you feel good about yourself and confident in addressing whatever came along. He did not seek out confrontation like John although he was much crueller. Barry was also a wow with the girls.

And then there was Jimmy, my good friend. Jimmy was from Glasgow and older than the rest of us; he was an ancient 18-year-old who shaved every day. He had large ears and walked with a strange gait. At first, I found him unintelligible as he spluttered in his strangled, mangled Glaswegian accent. I also thought he was stupid to the point of being backward; he just did not seem to understand what was going on in any of the lessons, asking the most pointless and ridiculous questions, and never knowing the answer to anything he was asked. In the early weeks I found him to be clownish and oafish; a simpleton who gibbered around the room doing monkey impressions or telling Beano-type jokes and shrieking with laughter as if he were a ten-year-old.

Then one day I found out that he was laughing at us all, that he was having huge fun – he made himself have huge fun at our expense. The revelation made me feel diminished. It happened one evening when the two of us went out to the James Street Vaults pub to cash a cheque. The James Street Vaults – known as the Jamie – was a small pub next to the college, which cashed cheques for cadets as long as they bought a drink. It was a neat idea that worked well and made sure the place was full every evening. We had several drinks on the proceeds of my cheque; I was becoming mildly drunk on Worthington E.

Jimmy was capering around as usual, squatting on a barstool and bouncing up and down making chimp noises, bumping into people and being generally irritating.

"For Christ sake, Jimmy! Why do you have to do that?" I asked in exasperation.

"Because ah've got the guts to do ut, which is mayre than ye," he answered, slapping his hands on the bar as he bounced.

"That's ridiculous. Acting like a monkey? You're crazy."

He sat on the stool properly and took a long pull out of his pint. "Ah'm no crazy. But ah'm no sad like ye."

"I'm not sad."

"Aye, ye'are." He looked at me. "Ah think ah'll call ye Humphrey."

"Why?"

"Because it's going t'irritate ye and embarrass ye and that'll do ye good."

We drank beer and smoked for a while, silently. I was irritated and embarrassed: "Why do you act like you do, Jimmy?" I asked with irritation.

He looked at me steadily though slate-grey eyes, smoke drifting out his nostrils. His face took a serious turn. "Ah'll tell ye. We all, ye all, we all act sa bloody serious. Concerned about how hard we are, how cool we are. It's aw shite. It's aw bollocks. People need a clown ta take their minds and eyes oot of the inside of their own backsides. And ah need to laugh at them all to take my mind off all ma bullshit and all the crap in ma life. Ma Da's a cripple: worked all his life like a slave for nuthin'; he's doodle-ally now, poor auld bugger. He can hardly make a cup a tea. Ma Ma' works 13 hours a day for nuthin'. Ah don't appreciate it, nor does my sister: we're too busy learning how to be assholes. Ma friends in Glasgee just want to get pissed and chant 'Celtic fa'ever!' and beat the shite out of Rangers supporters, and so do ah, the truth be telt. And they want to shag a lot and drink a lot and fight a lot until it's their turn, then they get hitched and have a flock of wee'ans and live in a shit-hole with a shite job and get fat and ugly and forget how to laugh and go home and hit the wife and hit the kids and blame everyone else for the stinkin' life they've got.

"And ah'm no goin' to be like that, Simon. Ah'm goin' to laugh and be a fool and be the fool and let my time go on way past the rest of ye all, watching ye practicing being sad. Sod that. Perhaps we'll all be sad one day, but ah'll be laughing long after the rest of ye."

We finished our drinks. I looked at him. I saw him in a new light. I looked at myself in the mirror behind the bar. I didn't think I looked sad and neither did I feel sad. Still, he made a good point, so I cashed another cheque and bought the next round while he carried on his chimping. I even gave a passable chimp impression myself later in the evening. Jimmy was a good man.

Barry, John, Jimmy and me went around as a foursome a lot of the time, occasionally with others hanging on the fringes. We weren't revered but we carried more cache than most of the other groups: John because of his charm and his toughness; Barry because he was clever and had a sense of menace that made others wary; Jimmy because he laughed at everything thrown at him and just didn't care; me? I don't know. Probably because I would never give up, I would always be there at the end and always get to the end of what I wanted to do. And I never let anyone down.

The other three usually had success with girls when we went out and I often became embarrassed because I lacked natural charm, sometimes ending up with the ugly leftover girl or, worse, as a solitary figure on the fringes, going back to the hostel alone. In defence, and to cloud the issue, I would drink more than the others and act outrageously, which they loved. Occasionally I got lucky too. All in all, the four of us went well together.

The classes were hard and the work was intense. There was none of the easing off of discipline that usually comes to students as they get older, nor any hint of the university-style lecturing with the greater responsibility for learning put on the student. This was high-pressure, hard, hard work. We wore full buttoned-up blues uniform and were put on discipline if we stepped outside the building without wearing a uniform cap. Every lecturer was 'Sir' and we stood up sharply when they entered the room.

The Jamie pub, the cadets' favourite watering hole. The pub is still going strong and is now a favourite of students at the University of Plymouth.

There was little reflective learning, little discussion. Information was crammed into us to be remembered, dissected and regurgitated. The mathematics spiralled into obscure calculus and spherical trigonometry, the underpinning of navigation. We were soaked in meteorology and naval architecture and hydrostatics, mechanics, maritime law and electronics. We learnt how to send Morse code, read charts, make charts; we learnt international conventions and agreements and business ethics. We were coached in the basics and then the detail of ship handling. We worked from nine in the morning until seven-thirty at night, with an hour for lunch and another for the evening meal. We were baggaged with projects and unfinished work that took us into the night.

In achievement, I was in the upper third of the class, which suited me well. Not too far down to be labelled as a dunce and hounded by the lecturers, not too far up so as to give too much expectation. Occasionally I was roasted around the edges for being a bit too casual and I was a bit wobbly with some of the hydrostatics and electronics, but usually I kept up with the work.

Barry was smart and sharp and had little difficulty with anything. The only time Barry steered himself into trouble was when his basic laziness got the better of him and he hadn't bothered to do the work; although when this happened he would pick himself up to mark in one evening's slog.

John had a quick mind but he was clumsy. Anything that involved precision and dexterity, such as cartography or naval architecture, was awful for him. His work was so bad that it was impossible for me to feign sympathy when I saw the awfulness of his scale diagrams.

After hours of laboured application on the cross-section of a cargo liner, John would show us the results with trepidation. Barry and I would hoot with laughter at John's childlike pictures; they were invariably hopelessly out of proportion and a cause of great hilarity to us. We loved to see the fruits of John's efforts. Our mocking would drive him into sullen and resentful mood, watching for an opportunity for revenge.

Jimmy had a lot of difficulty coping with the work. I was surprised by his problems because he was ahead of the rest of us in education, having taken his Scottish Highers, and I thought that we should all be trailing in his academic wake. Not so. He camouflaged his failings well by clowning and by making himself the class fool, but it was difficult for Jimmy and he struggled in most subjects. I never mocked him. Barry did.

On Thursdays we had communications, which we always looked forward to, because no one viewed it as real work – more as a sort of activity. We took the lesson in a crumbling building, still bomb-damaged from the war, set well away from the main college. Inside, it was rigged up with a bank of signal lamps for us to flash Morse code at each other, a magnetic flag board on which the international code flags were fixed, and a podium on which we had to perform semaphore. In a side-room was a mock radio shack, where we were drilled in FM speech for inter-ship and ship-shore, as well as the rudiments of long-wave and Morse sound transmission, to give us an understanding of the sparks' lair.

The class was taken by another CPO, Chief Robins. Chief Robins was ancient and wizened. He had probably been a hard man in his day but his fire had burned out long ago. For the first couple of weeks no one said a wrong word, because we were still dazed with the overall experience and blunted by the crush of work that was being loaded onto us. But as we found our confidence more, we identified how far we could go with our various lecturers. We could go far with Chief Robins.

It began at the start of one lesson when we all filed into the classroom and Jimmy swiped the Chief's trademark trilby off his desk, put it on his head and capered about the room. The Chief saw this and flapped about, waving his hands, asking for his hat back in a weak and pleading tone. Jimmy threw him the trilby. It landed on the floor at his feet. We all stood still. After a pause, Chief Robins picked it up. Poor Chief Robins started to have a rough ride from then on. Someone would grab his trilby at every lesson and it would get flung from cadet to cadet, while Chief said: "Come on lad, come on lads: stop messing about. Give me that hat back. Come on now."

We would act the idiot with the Morse lamp and the semaphore flags, sending nonsense to each other. Bell was put on the lamp for one Morse code session and sent: 'Sod off all of you.' We hooted. The Chief laughed. Someone stole the feather from his trilby. He turned up with a new feather the following week. Someone splashed ink on the back of his jacket. We drove him crazy by humming in class. It got worse as the weeks passed. Someone would always grab his trilby. Barry punched it flat at the end of one lesson. Dick answered his questions in a strange strangled voice, as if he were an imbecile. I stuck his register to the desk with chewing gum. A dog turd was placed under his desk.

Then, halfway through the first term, someone took his trilby and hid it in the flag locker, under a pile of semaphore flags. Chief Robins spoke to us sternly, demanding the return of his hat. We all sniggered. He shouted in a high, wavering old man's voice. We laughed. He started pleading for his hat, begging for it. We went quiet with embarrassment. He went quiet. He slumped in his chair, his head went down, his shoulders slipped and he started weeping. We sat in silence for several minutes; the only sound was from the old man. We filed out one-by-one. Jimmy retrieved his crushed trilby, straightened it up as best he could and laid in on his desk.

The next day we heard he had left. We turned up to communications the following Thursday, wondering who would take the class. Chief Rozer was there waiting for us, ramrod straight in his blues; his white dress cap on the desk in front of him. While we were all standing at our desks waiting for the command to sit like dogs, he stared at us, a blaze of aggression burning out of his eyes. He shouted: "Anybody wanna touch my hat?" No one replied.

Navigation was <u>the</u> intense subject. We had two double-lectures a week, taught by a grim-faced ex-master, Captain Daventry. All the lecturers were captains, apart from a few CPOs, who were chiefs. Daventry was the only one who had actually served as master though; the others were all ex-chief officers who held Masters Certificates.

Daventry was an authoritarian, and very clever. He expected everyone to be able to grasp whatever he taught and became impatient when we failed to do so. This made him a bad teacher because we were all nervous of ever asking any questions. And because of this, we struggled along in the hardest of all subjects, making heavy work of the ponderous mathematics and the yards of theory. At night, we brought work back to the hostel and laboured through it. The early 1970s were pre-calculator days and we had to *use Norries Tables* – a thick logarithmic almanac – to work out complex mathematical problems that were the grounding for navigation. We learnt page upon page of spherical trigonometry formula and then, when we had learnt them, Captain Daventry made us learn the mathematical proofs for them all.

Although I managed to keep my head above water during P1 23 and beyond, I studied navigation for two years before the penny finally dropped and everything slid into place. Once the different arms started to interlock, it all became clear and apparent and, as with all navigators, second nature. In P1 23 though, under Captain Daventry, navigation was hard graft.

The days went by. From Monday until Friday our time out was so short that every spare moment seemed precious, and every free couple of hours in the evening was a major occasion that we had to make the most of. So we went out into the night and drank and discovered the dens and dives and discos that served under-age drinkers and never closed. We came back for lights out and lay under the covers fully clothed when the senior cadet came round at 11.00 p.m., to check for missing bodies. Then we shinned out the window in small groups to climb back in at two and three in the morning and fall back into our bunks, drunk and exhausted.

We were pulled out of bed at 05.45 every morning except weekends and set to work on cleaning the place to inspection standard, then we went out and marched and marched in the rain and the sleet and the cold and then we worked again in class all day. And so it went on.

Saturday was the beginning of the end of the week. We loved Saturdays. The morning call was an hour later – 06.45 – and there was no drill. Chief Rozer's big Saturday inspection was taken seriously, because if you messed up on that then you were in for the weekend. Everything gleamed. There was not a mark on the floor or a hair in a sink or a smear on a window. The stair edges gleamed white as if from a TV advertisement. The place was cleaner than a hospital. Our Board-of-Trade-style beds were perfect to the millimetre. Even the senior cadet turned out to help on Saturdays, because it was his head too if the place failed. And God help us all if that happened. Chiefy found things wrong of course; 40 years of this had taught him everything there was to know. Usually it was a minor grumble that meant nothing: perhaps a small amount of grief for one person, or for an area cleaning team.

We only ever failed once: that was when a first-year engineer cadet's excesses from the previous night couldn't be held in and he rushed into the bathroom, just as Chiefy started his rounds, to vomit copiously in a sink, on the wall, on the floor, in a trail to one of the toilet stalls, in the toilet, all over himself. Then he collapsed and lay groaning in the whole stinking mess until Chiefy arrived. Chiefy walked in to the bathroom, paused, turned round, said: "Fail; Sunday inspection." Then went back to his apartment and banged the door closed.

We were furious. A Sunday inspection was held at 10.30 a.m., which meant that our sole day off was fractured and ruined. No lie in – just up at 06.45 and clean, clean, clean because Sunday inspections were five times more rigorous than Saturday inspections and everyone was made to fail in some minor way, no matter what. This meant that we had to spend Sunday afternoon in whatever penance Chiefy imposed: scrubbing the pavements outside, drill, washing out the dismal dank cellars, anything that was unpleasant and which took up most of the afternoon.

We thirsted for revenge and stripped the hapless engineer cadet naked then dragged him into a shower stall and held him in there with brooms while cold water soaked him until his screams turned to whimpers, then we covered him in soap powder and scrubbed him furiously with stiff bristle deck-brushes. Then we kicked him and slapped him as he ran naked and red-raw, bleeding through a gauntlet of blows until he reached his room. Everyone was boiling mad. We heard him howling in there for a long time. But that only happened once while I was there; usually we passed the Saturday inspection.

Saturday, after Chiefy's inspection, was 'real sailor time', as Chiefy said. We walked the mile to the Boat Centre, changed into our blue work clothes, then turned to, to man several old clinker-built whalers that had first been floated at the turn of the century. We dragged our whalers down the slip and sailed out into the sound in them, rain or shine.

For sailing, we were under the charge of half-mad Captain Polata. It was said that Polata had a nervous breakdown at sea and was invalided ashore. He was said to live in a tent on the edge of Dartmoor and catch his own food from the wild. He was said to talk to himself. He was said to have been a gun runner. He was avoided by the other lecturers, who disliked him for his strangeness. He was said to frequent the whorehouses off Union Street. We never knew what was true and what was invention, but they were good stories so we embellished them further for the next intake, as had probably been done previously for us. He was certainly an unconventional man who wore strange, ill-fitting clothes and went into long periods of silence, followed by frantic and frenzied activity.

We took our little flotilla across the sound and back every Saturday, tacking and wearing to Polata's orders. He sat in the stern of one of the whalers and used a loud-haler to shout commands to the rest of the boats. The rigging ropes were of sisal, which was rough on the hands and painful when wet. There were the minimum of blocks and tackles, so every rope that had to be hauled was a hard pull. We were told that gloves and coats were for sissies and soppy weekend yachties, so through January and February we held the icy ropes in our bare hands, while the water ran off and froze on our skin. If the weather really blew and the rain was hammering down, we were allowed to put on oilskins; but it had to be very severe. Sometimes the sea whacked into the old whaler so powerfully I felt my teeth judder, as the seas washed over the gunnels and we baled and baled while Polata shrieked at us through his loud-haler.

When we got back we had to haul the boats up the long slip by hand then strip them out and carry the big heavy orange canvas sails and hang them in the sail loft to dry. On warm and pleasant days, which we had from April onwards, Saturdays were wonderful. Sitting in the sun while the little boats pottered across the wavelets, smoking, joking, laughing, running our hands in the water; there was nothing better. But when it was wet and wintry and blowing, it was hellish; worse than a prolonged harsh scrubbing in a cold shower.

After everything had been stowed away, we sat in the sail loft and ate sandwiches for our lunch before going down for Chief Rozers practical seamanship lessons. For seamanship, we gathered in groups of three or four and garnered our fluency with rope-work: the enduring staple of seaman. We started by learning all the classic knots, bowlines, sheep-shanks, reef-knots, rolling hitches and others, before moving onto the fancy decorative knots like 'the monkey's fist' and 'the Turk's head'.

Most of us soon grasped the basic rope work, although once the lessons moved past that, someone either had an affinity or they didn't. I had little trouble on knots in general and easily picked up a good working knowledge of some of the more complex areas, such as splicing, stages, seizings and whippings. I only started to struggle when we moved on to the weaving of blocks and tackles and the rigging of derricks and lifting gear, where more often than not I would manage to entangle everything and produce unworkable gear. I looked forward to these seamanship afternoons though, and enjoyed absorbing an understanding of when to use manila ropes, or coir, or hemp, sisal or tarred ropes, ordinary lay, right-hand lay, plaited ropes, polypropylene ropes and all types of artificial fibre.

Jimmy was hopeless: all thumbs, the worst in the class for seamanship. Chiefy picked on Jimmy a lot for his Glasgow accent and held him up for ridicule to the rest of us. Jimmy acted the goat; Chiefy really disliked him for that. Sometime he ordered Jimmy up to the front of the class to demonstrate some complicated piece of work that he knew full well Jimmy would not be able to do. Poor Jimmy would fumble and fail while we all watched him with pity, until Chiefy finally sent him back to his place with humiliating gibes ringing in his ears. John and I tried to help Jimmy if we could, while Chiefy wasn't watching – although Barry would never help; he always thought it was hilarious to see Jimmy marched out to perform in front of everyone. But Barry was cruel.

☆   ☆   ☆

Saturday night had an almost desperate edge. We had all worked 70 hours from Monday through to Saturday and we <u>were</u> going to enjoy ourselves. As was the case for all young men in most parts of the world from time immemorial, this meant drinking, dancing and striving to meet girls to impress. Most of us were too young to be let into a lot of the pubs and clubs in Plymouth, so it became a conspiracy of disguise and manoeuvre and tactics of distraction to get into the places in and around Union Street. At the worst, when all else failed, we could always seek refuge in the Jamie or the Unity or Pennycomequick, where they would serve anyone who could stand up.

Freedom started at 5.00 p.m, when we were released from the Boat Centre to walk back to the hostels. We walked fast: we ran, sometimes, when it was cold and wet, because the hot water belonged to those who took the first half a dozen showers.

Then it was dinner in the dining hall, a grand end-of-the-week meal with everyone in a good mood. Several of the captains and chiefs were there on that day; Daventry from navigation, Polata from seamanship, Michaels from naval architecture, Curran from engineering, Drabble from meteorology, Chief Robins from communications (before he left), and of course our own Chiefy Rozer. They made a jolly racket at the top-table, along with the senior cadets. Usually, we were told to keep the noise down. But not Saturday evening; the whole hall bounced with the sound of voices. We talked, we shouted, we argued, we boasted. I loved Saturday evening meals.

Then we went out in pairs and groups, heading south towards town. John, Jimmy, Barry and me stopped in the Unity and all drank two pints of Double Diamond. We had a kitty and put in one pound ten shillings each. A pint was two shillings and sixpence in the Unity, although we could pay as much as much three and six in an expensive place. There were signs on the wall telling us how much that would be when decimal currency came in next year; half a crown would be 12-and-a-half pence – stupid-sounding money.

Our kitty should get us plastered, get us in the Top Rank club, give us enough to buy a couple of drinks for girls, if we struck lucky, and then leave enough for a bag of chips on the way home. It didn't get much better than that.

"Why does Barry get the kitty?" Jimmy complained. "He buggered off last week with it and we were all left in the Top Rank with nothing."

"Because I can count, that's why. Someone's got to order the drinks properly. You're not holding it, you're too thick. Besides, can I help it if the women drag me off?"

"Give it to Humphrey," said Jimmy. "No one ever drags him off."

Everyone laughed, including me, even though I was glowing with embarrassment at being singled out as having poor girl skills, as well as being anointed with Jimmy's irritating pet-name 'Humphrey'.

"Let Barry keep it," said John. "He's so tight, there's no danger of it being lost."

"Bollocks!"

"Bollocks to you too!"

We drank our Double Diamond and laughed at each other.

"Hey, freckles, come over here," said Barry, smiling his sly smile that all girls liked at a redheaded girl who stood by a pillar.

She came over and stood by us, smiling.

"So where's your three friends?" said John.

"I'm only here with my sister," she replied, indicating a shorter girl at the bar.

"Come and play the fruit machine with me," said Barry, while this lot charm your sister."

Later, John and I walked down to Union Street with our half of the kitty. Barry and Jimmy and the two sisters had gone off to the Barbican. We tried to get into the Cat Club but were refused entry. They let us in the Top Rank though, and we joined the crush, had a few dances, drunk more: drunk too much. We met Bell and Starling and Billy and Phil but didn't stay with them. I was sick in the toilets. I flushed out my mouth afterwards with Double Diamond and had a cigarette. My charm, feeble as it was, deserted me entirely, and I struggled to hold my own in conversation. Girls danced with me because John and I always interrupted a pair dancing on the floor, so one had to be with me. Towards the end of the evening, I fell over a handbag the girls were dancing around, scattering the contents. I thought it was hilarious; no one else did. I finished the night slumped on a stool by one of the tall tables near the edge of the dance floor. I was broke by then, so I lifted a pint of Double D from a group of lads at a crowded table but no one seemed to mind; they even cheered at me.

John was drunk too, which took the edge off his charm with the girls, but he ploughed on by himself, undaunted by failure. I watched him, marvelling at his persistence. I took a new tack and started to mock any girls who walked near me or who came dancing by. A couple swore at me, most ignored me. Then a dark-haired girl with short kiss-curls came up and slapped me hard, saying: "I hate pigs like you. You should be thrown out." I sat there blinking, my face stinging.

Then she said: "I'm so sorry, I'm so sorry, I didn't mean that!" and kissed me hard on the mouth. She tasted of Babysham. "I'm Stella." She was drunk. She sat on my lap. She apologised again. She told me I looked like Illya Kuriyakin *in The Man from Uncle*. I smiled, in what I hoped was a passable imitation of Illya.

I told her she looked like… Then I couldn't remember anyone, so I said: "My aunt," and we both screeched with laughter.

John walked up at that point and stood behind us awkwardly. She looked round; all three of us burst out laughing. Later, we walked back through the spring night; I was arm-in-arm with my new friend Stella, who lived in North Road, just past the college. John had enough change for one bag of chips, which we shared as we walked the dark streets. They tasted like the ambrosia of the gods, on the heels of our Double Diamond nectar.

Sundays were the best days, the very best. After the excesses of Saturday night I would sleep in late, until just before 9.00 a.m., at which time I would throw myself out of bed and bound across the road to the dining hall to catch breakfast before it finished being served. Most of the cadets arrived in the dining hall on Sunday as the clock was striking nine. Chiefy never took Sunday breakfast and few of the captains turned up to sit at the top-table.

Daventry usually made an appearance but seldom any of the others. On Sunday we had no inspection, no uniform, no drill, no lessons; just pure uninterrupted rest. Catching duty cadet on a Sunday was the cruellest event of all.

After breakfast I would wander down to Plymouth Hoe, the sea-front area, with some of the others and then walk around the Barbican, on the cobbled streets and alleyways, watching the Americans taking photographs of where the Pilgrim Fathers embarked on the *Mayflower*. Sometimes we would go the cinema, to sit in the stalls and wolf peanuts, whiling away the afternoon. A few cadets would just loaf the whole day, staying in bed until lunchtime then shambling around in the afternoon. I couldn't do that; couldn't lie in a hot bunk for hours and hours into the body of the day, even if I were hungover from Saturday night, which was usually the case.

I always telephoned my parents on a Sunday, usually in the early evening, telling them the sort of things that teenage sons tell parents – which was pretty much nothing. I certainly told them nothing of the wild antics that I was involved in. Usually I spoke to my mother, who generally answered the telephone. The news from home seemed as dull as the staid news I was reporting; perhaps they were also hiding wild antics from me.

Sunday lunch was casual; many people didn't bother to turn up, especially if the weather was fine. It seemed strange, in a daring sort of way, to eat in the dining hall out of uniform with no one serving the top-table. I felt a bit like a real student for a day, casting aside my true persona of a militarised unit within a militarised unit. After lunch we sat in the dining hall, smoking and talking, before drifting off to while away the afternoon, lying around outside on the grass if the sun was out, like lizards recharging.

On Sunday evenings, after the last meal, almost everyone was back in the hostel; people rarely went out on Sunday night. We all squeezed everything we could out of the day, relishing the freedom before in ended with a wake up shout at 05.45 the next morning, when the cycle of inspections and work started all over again. We watched TV on Sunday evening in the lounge or drifted in small groups from room to room, sitting on the bunks of the occupants, talking, joking, shouting, boasting, play-fighting, horsing around. We were like a huge delinquent family, headed up by Chiefy Rozer, keeping us all in order. There was a flavour to Queen Anne Terrace that, once tasted, could never be forgotten.

And the time went by. We had a fortnight's home leave after three months, between the terms. Jimmy and I sold our travel warrants and hitchhiked to Scotland to spend a couple of days of days with his strange and tough friends in Glasgow. We went to a football match at Celtic Park while we were there; Celtic won I think. I then spent ten days with my parents, where I noticed, as did they, the growing distance between us. I was keen to get back to Plymouth and arrived a day early. The Irish Shipping boys and the Iranians had stayed over the break and we all went out in the evening and got drunk, swaying home arm-in-arm, late at night, singing Irish/Persian/English songs together.

The second term marched on and the work became even more intense, but we were in our stride and had found our places. The sharp ones – Barry and Phil – led the field; the slow and the dim were by now firmly rooted at the back, including Bell and, sadly, Jimmy, with the rest of the pack strung out between them.

The 12-hour days were our routine; they were the norm, the standard. They were not a chore. We marched slickly, we ground out the work, we sailed smoothly, we made our Board-of-Trade bunks with geometric pattern and our top bunks were never thrown to the floor. We had the measure of the day and what it took, we had the youth and the stamina to be up before six, to clean, drill, study, study, study, then whoop into town and drink and play then sneak back expertly before light, catching a few hours sleep before the same again. My acquaintances became my friends, became my close-bonded compatriots that I would not forget.

The P1 24 intake of our second term looked like the children they were, fresh from home. The P1 23 experiment, of sending us to sea before college, was apparently not going to be repeated – there had been complaints from college staff about us: we were not pliant enough. A few new boys sobbed in the night the first week, down on their bottom bunks. Several were broken by the brutality of Chiefy and his senior cadet henchmen within the month, sitting meekly on their bunks in civvies on Saturday morning before leaving quietly for the station after inspection. The rest rode the storm.

Our exams approached and we knuckled-down further; the work piled on. During the exam week itself, the normal day continued unabated. We were still up at 05.45; we still had to clean the place and then drill before breakfast. The only difference was that we had no actual lessons, just a barrage of tests, to allow us to demonstrate our skills of regurgitation.

Then it was over. The papers were all marked internally over the next few days and the results for the intake of the 25 souls of P1 23 were posted piteously on the notice board for all to see on the Tuesday of the following week. We crowded round the board at lunchtime to see how we had done. Phil, Barry and Starling were first, second and third; I was ninth in the year. One of the Persians was a dismal last, which was a surprise to no one, because he had a basic difficulty in speaking English, let alone writing it. Ahead of him was an Irish Shipping lad, then Bell. Jimmy came in a respectable fourth from bottom, which was a cause for huge celebration.

The following two weeks were the last of the term and were taken up with a sailing regatta, a fire-fighting course, a medical course and a series of meetings with the personnel officers of our respective shipping companies.

The regatta was a farce: John's boat capsized, which was an almost Herculean task for a whaler; no one could believe it had happened. Whalers four and five were disqualified for cheating; going the wrong way around the outer reach buoy. Polata was in the stern of whaler number one, adjudicating and shouting through his megaphone, when it started to sink. The crew started baling like mad as the boat went deeper in the water. Then there were screams from Polata and he started thrashing about violently. We learned later that someone had pulled out the drain plug and when Polata discovered it he went wild and started to attack the prime suspect: Jimmy was the prime suspect. Our boat cruised across the finishing line with no competition left in the race, apart from the slowly recovering whaler number one, which was by then a quarter of a mile behind, wallowing sluggishly as the crew strove to bail it out. We cheered ourselves as we crossed the line, all big wide grins and whoops and play fighting. Barry was proudly at the tiller, with me, Bell, Phil and Persian Monty on the sheets.

The medical course was as gruesome as it had been built up to be. Chiefy was in charge, predictably, and he delighted in showing us a series of grisly war footage of severed limbs, exploding guts and barbequed bodies. We started off cracking ghoulish jokes but fell silent as the images intensified. It was truly awful. Phil passed out; falling off his chair and cracking his head open to allow an impromptu lesson from Chiefy as he patched him up. The afternoon was devoted to bandaging, burn dressings, shock treatment and other jollity. We learnt to inoculate humans by injecting oranges.

The following day we all took a bus to the other side of the city to spend the first of two days at the Fire Centre. These were great fun. The Fire Centre had a mock ship, together with various metal buildings which the lecturing fireman would fill with wood and rags and set on fire. There were also pans of oil that were set ablaze. We formed hose parties and marched towards the fires, one hose forming a giant spray to protect everyone from the heat and the other sending a powerful jet onto the fire itself. We experimented with different types of fire extinguishers – water, foam and chemical – took them apart, re-assembled them, set them off and then refilled them.

We all tried on the breathing apparatus. I strapped the oxygen bottle to my back and tightened the breathing mask over my face. The sound of my breathing made a harsh whistling sound through the filter. I walked up and down; I felt like an astronaut.

The fireman asked for a volunteer. We sensed a difficult or embarrassing task so everyone averted their eyes. Bell was selected; we sniggered.

The fireman said that the breathing apparatus set had a 30-minute capacity under normal breathing conditions. Bell's task was to climb up the fire tower – a 60-foot structure for high-level hose practice – and then climb down again. This was to demonstrate how exertion would cause the oxygen to be used up faster. Bell donned the gear and set off to our hoots and jeers.

"He'll take more than half an hour to get up there!"

"Keep the mask on. It's an improvement, you ugly sod!"

"Come on Bell! Run! Run!"

"Do us a favour and jump when you get to the top, Bell!"

"Yeah! Jump!"

"Jump! Jump! Jump! Jump! Jump! Jump! " We all chanted.

"Quieten down lads," said the fireman.

"I bet he passes out before he gets to the top."

Bell clambered up the ladderways and eventually got to the top of the structure, where he raised both hands above his head and did a dance. We howled. He climbed down and the fireman read the oxygen capacity off the gauge: "OK, lads: that's two-thirds empty, see?"

We peered at the gauge. "And the time he took was… 18 minutes, right?" We looked at our watches. "So, 18 divided by 30 is?" We looked at each other.

"That's about two-thirds, isn't it?" said Barry.

"Duhhhh," said Jimmy.

"No, it's not!" said the fireman. "Two-thirds would be 20 minutes. He used up the same amount in only 18 minutes."

"So, he used up an extra two minutes?" asked Phil.

"Yes."

"That's not much."

"Two minutes could save your life," said the fireman pompously. We looked unconvinced.

"That's nothing," said Jimmy, provocatively.

"It's two minutes. Two minutes could save your life." The fireman was getting annoyed.

"But he's just climbed up and down a bloody great tower," protested John, "and only used 18 minutes. What if he just stood there? The BA set would last for hours."

"It bloody-well wouldn't!" shouted the fireman. He was furious that we failed to be impressed. We all snickered. The day wore on. We slyly baited the fireman more and more. It was good sport.

I was wondering if Mr. Harman would turn up for my end-of-term personnel interview to tell me more horror stories, but in his place was an altogether milder man nearing retirement. I was unnerved and surprised that he had heard about the knife fight, which he quizzed me about in some detail. I didn't want the issue to flare up again so I affected a bovine dumbness about the whole affair, unable to remember any detail.

He read out the comments made about me from the various lecturers: Daventry thought I was a weak student who didn't try; Polata got me confused with someone else, saying that my Irish accent made me difficult to understand; Drabble of meteorology said I was seditious and a fool, which I found disappointing because I liked meteorology and thought Drabble liked me; Benson of engineering reported me as slightly above the median line, although lazy. Only Chiefy had a good word: 'A good cadet who will make a good officer.' Good old Chiefy; it sometimes pays to punch people.

I was asked who I wanted to sail with. A large proportion of cadets in P1 23 – 12 of us – were with the same London oil company. Of the remainder, three were with Irish Shipping, two were Persians and there was a scattering of general cargo lads who sailed with Bank Line, B&C, Reardon Smith and one or two others. I told him that I would be happy to go to sea with Jimmy, John and Barry. The four of us had discussed this beforehand and would all say the same; there would then be a good chance of some of us being sent to the same ship. We were looking at 18 months sea time before coming back to P3 23. Eighteen months meant two ships probably; two nine-month trips separated by six weeks leave.

I was told I would receive my orders within a fortnight and could expect to join my ship within the month.

On the last day, we collected a huge pile of work to be done over the next 18 months: six correspondence courses, eight modules in each course, all heavy gruelling stuff. We looked at it and groaned.

"That's what Sundays at sea are for, lads," Daventry told us cheerfully, as he passed out suitcase-sized packs of work. "You won't get back into the college unless it's all done."

No one could think of a smart answer. It seemed a bit unfair. We had studied ourselves into the ground for the past six months and were now going off to work ten hours a day for a minimum of six days a week and we had all this to do as well. There was a lot of muttering when Daventry left.

John (left with shaved head) and the author during the training at the School of Navigation in Plymouth.

On the last night, I planned to have a quiet time: a couple of beers in the Jamie then fish and chips on the way home, followed by an early night. My good intentions were hijacked by events, however – as were everyone else's – and I found myself being sick in an alley off Union Street at two in the morning, before starting to stagger back to the hostel. I met others on the way though, which perked me up, and then the whole of P1 23 seemed to be there. We formed a swathe, walking north through the town to our hostel, under the yellow street lamps through empty streets, arm-in-arm and singing into the night, into the next phase.

Age 17

I went back to sea for the second time a wiser person: my 17th birthday was a week later. I was not as wise as I thought I was, nor as wise as I needed to be, but I knew where to stand and what not to say. I was also beginning to know about the power of the sea… but I didn't know enough yet about people – about the dominance and power that some people held in life over others.

4

Ape

'Join SS *Vexilla* in Tabango. Flight booked to Manila 13.45 July 21 London Heathrow. Ticket and full joining instructions to follow' , the telegram said. I had never heard of Tabango. I looked in up on a map: it showed a small port in the western Philippines, in Leyte province. According to the encyclopaedia, it had a population of about 15,000 people. I telephoned the company to acknowledge and confirm and asked who I was flying out with: John, Barry and a senior cadet called Ben Holmes. We were due to leave in five days. A worm of excitement coiled and burned in me.

My two-week wait for a ship in my parents' house in south Oxfordshire had dragged. In later life I would welcome time to idle, but not then; it was a time of impatience. I went out at first light and walked and walked in the warm summer of that year, whiling away the time until the telegram arrived. I would walk the ten miles to Oxford, browse the bookshops and wander the churchyards then walk back. I went out every night. I went to pubs, usually. For the most part I went out on my own although a few times with groups from my old school but I wasn't close to any of them and they were going nowhere in my eyes. They seemed to be in my wake; fat, soft and inexperienced, learning to choke back a couple of pints of bitter before being sick; I was lean and fit and could hoover down beer non-stop. I was just about to turn 17.

One shameful night, which haunts me to this day, I walked the mile down to the town of Abingdon early in the evening and sat alone at the bar in the Red Lion, a pub just off the square, not wanting the company that was available, listening to the buzz around me, drinking lager, smoking, studying the upside-down bottles behind the bar, all dressed with their shiny optics. The place was crammed with RAF memorabilia: squadron plaques;

a propeller; photographs of groups of young men in front of aeroplanes all staring at the camera. The landlord had a huge moustache. The talk was of Northern Ireland, Qatar and a few other places where the British were fighting that year; the landlord rueing the lack of anything for the RAF to do apart from ferry in people and equipment. For no reason – apart from an overload of drink, almost certainly – I felt a wave of sadness wash over me: an RAF child who had gone to sea, marooned in a pub with a collection of old fools, bereft of plane or ship or decent company. Woe. I left when last orders was rung at 10.30 p.m. and begun the walk home. I decided to cut through my old school playing fields. And then, there it was: my school, right in front of me, with its' windows gleaming brightly in the moonlight.

I hurled the first stone at one big plate-glass swivel window in the science lab; it went right through the middle, the glass shimmered then fell out in a blanket, landing in the playground with a crash. I whooped. My next two missed, then I scored a hit on the top floor: sixth-form common room. I scrabbled in the dark for more stones. There were none. I fell over and cursed. Then I saw a club-like object sticking out from behind the grass roller – something left behind: a cricket bat; just the thing. I took the bat and whirled it round my head like a medieval flail and let fly, aiming for the group of long landing windows. I missed them by 20 yards, but the bat curved in an arc and smashed through the fan-light over the main door. I cheered. Someone yelled. I turned towards the sound. They yelled again, close. I ran. Several people shouted. They sounded closer. I could see movement in the gloom. They were closing on me. There was anger in the voices. I kicked up my heels and pelted across the sports fields, achieving speeds I had never attained during PE lessons when I was at that school. I heard the rumble of voices fall in somewhere behind. I flew through the night. I vaulted the fence at the back of the school then cut right and ran on along a lane for half a mile, before sinking down under a hedge. The voices disappeared. Goodbye old school and mutual good riddance. No reunions for me. Oh sweet sea take me back. I fell asleep and woke drenched in dew in the early hours. I crept home in shame.

We met at Heathrow on a bright summer morning, checked-in and squatted in the bar until the flight was called. Ben was aloof, being six months before the end of his cadetship. He was hoping to only do three more months as a senior cadet and then get an uplift to uncertificated third mate so he didn't want to get too pally with cadets he would probably be ordering around in the near future. There was an officer shortage at the time and it was common for senior cadets to be made up to uncert' third mate for the last few months of their time.

The BOAC flight stopped in the Bahrain to refuel and we were allowed off to stretch our legs in the airport terminal. There was no bar; the airport shops were full of junk. We boarded the plane again and landed at Manila 20 hours after leaving London.

Manila had the hugging humid feel of the Far East. I had been to school in Singapore for three years where my father had been posted to fly Twin Pioneer transport planes to the jungle strips in Malaya and Borneo; we had only left at the beginning of the previous year. Manila gave to me the familiar smell of… home.

We were met by the agent: he was a small, grimly-intense man wearing a gun, who delivered us to a fairly crummy hotel at the edge of Ermita, the dockland bar district. We arrived there in the mid-afternoon and were told that we would be picked up after breakfast the next morning and driven overland to Tabango. We subbed money from him before he left; he peeled off pesos from a massive bankroll. He didn't seem to count, just bunged us each a small wad.

Manila in the days before 1971 when General Marcos took over the country in a military coup was a spectacle to see. It was far too dangerous for the casual traveller; it was like the Wild West. Everyone – everyone – was armed with a knife, a machete, or a sword; or with a club; or with guns. The Philippines was a hard country to enter before Marcos arrived and it was hard to live in when you got there. There were more murders in the dockside Ermita district in a month than the whole of New York in a year; and this was the early 1970s when New York was being touted as Gomorrah, with its drug wars and street gangs and gun slayings dominating the news. People were fleeing New York, but they certainly weren't fleeing to the Philippines. The only people that went to Manila in those days were Merchant Navy seaman, American troops on R&R from Vietnam, and businessmen from America and Japan. The tourist industry stayed away – everyone stayed away unless they had to go.

The Filipinos are small and tough and mostly charming, but they can also be indescribably vicious and callous. Three thousand years of feuding warlords, a brutal climate, a mix of Spanish and Malay blood, and a century of US dominance interrupted by a cruel Japanese occupation, has given the people a curious cocktail of laid back *manyana* attitude and prickly pride that can suddenly detonate into violence. They can be sweet and generous, happy and laughing and sharing. The Filipinos are beautiful people and their nature makes you want to stay with them. But on the other face, a slum thug would approach a Westerner who had wandered off one of the main streets, giving him a radiant smile and an offer to show the local sights; but the next minute, the Westerner would be lying in the dirt, holding his bleeding face which had been ripped into by a razor-edged butterfly knife, his money gone, passport gone, watch gone, shoes gone... sometimes his life would be gone.

I loved Manila in the early 1970s. No one could fail to be excited by a town like that. As I walked the streets there was tightness in my stomach and a tingling in my groin and my mind was racing as if on overdrive. All the key drivers that make up our basic instincts were there: trepidation, challenge, lust. The sights and sounds and scents and ambiance were so spectacular that it was a thrill just to be in town.

The three of us – John, Barry and me (Ben stayed in the hotel) – walked wide-eyed down the main road through Ermita, dodging the 'Jeepneys' – the garishly decorated multi-customer taxis covered in lights and murals, festooned with religious statues, and built on the chassis of US Army Jeeps, as they honked and bullied their way through the tide. We were wrapped in a blanket of smells: the wet succulent air of the East, the scent of unwashed bodies packed together, strange spicy food fried in open pans in the street, garbage, sewerage, exhaust fumes, pollution, perfume, alcohol. All of it percolated together: the smell of a violent exuberant urban stew on a hot, hot day in a hot, hot part of the world.

The noise blasted us: the rapid fire *Tagalog* speech of the Filipino, high and shrill and rising further in pitch at the end of a sentence; the howls of the street hawkers; the roar and rumble of traffic; the din of a thousand drivers leaning on their horns; music thumping from bars, blaring from cars, from open windows; it was a battle of sound – to talk was to shout.

And the violence: this was truly a Barbary Coast experience. The bars, clubs, hotels and public buildings had prominent signs at the entrance, which read: 'All firearms, knives, swords and lethal weapons to be deposited at the desk before entering.' We walked about feeling naked with our lack of weaponry. A lot of the men had pistols tucked into their waistbands, in side-holsters, shoulder-holsters, some simply had one in their side pocket with the butt protruding in a casual manner. Businessmen of status had two guns, pearl-handled in shoulder-holsters, the butts jutting out from the edges of their jackets. There were guards everywhere: outside bars, outside shops, banks, office buildings, gas stations, schools, clubs – everywhere. Guards followed the people they were protecting, guards trailed behind their masters, behind their mistresses, behind school-children. When school finished there were fleets of guards with their young charges. The guards were really tooled up. They had pistols in side-holsters – some had automatics but mostly older revolvers – with a belt full of bullets, or speed-loaders clipped to their sides. Some had a secondary handgun in their belt or in a shoulder-holster. Most had pump-action Remington shotguns, which they carried over one shoulder, with a bandolier of cartridges slung around their body. They usually had a large knife strapped to their leg, and occasionally a machete on another belt, hanging low. That was the weaponry on show; there would also have been the reserves under cover: small pistols in ankle-holsters, flick-knives, butterfly knives, razors, brass knuckles, saps, telescopic metal security clubs. When a troop of guards came towards us, we moved to one side. Just as the Roman citizens had done 2,000 years before when the *Praetorian* stared a citizen in the eye and strode towards him, hand on *gladius*. Nothing changes in man's dominance of man.

During the afternoon and evening we were in the Ermita bar area, there were two stab-bings – casual affairs where the heat of the argument led one of the protagonists to abandon the power of discourse and reach for his butterfly knife. We actually saw the first one, but I didn't realise it was happening until I was told about it afterwards. I just thought it was two people scuffling in the back of the bar. It took place in a grim, noisy bar called 'Ozzies', and happened at the back, shortly after we walked in. Two Filipinos started going at each other, screeching and threatening. One punched the other, who crashed back against the wall. We cheered, eyes swivelled towards us, we looked at the floor then turned back to the bar and missed what happened next. The one who had been punched came back at the other, who stabbed him in the side: he fell to the floor moaning. The bar owner was Australian: he shouted at them, then went over holding a wooden broom handle and laid into both, beating the knifeman across the face and shoulders until he fell, then rounding on the bleeding victim and giving him several clouts across the side of the head. One of the bar-girls came up to the owner and excitedly explained her version of what had happened; the Australian turned back to the attacker and started kicking him viciously. Someone pulled off the shirt off the man who had been stabbed; he was punctured just below the ribs. He made a lot of noise but there wasn't much blood. A makeshift bandage made from his shirt was wrapped around his wound and he was given a drink. The other was thrown out into the street, still bleeding; he lay prone in the dirt, people walking over him. Ozzie, the Australian bar owner, told me this after the event.

The second stabbing was more a slash-and-stab affair and happened across the street from us. A Scottish sailor recounted what happened: a big fat man and a small skinny man were waving their arms and leaning into each other's faces. The size difference made it comical until the small man pulled out his knife and whipped it across the big man's cheek, opening his face from ear to mouth, then jumped on him and clung on like a monkey, stabbing away at his back furiously. A group of guards standing nearby piled in to cause a scrum that burst off the boardwalk onto the street in a clamber of noise. The Scot decided that this was not a place to rubberneck and came across the street to our bar.

Later, after the sun went down, we heard sporadic gunfire, usually two or three shots at a time followed by silence; the event being presumably settled.

A typical bar in Manila at that time was cool and loud, with a long bar, neon-lit behind, two or three people serving, and a row of faux leather stools lining the front. The room itself was unlit and got darker the further back from the bar, until, at the extremities, the people were just gloomy shadows. There was a stage at one end of the bar, on which the girls would strut around and dance, usually badly, to booming Western music. Mainly they wore bikinis, or just a few odd spots of clothing. Some took their dancing seriously and strived to produce steps and moves that were intended to be meaningful and erotic, their faces gripped in concentration. Others took the whole thing as a grand game, charging around the stage, taking their tops off and waving them around, yelling at the crowd, whipping us all up. Sometimes the stage would butt onto the bar and the girls would prance along the bar top, kicking over ashtrays and drinks if you weren't careful. The clientele were mostly seaman, some US soldiers, and a few odd travellers, who all whooped and howled and drank cold beer as fast as the glasses could be refilled. Strutting around the bar-floor were the girls who were in between bouts on the stage, or who didn't perform, striking up talk with the customers, badgering for drinks – which were overpriced, but not by that much. They danced with the customers, laughing and flattering and clinging on. It wasn't until the end of the night that someone told me they were all prostitutes. Happy prostitutes though, it seemed. We got back to our hotel in the early hours, flushed with the experience and the beer.

The next morning we left after breakfast for the long drive across-country to Tabango. The agent drove us in an old, massive American limousine. The car was too ancient for air-conditioning so we had the windows open throughout the seven-hour trip. I had my arm on the window edge for most of it, and when we arrived it was burnt crimson. We were mostly silent, wrapped in our hangovers; we watched the verdant green country go by, shimmering in the heat. We caught the ferry over to Leyte in the late afternoon and arrived at the *Vexilla* half an hour afterwards.

The *Vexilla* was the same class as my first ship, the *Valvata*, and similar in most ways, except that she was much older, more battered, and had a Hong Kong Chinese crew. She lay

The SS Vexilla *at sea (www.fotoflite.com).*

alongside a rickety wooden jetty, pumping black oil ashore through big rubber hoses into a single storage tank. There was little movement, either on or off the ship; just a few small groups of men sitting in the shade, dozing. We wondered about the chief mate: the most important person in our microcosm life.

Ben knew who was arriving to take over as chief mate: "It's LJ!" he said.

"Do you know him?" asked Barry.

"Everyone knows LJ," relayed Ben.

"What's he like?" asked John.

"LJ Wilson. Lionel, I think his first name is: bit of a bastard, as I understand, but then I've never sailed with him," was the reply.

"So tell us what you do know about him then, Ben," I urged.

"Well, he's tough. He's a bit mad. He's been with the company since he was an ape. He thinks he's funny. He likes cadets, the more the merrier. He'll work you like dogs, though."

"Not you?" said John.

"Nope. I'm senior cadet. I'll be on the bridge while you poor sods are down on deck covered in crap."

"Happy days," said Barry.

We climbed the gangway with our bags. The chief mate, who was on the *Vexilla* when we arrived, was a small, cynical man who mostly ignored us. He was going to be leaving at the next port, to be replaced by LJ. We repaid the compliment and mostly ignored him back – unless he snapped an order, in which case we hopped to it.

Chinese crew ships were a different phenomenon to white crews. Most officers preferred Chinese crews because they gave less trouble, didn't fight among themselves much, were generally more subservient, and usually did what they were told. This contrasted with many white crews, who got drunk whenever possible, argued back, were violent and didn't miss an opportunity to do-down an officer. Most Chinese crews at that time were from Hong Kong and seemed to provide a better environment for the cadet, because they were more polite and had no particular desire to mock or demonstrate that they knew more. They treated the junior cadets with a sort of avuncular glee and were respectful towards the more senior ones.

A few of the crew leant on the rails by the gangway, dressed in blue work clothes and caps. They watched us board, smiling broadly. A couple had gold teeth. None were particularly young. One came up to us and spoke a kind of hurried pidgin English:

"You cadet? You cadet? Ahh, me AB. Me Chung. You cabin that way," gesturing towards midships. He rambled on: "This good ship. Number one. Plenty good chow. Good chief mate. Number one. Good captain. Number one. Good ship. Yeah. Number one."

We smiled brightly. I wondered if there was something wrong with him.

Ben responded, twisting his features and elongating his features as he spoke: "Good ship, eh? Number one, eh? Where-for next port? Hong Kong? Singapore? Which man bosun? How long on ship now? One year? Two year?"

"One year now. One year. We go Singapore now. After leave here. Singapore number one. Number one place."

"Yeah. Singapore good. Singapore number one. Which man bosun?"

"Chin Yee bosun."

"Chin Yee? Ohh. Good man. Number one. I know Chin Yee. Sail with him long time."

"You know Chin Yee?"

"I know Chin Yee long time. Good man. Number one."

"Ahh. Good. Good number one."

We looked on in mild bafflement as Ben and Chung had their garbled exchange. No doubt we would master the language in due course.

We crunched across the rusting deck and along the flying bridge to our home for the next nine months. A happy looking steward in a vest and blue-chequered trousers met us at the entrance and guided us to the first cabin on the starboard side: two single bunks, a sink, two lockers, two portholes. Barry threw his bags on one bunk, John claimed the other. They grinned at me. I grimaced, I was stuck with Ben. Ben grimaced; he was stuck with me. The steward took us to the next cabin, which faced forward. It was identical to Barry and John's, although had a better view. I slung my globetrotter suitcase on one of the bunks; Ben went to do the same on the other, but the steward touched his arm and said:

"You senior cadet. You go fourth officer cabin." He gestured for Ben to follow.

Ben looked at me. I looked at Ben. We both smiled. Neither of us had been looking forward to sharing with the other. None of us knew the ship would have an extra officer's cabin. I went to share my good news with John and Barry; they looked stricken with jealousy at me having my own cabin for the trip. I tried to look blasé about the whole thing and went to unpack.

LJ Wilson was a pompous man, although a good chief officer. He was short and stout with many mismatched bits. He had a large dome of a head, pallid and almost bald, with wisps of blonde hair clinging to the edges. He had minute ears and bug eyes. His feet were tiny, almost dainty, although his hands were huge, like great hams.

Shortly after he came onboard, he gave us a mighty lecture in the ship's office for about an hour. He was very pleased with having us onboard; things probably couldn't be better for him. Ben would take his watch, the four-to-eight, which meant he could nominally supervise while getting on with other things. He now had three apes who weren't first-trippers. One would go on each watch in port to do all the ullages and tank changes and there would be three available to take the temperatures at sea, leaving the Chinese crew to be more gainfully employed. We would also take a watch on the bridge when approaching and leaving port, reverting to day-work when we were back at sea, where we would labour on deck. Saturday would be a study day if there were no important jobs to be done. Sundays mornings at sea was inspection time, which meant that we had to spend half the morning scrubbing out our cabins. Sunday afternoon was free, unless Saturday had been a work day due to overload, in which case we would study on Sunday. He didn't mind if we swapped watches in port so that the others could go ashore, although he didn't expect to see anyone working more that 24 hours in one stretch unless things became really busy. It all sounded pretty fair to us.

I was put on the twelve-to-four watch with the second mate, who I found to be a loud and friendly man. He seemed quite old to me, perhaps 26 or 27. On the first watch he told me to call him by his first name, Joey, unless the mate was in earshot, in which case I should call him 'Second Mate' or 'sir'. I liked Joey, at first. He told entertaining tales of his time in general cargo ships; of all the weeks he had in port; of all the places he had been to; of all the adventures he had had; of the hundreds of women he had slept with. As time went by though, I grew to distrust him and then dislike him. One minute he would be happily chatting away, then the next he would suddenly stop and start screaming at me, calling me an imbecile and ordering me to go and do some foul task. Later he would sidle up and say: "Sorry, Simon; the mate was watching. You know how it is." Often the mate or the captain was watching, but I still didn't see any call for such a change. Sometimes there was no one watching and he just made believe there was. We would rotate the watches in each port and I exchanged views on Joey with Barry and John: we all agreed he was a poor officer. LJ didn't like him either and occasionally gave him a public roasting, which made us smirk.

If you are going to be an ape, then the Far East on a Chinese crew ship is not a bad place to be. The *Vexilla* was a happy ship and our run was as far north as Japan, where we called at Yokohama, Kobe and Osaka, and as far south as Jakarta in Java. In between we called at Pusan in South Korea, several ports in the Philippines, Hong Kong, Sarawak and Singapore. Singapore was our home port and where we loaded for each voyage, dropping our cargo at the various places we then visited. Occasionally we would have a run across to India and Sri Lanka, calling into Bombay, Madras, Calcutta and Colombo. Once we went right across the Indian Ocean to southern Africa and docked in Lourenco Marques in Mozambique and Durban in South Africa.

The weather turned wickedly cold in Japan and Korea in the winter months, though for most of the time it was warm and balmy and we wore tropical white uniforms. On deck when we were working, we just wore shorts and were burnt as brown as nuts after a few weeks.

We worked alongside the Chinese crew; chipping, painting, cleaning, oiling, mending. Many chief mates kept their apes ground down at all the unpleasant jobs without stopping – 'To toughen their character', they said, but LJ tried to vary our work so as to try and make reasonable sailors out of us.

We spent a lot of time with the 'Casab', who was the Chinese version of the British deck storekeeper, in charge of wires and ropes, paints and all the ships tools and deck stores. Casab honed the splicing skills we had learned from Chiefy Rozer; he had us cut out the rope burns and then short-splice the big polypropylene mooring ropes. We spliced eyes in the fire-wires and rigged work stages to hang down the side of the accommodation for painting parties to sit on. We sewed canvas sleeves round the cork lifebuoys, then painted them in red and white quarters and stencilled the ship's name on in black letters. He had us hauled up the masts on small bosun's chairs, for us to then slide down the wire stays, held on by a shackle, greasing them with white lead as we descended. No safety harness. I was never a great one for heights and I enjoyed the experience less than Barry and John, who hooted at each other as we swayed and rocked on our 2-foot-by-9-inch platforms, 100 feet above the South China Sea, the *Vexilla* lolling slowly side to side in the deep swell.

Sometimes we were given to the third mate, who would work us in his areas of responsibility. The third mate was responsible for all the safety equipment on the ship: lifeboats, breathing apparatus, fire hoses, fire extinguishers and all the related gear. We sanded and oiled the oars, scrubbed out and painted the boats, changed the fresh water, aired the sails and rigging and packed everything away as it should be. We surreptitiously stole spare barley sugar from the lifeboat stores and gorged ourselves until we felt sick.

All the time, we became stronger, fitter, browner, quicker, more skilled at the work we did.

When the ship was loaded, we took the temperatures on a daily basis. The weather was occasionally blowing, causing the sea to break and rush across the deck, at which time we had to run and dodge as we fled for safety to the higher points. As the weeks wore on, the three of us could do all 30 tanks in 30 minutes, dropping thermometers down six tanks at a time, then going back to read them one-by-one. We would memorise all the readings.

We were also introduced to a new job; one that was particularly ghastly. Starling and I had been spared this task on the *Valvata*, although I remember the crew having to undertake it, to much moaning and groaning. I don't know why the *Valvata's* mate hadn't included us at the time; perhaps he thought we were too young and inexperienced and the work was too hard and dangerous. The job was tank cleaning.

As a tanker pumps out its oil, it gets higher and higher in the water. Eventually it would reach a point of instability and run the risk of toppling over. To prevent this happening, some of the tanks are filled up with sea water as ballast, to put weight back into the hull. When the tanker is empty of oil, it has about a quarter of its tanks filled up with sea water ballast. This water is filthy because it mixes with the oil residue and sludge that is still in the tank.

Tank cleaning in those days came in three stages. First was the steam clean: boiling hot water was blasted into the empty tank through big heavy hoses, six inches in diameter, on the end of which were huge brass spinning nozzles, which sprayed the boiling water at high pressure onto the tank walls. We had to lug these scalding hot hoses across the deck, lower them down, four to a tank, leave them for 30 minutes or so, then lower them further, wait 30 minutes, lower them further, and so on. When a tank was declared done, we heaved everything up on deck and moved the whole apparatus to the next tank to start again. The water blasted in from the hoses was pumped over the side as it collected in the bottom of the tank, whereas the thick oily residue, which floated on the surface because it was lighter than the water, was pumped to the slop tank, a permanently filthy place that was pumped ashore when we reached Singapore.

The next stage was the venting. Big air-driven fans were attached to manhole covers to suck up the poisonous air from the tank. We turned off the fans at regular intervals and tested the air with an oxygen monitor that we lowered into the depths, waiting until the readings indicated the tank was fit and safe for human descent.

Then came the worst part. Clad in boiler suits, hard hats and wearing rubber gloves, we descended into the hell of the tank, all the way to the bottom, where, in between the frames, there was a foot of thick black hot oil sludge. We used scoops to shovel it into buckets that were lowered from the deck; when the buckets were full we yanked on the rope. The bucket was pulled aloft, its contents emptied into the slop tank, and then lowered again for us to refill.

Tank digging was as bad as any Roman slave pit could have been. The heat was unbearable: we were grilled like steaks by the hot, hot steel of the tank walls, which had been blasted for hours by near boiling water. We skidded and slipped over constantly on the treacherous muck until we were as black as the sludge itself. Every pore and orifice became clogged with oil sludge. The boiler suit was scant protection against the filth; we might just as well have gone in naked. The only reason we wore the suits was to minimise burns from the red hot steel works. Every now and again, a pocket of gas would rise up from the sludge and we would reel with dizziness; I had visions of collapsing and expiring in the mire. If there were too many collapses, one of the CPOs (either the bosun or Casab was always with the digging party) would send us all to the surface while the tank was given another venting.

Once the tanks were clean, we had a respite while the ballast was changed. Fresh seawater was pumped into several clean tanks, which allowed the dirty ballast from the uncleaned tanks to be discharged. With limited regard for the environment in those days, this discharging was done direct into the sea, on the basis that the oil would have floated to the surface and therefore most of the tank would be filled with clean water. This seemed partially true to me. One of the cadets was posted on the poop deck to call out when the discharge turned from dirty water to oil, at which point the oily residue was diverted to the slop tank. Once the dirty ballast tanks were empty, we had a new set of tanks to clean.

The cleaning process for a 30-tank ship like the *Vexilla* took four days and nights, weather permitting. It was the vilest job I ever had to undertake by a country mile. I would have gladly cleaned out 100 German toilets rather than suffer a full tank clean on a black-oil tanker. It my time on the *Vexilla*, we cleaned all the tanks on six occasions.

While the sun shined at sea, we always worked outside; the staple jobs being chipping and painting, holystoning, cleaning up oil patches and carrying out our temperature duties. We could usually bank on a skilled day on ropes and wires every couple of weeks, together with the dreaded tank-cleaning about once a month. When the weather turned and the sea was up, we were either given a storeroom to paint out, a water tank to scrape and paint, or were given to the Casab as tools for him to work.

The day started with a call from Ben at 06.30. He was sent down from the bridge by LJ. We washed, dressed in uniform, and went along for breakfast at 07.00. Breakfast was always big: juice, kippers, kedgeree, bacon and eggs, toast and tea or coffee. We needed our fuel. The Chinese steward was always pleased to see the three of us and fussed around to make sure we had what we wanted. At 07.40, we took it in turns each day to go up to the bridge and receive our day's work from LJ. The bosun was just leaving when we arrived. Sometimes LJ would just say: "Turn to with the bosun," and that would be that: off we would go to work with the crew. Mostly though, our orders were a little more specific, our work requirement a little more precise than that of the crew, so we could be held to account. LJ told us, repeatedly, repeatedly *ad nauseum*: "You have to be able to do every job that a ship has to offer; you have to understand how to do it; you have to understand why it has to be done; you have to have done it; you have to have done it better than any crew-member would bother to do it. This is why I give you all these jobs. It's for your own good."

Sometimes, stuck in the dark depths of a filthy tank, knee-deep in oil sludge, blinded by muck and scrabbling in the slimy residue for our boots that had been sucked off into the mire, we struggled to believe it was all for our own good. But that didn't stop LJ from reciting his daily mantra.

We turned to at 08.00, not a minute later. If LJ knew we were late, then punishment swiftly followed: usually a banning from the bar, replaced by an hour's extra study time after dinner. LJ always, always knew if we were late, no matter where we were working. 10.00 was morning 'smoko'. Barry and I smoked, John didn't. We either sat on the floor of one of our cabins or squatted on the poop deck with the Chinese. Outside smoking was only allowed if you were aft of the funnel. Smoko lasted 20 minutes: just time for coffee and tinned milk, and one cigarette.

Lunch was from midday until 13.00. We were only allowed to have 'dirty chow' if the day's work was one of the horrors: tank cleaning was a valid excuse. 'Dirty chow' entailed cleaning our hands and then getting a plate of food from the galley and eating it on the poop deck. Dirty chows were only allowed with the express permission of LJ, which was very rare. Normally, we had to shower and change into uniform and eat in the dining saloon. If we rushed, we could squeeze in a very quick beer in the bar beforehand. Officers had fridges and were allowed to keep beer in their cabins. Cadets didn't have a fridge and were only allowed to drink in the bar; but sometimes we secreted cans in the cold air blowers. Lunch was three courses followed by coffee but we never had time for coffee as we had to be back on deck for 13.00.

The afternoon work was from 13.00 until 17.00 with a 20-minute smoko at three o'clock. We finished at 17.00 and then all three of us had to report back to LJ and have a 20-minute meeting to explain and discuss everything we had done that day. If there was anything he was unhappy about, we had to go and repair the problem. We could generally bank on him being dissatisfied on one day in every three. Most of our days ended by 17.30, although sometimes we were still at it an hour after that.

Once, John had to work until 20.00, for smirking when LJ spilled his coffee down his freshly-laundered tropical whites during the after-work debrief. Barry and I struggled to keep serious looks on our faces while John was roasted by LJ's fiery blast before being sent to sugee the deck-head on the poop. Barry and I cleaned up then went down kept him company, sitting on the bits, watching, smoking and drinking cold Tiger beer we had brought from the bar, making fun of his sugee work as he scrubbed his detergent mix in vain over the years of accumulated grime on the deck-head. We offered helpful advice and John got angrier and angrier, to our delight. John's meal was put in the pantry hot-press, a sort of warming oven, although Barry went in after we had dinner and ate John's chicken portion, leaving a gnawed bone sitting in a mound of gravy and vegetables. John's plaintive howl when he finally got his dinner, dog-tired after his 12 hours of labour, was both heart-rending and hilarious.

In port, everything changed: a different sort of work, more frantic, driven by the lash of commerce. Arrival took place early in the morning, more often than not at first light, between 06.00 and 07.00. Like most tankers, we were only in port for two reasons: loading or discharging. Loading meant connecting huge rubber hoses to the deck manifolds, with the shore pumps then blasting in the oil to fill up our tanks. Discharging meant the ships pumps sending the oil the other way, to fill up the shore tanks.

Us three cadets were each put one on of the three watches: twelve to four, four to eight or eight to twelve. The first job we had, once we were moored to the quay, was to go round and drive large wooden bungs into the deck scuppers. That way, if there was an overflow, the oil would stay on the ship, rather than run off and pollute the harbour.

The cadet who caught first watch would then go round with the duty mate and set up the pipes. The whole ship, above deck and below, was a mass of inter-connecting pipes, so that each tank can be set up to receive or send oil. A loading plan was drawn up by the chief mate and then the cadet and duty sailor, under the guidance of the watch officer, had to wind open all the valves, using big hand wheels 3 foot across, 30 turns apiece. The first time I had to do this, I simply couldn't finish opening the valves – they were too stiff and I wasn't strong enough. It seemed to me that I would need to turn into some sort of Goliath before I would be able to turn one of the wheels fully up the spindle. Three months into the trip I could open and close them all day.

When a tank was filling to the top, we performed a ritual called 'topping off'. This was a crucial stage that couldn't be allowed to go wrong. Topping-off sticks were 6-foot wooden staffs, marked in feet and inches, with a cross piece that came to rest on the lip of the ullage pipe. The stick would be lowered into the tank and lifted up so as to read the reducing space left in the tank. The ullage pipe was 12 inches high, which meant that the tank had to be closed off when the reading was about 15 inches. The duty officer would scream, "Now! Now!", and we would spin the great wheels shut as fast as we could. At the same time, the watch sailor would work on another wheel to open the new tank to be filled. The perils of getting this wrong were catastrophic: if the tank was not closed off in time, a geyser of oil would erupt out of the ullage pipe, blackening everything in sight, raining hot oil down onto those on the deck. If oil was hot enough to pump it was hot enough to hurt when it rained on you. If oil escaped in the harbour, the ship would be fined and the chief officer could sometimes be arrested. Topping off times were always tense.

In between these high drama moments, the cadets' slog during port time was to take the ullages, keep the moorings at the right tightness, watch the gangway, and carry out all the generalities of loading/discharging work. When discharging, we were sometimes only in port for a few hours, pumping out three or four tanks to keep some small town going, before setting off further up the coast. In these cases, the combined clearance time in and out of port was often longer than the actual pumping time.

Although the watches were four hours on, eight hours off, we would often agree in port that one of us would do a double watch to give a decent break to another cadet. When it was turn for a watch-off, I would finish the four-to-eight at 20.00 and go ashore in the knowledge that John or Barry would carry my four-to-eight in the morning stint, giving me a full 20 hours off. You can do a lot in a 20-hour shore run: be ashore by 20.30, drunk by 22.00, in an array of seedy dives until 02.00 in the morning, back by 03.00, sleep until 08.00, shake off the hangover by 10.00, then ashore again for leg-stretching, sight-seeing and souvenir-seeking, back by 15.30, back on watch by 16.00.

A typical stay in port was between 24 and 36 hours: by the time we sailed away, all three of us were shattered – the ones who made it ashore had overindulged and the one who had stayed aboard had overworked. We felt ourselves slump on the rails as the ship slid out of port, we were heavy limbed and our minds were dulled. All we wanted to do was sleep the heavy sleep of old ill men. I learnt to sleep standing up, wedged against the bulkhead, my mind switched into the dead zone, my body shut down, a small part of my mind on standby to react to a shouted order.

LJ's rule was that if the ship left port and we were stood down before 02.00 then we turned to at 08.00 for a full day's work the next day. If we were stood down between 02.00 and 06.00, we turned to after the morning smoko at 10.20. If we were stood down after 06.00, then he felt we were up and working anyway, so we had to just carry on with the day's work. This was hard graft by any standard. As I became stronger, I gained the strength and stamina to carry on like this, but importantly, my youth gave me the capacity to recover quickly, which was what really counted.

We got on well, the three of us, considering the confinement, our low station in life and the pressure-cooker work schedule. We argued a lot, plotted against each other from time to time, and were quick to laugh cruelly at any misfortunes suffered by either of the other two. Although we would goad each other, we rarely fought: I did have one nasty scrap with Barry on a Sunday afternoon over some petty joke that got out of hand. Barry must have been in a sensitive mood because he had lunged at me in anger, in response to my jibes. We scrabbled and grappled and punched at each other, the tempo and tempers rising. I knew that when the red mist came down on Barry, he became vicious and dangerous, and so I ended up holding him in a head-lock, fearful to let go in case he went berserk, perhaps even reaching for a weapon of some sort to try and do me serious damage. He was spitting mad and I thought it best to try and choke him into unconsciousness. I squeezed and twisted and yanked on his neck for all I was worth but it only made him rage and twist even harder. We were in my cabin and we thrashed around, wrecking the place. John sat on the spare bunk, grinning and enjoying the show, egging us on. After several minutes I couldn't hold on any more and I flung Barry to the deck and tried to kick him to keep him down. I missed and slipped and crashed down next to him. We grabbed onto each other and rolled out into the alleyway, wrapped together as if in some cartoon sketch; then Barry's grip went slack. I thought I had killed him. I sat up. He was lying there, not dead but shaking with laughter. John was in the doorway of my cabin, bent over and holding his stomach, he slid to the floor too. I felt the mad world we lived in was going madder, I lay back and we all laughed out loud together. The Chinese steward walked past, stepping over us, looking puzzled.

What we had between us was a bond; an unbreakable bond, camaraderie. A mutual feeling that would hold for life: if we met in 40 years time it would still be there and we would know each other again in an instant. Most people never experience camaraderie. Many try to produce it or reproduce it in clubs and groups and societies, but it is generally too contrived to work. A rugby club brings men together and instils a certain amount of *espirit de corps*, a City drinking den excludes those who do not operate within the pressures of the business world, a boozing and fishing weekend is fine too, and a club where men meet every week to talk and drink and agree to do foolish things for charity is admirable. But true camaraderie is given birth out of young men living together and growing up in extreme environment. John and Barry and I worked together, four times as hard as most people in conditions that would never be tolerated in mainstream society. We lived together, ate together, we worked when we were ill because we were not allowed to be sick, we played together, explored strange and dangerous parts of the world together, got drunk together, rescued each other, fought for each other, spent our money on each other, used each other's possessions, wore each other's clothes. Our camaraderie took shape out of young men coming of age and forming their morals and views, and then taking their stand in the world. We stuck together because we had to. We couldn't go home at night: we were home.

We were sitting on the deck of the fo'c'sle (forecastle) one afternoon. The three of us had been greasing the dogs – the swivel handles that locked the watertight doors – for all the fo'c'sle doors. We had to take off the dogs that were jammed, which was most of them, soak the movements in kerosene, scrub the shafts with a wire brush, grease everything, then put it back in place. It wasn't a bad job, amongst the jobs we were given, and we could take all the dogs that had to be repaired up on deck and sit in the sun in our shorts while we worked.

When afternoon smoko arrived, it seemed too nice to go back to the accommodation block to make coffee, so we stayed in the sun and leant over the bulwarks and watched the dolphins riding the bow wave – dozens of them, aquaplaning ahead of us. A fat-bellied aeroplane went past, low overhead, RAF roundels on the wings. I had been living with my family in Singapore 18 months beforehand, so I vaguely knew about the RAF flying patterns in that part of the world. I suspected it was heading for Singapore out of Kuching, my father's old Transport Command squadron. I watched it wheel towards the southwest, climbing into the blue sky, heading towards the gathering thunderheads. I felt a sharp twist of nostalgia for those simpler schooldays when I lived with all the other RAF children and could run to the warmth and comfort of my parents when anything happened. Could my life now be any more different?

We were in ballast on the run in to Singapore, going through the Api Passage off Kuching, due to be in Singapore late the next day. 'Singapore' meant Pulau Bukom, the island a mile to the south, crowded with oil tanks and pipes, a dozen tankers tied up bow to stern, with many more anchored in the roads, waiting for a berth. With luck, we would catch another cadet from P1 23.

"I think Des is on the *Halia* and that's on the Singapore Hong Kong run," I said. "I wonder if she's in."

"Yeah, could be," replied John. "Phil's on the *Hadra*: she's around this part of the world too."

"Who's working Singapore?" Said Barry.

There was silence while we worked it out, manoeuvring for position.

"I did Manila," I ventured. Manila was the last place where there was time for a run ashore.

"That hardly counts," said John. "We were only there ten hours."

"Of course it counts." I replied. "I did the whole ten hours and the two of you went to town."

"Singapore's different," said Barry. "We'll be there a couple of days and everyone wants to get ashore in Singapore."

I bristled, sensing a conspiracy. "Just hold on. Are you two expecting me to flog myself to death in Singapore so the two of you can swan off up town? Forget it! I've just done Manila – ten hours or not, I did it and it's my turn for a run ashore."

The dolphins veered away from the bow and started leaping out of the water on either side of the ship. There was a dozen or more, jumping in unison. We watched them without speaking for a bit. Barry said: "Let's draw straws."

"You two straw straws," I replied huffily. "It's my turn to get off the ship and go out on the town."

"Come on Simon," pleaded John. "Everyone wants to get off in Singapore. Let's just work out a split we're all happy with."

The bosun shouted from the foredeck that smoko had ended and we squatted down to continue working on the dogs, bickering as we did so. We washed and scrubbed away, laying the clean dogs in a line on the deck, with all the component parts by each one, ready for greasing up.

"Look at that," said John suddenly. "What's going on?" We looked aft: great gouts of thick black smoke were belching out of the funnel.

"We're slowing," said Barry.

We stood up and looked over the side. The *Vexilla* was reducing speed, slowing right down. The vibration had ceased, the wire stays no longer wobbled back and forth, the white of the bow wave disappeared and the *Vexilla* slowed, and slowed, and stopped. The ship lay in the gently rolling swell and wallowed. The black smoke stopped. Everything was very quiet. There were no alarms. We had obviously broken down. No point in going aft to find out what was happening; we would only get into trouble with LJ. We squatted back down and carried on with our dog work.

"Wouldn't it be great if the engines are knackered and we have to go into dock," said John.

Barry and I laughed and agreed.

"Some problem with the bearings apparently." Said LJ. We were standing on the bridge wing with him at the end of the day. The ship was still stopped, rolling gently in the western swell.

"So what happens now, sir?" I asked.

"The chief engineer is down there with his team. He'll jury rig something and we'll crawl into Singapore."

"And… then what?" inquired Barry.

"I expect we'll have to go into dock."

"Dry dock, sir. In Jurong?" John asked. Jurong was round in the north end of the island, away from the town

"Probably," replied LJ. "Either that or the floating dock in Keppel Harbour. It depends on what needs doing. It looks like a big job."

"Er, how long are we likely to be in dock, Sir" I asked, as casually as I could.

"If it's Keppel, then probably only three or four days. If we have to go into dry dock in Jurong then we'll end up blasting the hull while we're in so it will probably be a week or more." We eyed each other in disbelief. It seemed we were facing a choice of three or four days in port with no cargo work or a week or more in port with no cargo work. "Some fun for you boys by the look of things," said LJ, with a twinkle in his eye. "This sort of thing doesn't happen often. Better make the most of it."

It was Keppel. Right on the Singapore waterfront. Four days.

The ship limped into Singapore at walking pace three days later and spent two days in the roads off Pulau Bukom Island, being tank-cleaned by a shore gang. It was far more thorough cleaning job than we would normally do at sea, because every suggestion of gas had to be vented from the tanks. A few sailors expiring from the fumes or a minor explosion at sea was one thing, but for this to happen in the dockyard was quite unthinkable.

The three of us spent the time on inspection rota with the deck officers, recording any deficiency that would now be dealt with while we were in dock. The company superintendent flew in; he stayed in the ship's hospital. Although the super spent most of his time in the engine room looking at the damaged bearings, we toured the decks with him for half a day while he inspected all parts. He was an old school ex-master who treated us like serfs, snapping his fingers and barking commands; even LJ seemed faintly embarrassed at his imperiousness. We plotted a minor accident – although the opportunity never arose.

Once the ship was certified clean and safe to dockyard standards, we were towed into Keppel. The *Vexilla* was manoeuvred and carefully housed in the floating dock. Swarms of workers poured onboard to rebuild the broken engine parts, shore power was connected, and we were all moved off to stay in Connell House, the seaman's mission in Anson Road, while the ship's electrics, sanitation and air-conditioning were also taken apart. The air-conditioning was an afterthought to the ship and had been progressively added over the years. Our cabins enjoyed an almost un-noticeable trickle of coolish air through the vent – it was cooler to keep our portholes open, when weather allowed.

Our working day during the dock period called for us to arrive at the ship by 08.30 and stay on the coattails of the third officer, on call from LJ if anything arose. We spent most of the time watching the dock workers, and we ran minor errands from time to time. Local dock labour rules prevented us from being able to carry out any real work, to our delight and LJ's irritation. We went back to the dock canteen for lunch and ate *nasi goreng* with the Chinese workers. We finished at 17.00 and walked the half-mile back to Connell House. We were actually having a normal life. We were even given a day off each to do with what we pleased.

The Connell House seaman's mission in Anson Road was a step back in time. It was a big grey-white colonial building, built not long after Sir Stamford Raffles founded Singapore in 1819. The building had pillars and high ceilings, fans and quiet polished corridors, green and gentle gardens. It was pulled down in the 1980s, but back then it was a two-storied, galleried, regency-style, built in a rectangle around inner courtyard gardens, with the balconies for the better, upper-floor rooms overlooking the gardens and the ones for the lesser rooms overlooking the streets. The east-wing rooms were for officers; the west-side was for crew.

The bar ran along one of the lower-middle sections, cool and dark with white walls, shuttered windows, big plants and dark wood. It was an oasis of continuity, always the same sounds: a low murmur of conversation; the clink of ice and glass; the flat whoosh of air from the big fans. It was a common bar for officers and crew, although decorum dictated they gathered at different ends. The better end was the one with the bar-top fan. Adjoining the bar was the dining saloon with its polished floors, rattan furniture, big wooden ceiling fans and ghost-quiet waiters.

Barry, John and I had a room each. Mine overlooked the mad-dog noise of the market, which howled up at me when I opened the louvered wooden doors to stand on the balcony, a thousand market odors, traffic fumes and the stink of people blasted upwards, overlaid with the pervading sickly-sweet stench of the durian fruit, which was being pushed by hawkers.

Down the corridor were the communal washrooms, tiled and echoing. The urinal was a long porcelain tank, and in the communal showers I was flayed with cold water which felt as heavy as if it were plunging from a waterfall. The largest population of the mission was British sailors, followed by other Europeans – predominantly Germans, Dutch, Scandinavians and French. There were a few Russians and Indians. I stayed in Connell House several times and always enjoyed it.

On my day off, I took a bus to Katong, where I had lived 18 months previously. There wasn't much change; this was before Singapore was developed into a megopolis. Then, it was a busy bustling exciting place, chock-full of all the races of the East and beyond: the Chinese majority were mostly from south China although there was a good representation from the northeast. They existed side-by-side with Malays, Tamils, Sikhs, Filipinos, Europeans and several-dozen other races around the edges. Singapore was a place of noise and movement and wet clamming heat that erupted into rain in the afternoon when the thunderheads rolled in from Sumatra.

Although there was no great change, I noticed the small things as the bus rolled along the East Coast Road through Katong district: the filthy shop fronts in Joo Chiat Road were being spruced up, the streets looked a bit cleaner, the open drains had less rubbish in, the Palace cinema had changed from English films to Chinese, the Grand Hotel had closed. I left the bus and walked to my old house, taking the short cut between small noisy houses that backed onto each other, tightrope-walking along the edge of the open monsoon drains, as I did as a boy. A boy? When did I become a man?

My house looked the same. I felt I could have walked in and sat down and nothing would have moved on. I could feel my father's presence in baggy shorts and a checked shirt, wearing brown plastic sandals, smoking and drinking a glass of Tiger beer; my mother in a blue print dress, my brother Peter on the balcony, firing his air rifle at the goldfish in the neighbour's pond next door. A heavy Malay came out onto the front veranda and looked at me curiously as I stood staring through the barbed-wire-topped fence; I smiled and moved on. Important to move on.

I caught a bus back to town, disembarked near Rochor Canal, and spent the afternoon wandering the Thieves Market, where I bought an old British Army penknife. Later, I walked across town to Orchard Road and went ten-pin bowling by myself, before heading back up to Connell House mission to shower and sink cold beer in the bar, in preparation for the night.

5

Drink

There is no getting away from the fact that drink played a big part in life at sea. It was the glue that held us all together. Over the years, I've been lectured about the ills of drinking so many times: by religious teetotallers, by healthy abstainers, by wise people, by stupid people, by fools and blowhards, by ex-drunks, by people who were drunk at the time they were lecturing me, and by people or who were in between sober and drunk. I know the bad things drinking can bring in its wake and I know the problems it can cause. I have seen people lose their way, lose their money, lose their ship, lose their friends, lose their job, lose their wives, lose their minds, lose their liberty, lose their lives.

We all knew this – those of us who drank, which was most of us – and mostly we laughed about it. We laughed because the other side of the coin was so much sweeter. It was the bonding of our lives, it bound us together; it was our substitute for everything that we couldn't get because of what we did. We had no home to go to for six or eight or 16 or 18 months. The hive of our home was a small cabin, 9-foot by 6-foot with a glass porthole and a hard bunk. The bunk was to sleep in, the cabin was to hide in, the ship was to live in – the ship was our home. To cope with this place – this place where we worked like mules, like slaves – we drank and this rounded the edges of our lives and made everything that much more tolerable. A grim day, dirty and hard and blazing hot, beasted by the mate, screamed at by the captain, bullied by the bosun, jeered at by the crew, humiliated by the officers, became an altogether different place when we were on the outside of half a dozen Tiger beers. It became not just tolerable but... a place where we wanted to be, a place of deep and binding camaraderie.

When we sat in the bar drinking until early into the morning, those of us left who were left at the end – me aged 17, the captain at 58, Sparks at 35 – we would be bonded, not as friends, not as 'ignore-the-rank' buddies; we were just bonded beyond the barriers of age, because we lived an extreme life that few people ashore would understand – and because of that we were close. I did not like all the people I sailed with but I always felt closer to them than I would have felt with friends of my own age from my earlier life.

People of different ages and disparate backgrounds would go ashore as drinking companions, as if it were the most natural thing. Drink could cause a sudden flare up, which sometimes tipped over into violence. People fell out a lot through drink, although it was generally forgotten the next day – unless there had been a major humiliation or if someone was showing visible injuries.

The bar was the place to be; the place we all gravitated to when we were in between working, sleeping and eating. Occasionally, a steward would serve, although most of the time it was an honesty bar, with a book on the bar-top where we marked down what we took. Our drinking was daily and heavy. The three of us apes squeezed in one or two beers at lunchtime and worked towards that point in the late afternoon when, filthy and sweat-streaked and burning, we would fall into the showers and hurriedly scrub, and then dress – still damp – in our cool, white tropical uniforms and almost run down the flying-bridge to the bar.

That first cool, cool, Tiger or Amstel or Carlsberg or Anchor or Kirin or San Miguel went down, down, down like some sweetness dropped from heaven. We would spike open the tops with the can-openers we carried slung on string around our necks (which was the fashion in the East in the early 1970s), and drink from the can, unless there was a senior officer in the bar, in which case we used a glass. The first third would go down with a pleasure like nothing I can describe. Then I would pause and light a Rothmans cigarette with my Ronson lighter and pull the smoke deep, deep down into my lungs and wait, with my eyes half-closed, then let it ease out gently. Then I would drink the rest of the beer in two or three swallows and open another.

Dinner was at 18.30 and, with speed and luck, we could be in the bar by 17.30, where we could generally expect to push down half a dozen beers before dinner. Joey, the second mate, would always be in there when we arrived, his watch having finished at 16.00. He was usually mildly drunk by then, working his way towards that more satisfactory state beyond tipsy but before you start to stagger and slur, where you are witty and good company and feel witty and good company, and feel life is good and you are on top of the world. The third engineer was also there – he held the parallel watch to Jerry in the engine room. Then there was the third officer and the fourth engineer, who each had the eight-to-twelve watch: although they drank before dinner, the expectation was that they would be in good and sober order for the start of their watch. The bar filled up before the evening meal: the captain, chief engineer, chief steward, a couple of fivers, the sparks, the engineer cadets. It was all very loud and smoky and noisy and jolly. At 18.30 the saloon steward walked past the bar, beating the dinner-gong, and we squeezed in one more drink then went down to eat.

The bar on the *Vexilla* was much the same as other bars on ships built in the early 1950s. Ships of that age were not built with bars: the one on the *Vexilla* was the converted smoke room. The older officers still tended to call it the smoke room. In smoke-room days, the officers would gather for cards and a glass of something before dinner and would retreat back there afterwards for brandy and cigars. As the 1960s arrived, the officers drinking appetites were given freer expression and bars were built into the smoke rooms.

The *Vexilla's* bar had been sturdily put together by the ship's carpenter several years ago and was L-shaped, built of varnished hardwood. Three people could fit behind it, where there was a big fridge containing the beer, mixers and soft drinks; along the bulkhead was a row of inverted spirit bottles perched on fat delivery optics. Stacked under the bar surface were several cases of beer, ready for replenishing the cold stock. In front of the bar were half a dozen swivel stools, bolted to the deck, with red plastic seat coverings and chrome backrests. The glasses were in an open-fronted cabinet fixed to the bulkhead, caged behind roll bars.

In the main body of the room, which was about 30 foot by 20, there was a scattering of armchairs and two flip-top card tables. It was light and airy, being on the starboard-forward corner, with three brass portholes forward and four down the starboard side. There was a darts board, a shove ha'penny board and a pull-down screen where we showed the films. A doorway at the end led through to the table tennis room, which was lined with shelves and was also where the ships library was stowed.

It was rare for someone to be banned from the bar. I was once and so was John, on both occasions after making shameful fools of ourselves. In John's case he vomited in the corner of the bar late one night, in the bin, causing a huge outcry. Everyone decamped to the second engineer's cabin to escape the stench. Tellingly, John was also allowed to come, although LJ banned him for three days the next morning. As for me, I was drunk one evening (we all were) and having an excitable argument with Sparks, I gesticulated with my arm to illustrate some point – I forget what it was: I forget what we were even arguing about – and knocked his and somebody else's drink over. They howled with rage and Sparks pushed me savagely in the chest, calling me a bloody idiot. I fell back and bounced against the glasses cabinet and fell on the deck: the cabinet came off the bulkhead and crashed on top of my head, spilling out broken glasses. I was cut and hurt and bleeding and covered with broken glass. Everyone shouted that I was a clumsy fool. Then we all laughed. I had a three-day ban.

Of the three of us, I probably drank the most. We more-or-less continued as we had left off in Plymouth: Barry drank the least; John lurched into occasional wild binges; whereas I would just drink a lot, steadily. On a running average, I would be ahead in consumption most of the time, John a close second. I never felt that I had a 'drink problem' any more than anyone at that age did; I was just enjoying myself. I read *John Barleycorn*, Jack London's cautionary tale of drinking, while I was on the *Vexilla* and wondered why he seemed to be so warning in his prose: he seemed to be taking it all too seriously. I took the time to note however, as all drinkers did, that though a lot of the people around me seemed to have a drink problem – I did not.

The third engineer had a problem, to my eyes. He trembled most of the time; sometimes he shook. Quite often he would be in for breakfast, thoroughly plastered after coming off watch at 04.00 and drinking in the bar until 07.30. Sometimes Joey would be with him, although not often because he had to be on the bridge for 09.30 to check the day's navigation. On the occasions they did both turn up for breakfast, they would be loud and raucous in the dining saloon as they wolfed down bacon and eggs while carrying on drinking beer from cans. They always made sure they were away by 08.00, before the captain and chief engineer arrived. The third engineer looked old to me, about 40, with his beard and stringy hair and bad skin and grimy, wounded engineer's hands, but I found out he was only 26. He was from the Western Isles and spoke in a gentle burr that became more difficult to understand as he became drunker and drunker. Sometimes, when he was completely gone, he would lapse into Gaelic and start singing and then fall into weeping.

The Old Man too: he had a problem. He was a gin drinker, with a ritual of sitting in the same place – end bar-stool by the porthole – at the same time, every day. At lunchtime he would arrive at 11.45 on the dot for his first drink of the day, or at least his first public drink of the day. He always had a tall glass full of ice with two slices of lemon, a double gin and a few splashes of Schweppes to fill it to the brim. The optic capacity was a fifth of a gill, bigger than the standard UK sixth. A double was therefore a hefty measure. He would have three before lunch. In the evening he would arrive at 17.30 and could be relied on to have four doubles. After dinner he would go to the bridge to chat to LJ, watch the third mate take over the eight-to-twelve watch, write up his night orders, and be back in the bar by 20.30. His post-dinner drinking varied: if it was a film night then he would have one before the start, one at the end of each reel, and a couple at the end. All-in-all, the Old Man could be relied on to polish off a bottle of Gordon's a day – unless there was a celebration of some sort, in which case it would be a lot more.

The Old Man didn't become incoherent or foolish like me and the other younger ones onboard when he drank; he became a bit more pompous, he talked a lot more, and became a bit kinder I suppose. He also became much less intimidating late into the evening, although I suppose this was probably mostly due to my own inebriated state at that time, which caused me to become braver in the way I spoke to him.

The chief steward – he had a significant problem. He was a short man, slightly bitter and slightly vicious. Although he was an officer – a two-striper, nominally equal to the second mate and the third engineer – he was an officer on the fringes. The deck officers and engineer officers were trained, were professional people. The chief steward had a background of serving meals in the saloon, making bunks and cleaning cabins: the stewards were the least-admired group of ratings on a ship, below the sailors and the engine-room workers, the firemen. So, when a steward climbed up the greasy pole to become chief steward – an officer – he was never really accepted. In my experience, the chief steward of a ship usually tended to develop a friendship with the sparks – another loner; another outsider. The sparks, however, had a lot more respect, being viewed as an educated man – the chief steward was at the bottom of the status pole.

The chief steward on the *Vexilla* had a habit of bullying his stewards. I once saw him grab the midships steward by his collar and bang his head against the bulkhead until he howled and wept. This was because he had done a poor job cleaning the hospital. The chief steward drank all day, shamelessly and visibly. I would often pass his cabin in the morning on the way back from breakfast and he would be sitting in his cabin with the curtain open, his ledgers spread out in front of him, a glass of neat scotch on the desk.

It was during the runs ashore that we excelled in our drinking. Our four-day-five-night spell in Singapore while the *Vexilla* was in Keppel dock was a prime example. On the first night, I met John and Barry in the Connell House bar at 6.00 p.m., after my day off in town. I was sitting in the cool of the big fan when they came in. We sank Tigers for an hour while exchanging news of the day. Mine was generally uninteresting to them. The only thing I had bought was a chunky fat-bladed penknife from the Thieves Market in Rochor Canal Road; I had found it attractive because it had a marlin spike and a War Department stamp on the handle.

Their story was altogether more entertaining: the bilge cleaners – a grim band of Chinese ladies in their 40s and 50s, whose job it was to go beneath the engine room plating and swab out the oily bilges with cotton waste rags – were selling themselves to the crew for 30 Singapore dollars a turn. That was about four pounds sterling at the time. They were taking shifts in one of the sailor's cabins and most of the crew, according to John, were finding time to visit.

Barry started goading John, accusing him of surreptitiously sneaking into the cabin and shagging one of them. John began denying this vehemently, to such an extent that I began to wonder whether there was any truth in the accusation. I thought it would be good sport to side with Barry to try and wind John up, although John was always good at manoeuvring and was skilled in turning a situation back on his accuser. Our arguments were generally good-natured and, if they did get out of hand, things returned to an even keel fairly soon afterwards.

Eventually, we exhausted the potential of accusing each other of deeds we may or may not have done and went through into the dining room, in high merriment, and ate plates of *nasi goreng*, packing our stomachs with rice and grease, followed by a choice of treacle pudding or jam roly-poly, washed down with beer. The dining room was half-full: a table of noisy Germans, a table of noisier Dutch, three Scottish ABs who argued loudly – paid-off early from a Ben Line ship for some misdeed, from what we overheard.

Elsewhere, scatterings of twos and threes – mostly Europeans, some Indians, a few Orientals. The waiters slid past silently, the big wooden ceiling fans went whoosh, whoosh, whoosh over our heads, the louvered shutters were open to the heavily-scented gardens, and the muted traffic noise joined the clink and clatter and the stew of our conversations.

Afterwards, we walked in the gardens under the dark equatorial night and smoked and talked of all the grand things we were going to do, of mischief, of debauchery. We talked of those on the *Vexilla* we liked and those we didn't. We talked of LJ the mate and Ben the senior cadet, who had managed to get a set of fourth mate's epaulettes to wear. We wondered what the Old Man was like as a cadet and speculated whether he was a crawler or a shagger or an oaf or a party man. We laughed and walked out of the gardens and into the Singapore night.

☆   ☆   ☆

There was a row of bars in lower Anson Road – about ten in a line, catering to sailors. We went in. We didn't want to disappoint. We wanted to be catered to. We put our heads in several before settling into the Champagne Bar. The Champagne Bar didn't sell champagne, although it would sell flat Asti Spumante in its place at an extortionate price to anyone drunk or gullible enough.

The typical Singapore sailor bars at that time conformed to a common standard, the Champagne Bar being no exception. They were dark with polar air-conditioning and had a juke-box, which the customers were encouraged to feed and which played the records of the day. We poured in the coins and all the sounds of the early 1970s washed over us: Edison Lighthouse's *Love Grows*; Jackson Five's *I Want You Back*; Norman Greenbaum's *Spirit in the Sky*; Christie's *Yellow River*; Mungo Jerry's *In the Summertime*; *All Right Now* by Free; Simon & Garfunkel's *Bridge Over Troubled Water*; Lee Marvin's *Wandering Star*; Rolf Harris' *Two Little Boys*.

The bar ran along one wall, dimly lit from behind with pale green lights. Round stools with black plastic-covered seats were along its length and curled round one end. At the end sat a big Sikh, who smiled pleasantly if you caught his eye. He sipped a colourful drink and surveyed the room. His real role was to be unpleasant to anyone who stepped out of line and he carried a three-foot club to aid his efforts.

The *mama-san* served behind the bar. Fluent in several languages, blousy, bossy, shrill, garishly dressed, chain-smoking, shrewd eyes, *mama-sans* were what some bar-girls became when they were too old to flatter – if they were clever enough and tough enough to run the staff. Most weren't. Those that came through from bar-girl-cum-whore to *mama-san* were tough, tough people. This *mama-san* laughed a lot and shrieked at the other girls in the bar. The other girls in the bar were all younger, probably between 17 and 25, although I found it difficult to tell the age of Chinese girls, especially in the dark, when I was half drunk. Their job was simple: take as much money from the patrons as was possible to do.

When we walked in, they descended on us like a flock of aggressive sparrows, chattering, flitting about, pulling at us, squabbling over us, two competitors pulling at either arm. There is no 17-year-old male alive that doesn't like being fought over by a pretty woman.

The girls were mostly dressed in Chinese-style print dresses, split up the sides to the top of the thigh. They were drenched in perfumes and had their hair pulled up high and held back with clips. Flawless skin. They all looked gorgeous, even the ugly ones, as we always said later.

We sat in a line at the bar for a bit, while the *mama-san* put three cold Anchor Pilsner beers in front of us, with frosted glasses pulled straight from the freezer. The girls leant against us and cooed for drinks themselves. We bought them small shots of coloured water at $10 Singapore a time, which they threw back in a gulp and asked for more. They did their best to be entertaining; they worked hard at it and had to be admired, telling us how handsome we were, how rich we must be, how clever we were, how much I looked like David McCullum, how John looked like Dean Martin, how Barry looked like Sean Connery. We laughed and were easily flattered and bought them drinks. We carried on feeding the juke-box and danced to Diana Ross and the Supremes and whoever else came on.

The *mama-san* placed a continued flow of fresh bottles of Anchor in front of us; new ones instantly appeared when the level fell below the label. We decamped to a table in the corner where the girls hugged us and stroked us and told us we were so funny and so handsome and so clever and took our money for the juke-box and took our money for their drinks and took our money for tips.

At 11.00 p.m., we said our goodbyes. They laughed and twittered and begged us to stay and we promised to come back and we left much poorer and walked to the harbourfront to find a taxi.

"I'm starving," said John, as we walked up Anson Road.

"We'll have something when we get to Bugis Street," I replied.

"So what about this Bugis Street then?" asked Barry. "You been there, Simon? You used to live here."

I had never been to Bugis Street, but I wanted to appear more informed than I was: "Well... sort of."

"What do you mean, 'sort of'? You've either been there or you haven't," said John.

"Well, I've been past there." They looked at me sceptically. "In the day-time, actually," I admitted. They looked even more sceptical.

"The place only properly opens after midnight. You know as much as we do," said Barry.

"I know a lot of people who've been there, so I know a lot about the place." They looked at each other.

"Stop digging, Simon." John advised.

A black and yellow Morris Oxford taxi pulled up and we climbed in.

Bugis Street was a small connecting road in the middle of Singapore city, between the larger thoroughfares of North Bridge Road and Victoria Street. Late in the evening, after eleven o'clock, wooden tables were set up and gas lanterns lit and the place started to come alive. Beer-sellers arrived, supplying big bottles of Anchor and Tiger, iced down in metal bins.

The food merchants flashed up their charcoal fires and laid out spiced duck, soy-sauce-soaked chickens and bright shellfish, all ready for cooking, preparing the huge iron rice woks for *nasi goreng*. Wandering merchants hawked their wares in trays slung from their necks: cigarettes, cigarette-lighters, postcards, tacky souvenir flags, badly-made plaster statuettes of dragons and ancient figures from China's past. The noughts-and-crosses boys turned up; small lads who carried small blackboards and chalk and who would badger you to play for a dollar. They would never lose; the best you could ever do was draw.

Old men hawked rambutans, small spiky and conker-like, which peeled back to reveal soft white fruit inside. Durian salesman wandered through, the hoarse cries competing with the rambutan men: "Duuuurrriiiiaaaaaannnnnn! Ahh, ahh, ahh. Duuuuurrriiiiaaaaaannnnnn!"

"Raaaaaaam-boota! Raaaaaaam-boota! Raaaaaaam-boota!"

Durian is a foul-smelling melon-sized fruit that cannot be abided by most Europeans. It has an all-pervading sickly-sweet, rotting smell, like sour vomit, that seems to be attuned to the gag reflex. I was often told that it actually tasted quite nice, although I could never bring myself to put a piece near my face. They were other fruit hawkers selling melon, lychees and juices, all howling their own tunes, but the rambutan and durian men were kings.

We arrived at about 11.30 p.m., and the place was starting to fill. There were several people from the *Vexilla* and we took a table next to the third mate and second engineer and two Germans they had fallen in with. They were all bright-eyed and red-faced and noisy: we fitted together well. We ordered ice-cold Anchor beer for John and I; Barry had switched to rum and coke.

The noise started to swell: loud conversations punctuated by shouting, laughing, cursing. All the table were taken by Europeans: British squaddies form Selarang barracks, British servicemen from the Changi and Seletar R.A.F. camps, Australian soldiers from the Anzac detachment, Merchant Navy seaman – mostly British, Dutch and Germans, and a few Americans on R& R from Vietnam. All men. Mostly young men; mostly young men who wore uniform for their jobs, dressed now in slacks and short-sleeved shirts and light shoes. Occasionally an adventurous tourist would come through, but not often.

At midnight the show began. The first of the most incredible-looking Eurasian women came sashaying between the tables. Dressed to kill, made up to extreme, big hair in every colour. We were agog. One passed our table and bent down to kiss John on the top of his head, then running her fingers over Barry's short stubbled crown before moving on. Another picked up my bottle of Anchor, took a short swig, winked at me and walked off.

"Are they...?" asked John.

"Yes! Oh course they are!" I replied. More drifted in – 15, perhaps 20 – all gorgeous, fashion plate gorgeous, magazine gorgeous.

"I've heard some aren't," mused John.

"They all are," snapped Barry.

And they all were: they were men. Or at least, they were transsexuals.

They were known as '*ki-ti*': men with various degrees of treatment and surgery to half-turn themselves into women. They took hormones and had breast enhancements and this, along with the fact that Asian men are generally more slender, smoother-skinned and less hairy than Europeans, made them extremely convincing women – particularly when most of their audience was drunk, when it was night, and when they were made up and bewigged and dressed to the nines. They all prostituted themselves shamelessly. Stories were rife of soldiers and sailors going off with a *ki-ti*, convinced that he/she was in fact a woman, to encounter a fright later on when the clothes came off. It was even worse when someone woke up in the morning lying next to one and had to address the reality.

The crowd went wild as the *ki-tis* made their way through, sitting on peoples laps, drinking their drinks, eating their food, coercing and inveigling and tempting the easily-led into coming back with them.

At 2.00 a.m., the fights started. The first was three tables away from us: half a dozen Dutch sailors steamed into a table full of British squaddies, brawling over the affections of a couple of *ki-tis*, who had apparently left one group to join the other. The fight was noisy and brutal: they fought with fists and heavy wooden stools and bottles, the squaddies head-butting whenever they could. Chinese stallholders joined in to try and separate the combatants, which made it an even bigger event. Tables crashed over and we had to grab our drinks and vacate ours as the battle spilled wider. Fighting twosomes rolled on the ground in the beer and food and broken glass and filth, locked together, trying to do as much damage to each other as possible. Eventually it was over, broken up by the Chinese stallholders, by others who felt they should separate the factions, by exhaustion and, in some cases, by grievous wounding and near unconsciousness. Neither side could claim victory. Each party, bleeding and wounded and groaning, was given a fresh table at opposite ends of the street. The battle-site was spruced up, table and stools put upright and then given over to eager new arrivals.

There were sporadic flare-ups from then on, although we didn't see one as brutal as the Dutch verses the British. Mostly, these fights were heralded by loud oaths and the sound of smashing glass, followed by thuds and smacks and grunts and curses, then a flooding in of Chinese stallholders before it all died down. No one was ever evicted from the street for fighting, merely moved to the back of the class.

At about 3.00 a.m., we ordered steamed crab claws. A photographer came by and took a Polaroid picture of the three of us, glassy-eyed, hunched over our shellfish among a sea of empty beer bottles. Barry was elegantly giving the V-sign as the shutter snapped, which caused John to fly into a rage and shout at Barry for spoiling the picture.

Shortly afterwards, I visited the fabled Bugis Street toilets, which were internationally renowned for their vileness: water dripped from the eves; slime slid down the walls inside and out; the air inside was fetid; and the stench unbelievably foul. There were no lights, just a dim paleness filtering from the gas lamps through the permanently-open doorway. People mostly just stood in the open doorway and started urinating in the general direction of what was believed to be the urinal. People who wanted to defecate either had to be very brave or desperate. Those poor souls who couldn't wait felt their way deeper into the gloom and squatted where they could, dumping their goods God-knows-where. Occasionally, someone would fall over as they squatted, causing them to howl and curse and eventually emerge smeared with piss and shit and slime and every other revolting paste imaginable. The scurry of rats was endemic. I could not bring myself to go near the doorway and instead urinated against the wall outside, like most sensible people. Two grunting forms made the beast-with-two-backs in the pitch dark shadow a few feet away. Man and woman or man and man-woman; I didn't want to know.

By 5.00 a.m., we were too drunk to continue speaking and sat slumped on our stools, watching the strange world we were in start to wind down. The food stalls were putting out their charcoal and the tables were being put away as they were vacated. Buckets of water were being thrown down to swill the night's excesses away into the monsoon drains. Beer was still being served, although trade was much slacker now.

We caught two trishaws back to Anson Road, John and I shared while Barry slumped in his own one. As the wind caught our faces, we livened up and cajoled the ancient men who were peddling into a race, which they entered into with some enthusiasm in anticipation of a tip. We careered through the empty streets in the pre-dawn, seeing the early starters scratching and stretching on the pavements. Barry won by a long way.

I fell onto my pillow at 6.00 a.m., for two hours of saturated sleep before rising for the day's work. As I sank into the darkness, I felt a stab of envy for John, who had his day off and could lie in and take several hours heavy slumber.

When the *Vexilla* slipped out of Keppel in the early morning several days later, I felt a certain relief. I needed sleep and a break from the succession of nights that went on in wild relief until breakfast was approaching. I wanted the clean sea air in my lungs and I wanted hard work to flush

From left to right: John, the author and Barry in Bugis Street Market, Singapore late one night.

out my system, I wanted to sleep for seven unbroken hours, I wanted an evening where I would drink no more than half a dozen cans a beer and smoke no more than ten cigarettes. I wanted the hot sun on my brown back as I sweated on deck. I wanted all the poisons leeched out of me.

We steamed the four miles across the crowded Singapore harbour, weaving between the ships at anchor, to Pulau Bukom, the big oil refinery loading port of the Far East. The *Vexilla* must have been the cleanest ship on the island when we arrived. All the tanks sludge-free – even the engine room bilges were clean.

The loading plan was to take a full black oil cargo for Japan.

As I drank within the drinking society in which I lived, from time to time I thought of my father. Was I him? Was I becoming him? He was a second son too. Second sons are supposedly driven people, driving themselves to catch up with the first son. We second sons strive harder. We act more outrageously. We are often accused of under-confidence, which we hate and deny. We take ourselves too seriously. We try to be the best at what we do. We usually accomplish more than others. I accomplished more drinking than Barry and John. Barry was an only child; John had an older sister – scant competition for a second son. My father drank too.

For as far back as I could recall, I always remembered my father drinking. I don't mean he was staggering around the place drunk, I mean he was a drinking person. He loved pubs, he loved the officers' mess, he loved bars of any kind, he loved the company of men drinking together, standing by the bar drinking and smoking and talking man-talk: loud talk, blasts of raucous laughing, the telling of tales, the telling of stories from years back about the things they and their friends had done. Most of the stories involved drink, involved being in bars, about being under the influence of drink or in search of drink, of groups of men who drunk together. I inherited all that from my father, although I didn't have his loud confidence when I was young; perhaps he didn't have it either when he was young.

When I was a boy, perhaps about ten, my father was stationed at the Central Flying School at Little Rissington in Gloucestershire. I remember we used to go shopping on a Saturday morning to Stow-on-the-Wold. The morning would conclude with my father and mother telling Peter and me to stay in the car while they went for a quick drink in the Red Lion in the square. Often we would sit there for a couple of hours, bickering and squabbling, until they returned, sometimes with a bag of sherbet lemons for us, to assuage their guilt. Saturday lunchtimes in my mid-childhood were the only regular time when my father drank with my mother. The other occasions would be when they went out to functions at the officers' mess – my father resplendent in his mess-kit: short jacket, starched shirt, black tie, medals; my mother glowing in a long dress and jewels, back straight, like a princess. When I was very young they went to parties a lot, fancy dress sometimes: the King and Queen of Hearts; Dracula and his bride; once as a caveman and his... I can't remember what my mother's role was then: cavewoman I suppose. I just remember my father in animal skins, wigged and bearded with ghastly false teeth and a massive club, chasing after us boys, grunting and banging his club on the ground while we ran and squealed with delight and a bit of fear. Peter and I would be left alone at home while they partied. We would see the photographs later: groups of men and women in strange costumes, all holding drinks, all smoking, all grinning at the camera.

My father told a lot of war stories. We loved his war stories. Peter and I would sit cross-legged on the floor while he told us of being a bomber pilot in the early part of the war, based in the Middle East, somewhere near Alexandria I think. He flew Wellingtons to bomb places in southern Europe. He was 19. His drinking stories in Alex were fabulous: drinking all day in seedy bars, drinking all night in glamorous nightclubs, drinking in the mess between missions, getting attacked in the street by the local Egyptians in the early hours after a drinking session because he said the 'Gypos hated the British, losing a day in his life after drinking some grim home-made brew. He used to tell us a story about a film that was being shown at the local cinema in Alexandria which featured the British being thrashed by the Arabs in some conflict in the Middle East; the cinema was packed out and the audience of locals were enjoying seeing the British getting what they deserved. As the tempo of the film picked up and the British came off worse and worse, the audience became worked up to a fever pitch: "Kill the British! Kill them! The dogs! Yes! Yes! Hurrah! Yes! Kill them all!" and suchlike they screamed, leaping up and down and stamping their feet and cheering. Then the whole balcony collapsed under the weight of it all, killing dozens, wounding scores. My father and his RAF chums thought it was a real hoot at the time: "Dirty 'Gypos: that'll teach them!" They toasted the hilarious rough justice of it all. Peter and I laughed. Tragi-comedy.

Later in the war he was a fighter pilot. He was then 21, strafing German troops and trains during the invasion, fighting with *Messerschmidts* flown by other 21-year-olds, duelling in the sun in the hot summer of 1944. And in between all of this, the parties and the pubs and the officers' mess. He was shot down once and bailed out of his Hurricane over the channel. He celebrated his survival and homecoming with a massive beano in the mess. He was given a week off to recuperate from his escape before being given a new Hurricane and sent back up into the sky to fight Germans again.

My father was no different to the others of his generation who wore uniform and went to war for several years. Drink was their release and their safety valve; it was what they did between the horror and the fear and the numbing boredom of waiting for both. To the other armed forces, my father was a 'toff" a 'Brylcreem boy' a 'sky-blue-khaki-boy'. The RAF were loved and hated and envied and pitied by the men on the ground. They didn't have the drudge and slog of the Army; they had high-speed terror and a quick, loud death if they were too slow as they blew up and crashed to earth. They had a low survival chance. They were all young men; they knew that lots of them would die, lots of them. They climbed into their planes with their leather helmets and goggles and scarves and they grinned and waved and flew off to die. They all wanted a quick death; nobody wanted to burn. And in between they drank and partied and acted outrageously because they believed they would all die soon and so they deserved to sing and drink and be foolish. People tutted and frowned, but everyone agreed that was what they should do. And for those that didn't die, they had built the drinking gene into themselves and acknowledged the all-importance of camaraderie, of the bond of men who drink together. Everything in my father's life revolved around drinking and the social acts that went with it and we, as his children, learnt the importance of it too.

So, when I went to sea and wore a uniform of my own, I knew how to act when it came to drinking: it was already instilled in me.

Drink nearly killed me in South Africa. No, that's not true: I was almost killed in South Africa when I was drunk and it wouldn't have happened if I had not been drunk. John and I were ashore in Durban and were having a grand time. We drank Castle beer until we were dizzy and bloated and then switched to rum. In our sodden state we decided that life at sea, while being good fun, was not exciting enough for two young bucks such as us – we resolved to do something about it.

At the time, the bush war in Rhodesia was in full swing and I announced that I had a hankering to join the Rhodesian Light Infantry and we should both travel north and sign up. I painted an image of myself skulking menacingly around the jungle in bush gear, tracking down the guerrillas. John's plan was vague and seemed to be to simply strike out into Africa and go on some grand trek, wandering the land, having adventures. Either way, fighting guerrillas in the jungle or seeking unknown adventure on the plains of Africa both seemed like great ideas and off we set, staggering up West Street, looking for our adventures.

After a few hundred yards we stopped to refuel and went into a dark and noisy club. We sat at a table near the singer and ordered more rum. We spoke to a young South African who was sitting on his own nearby. He joined us. We told him our plans. He seemed impressed that we had a grand plan, although not so much with our actual choices. We drank more rum. We honed our plans with the help of the South African and worked out how to get to Rhodesia, drawing maps for each other on beer mats. We drunk more rum. The South African knew of a better club. We all had difficulty walking. We piled into his car, which was parked outside. We roared off, haring down West Street through one red light, two red lights, then three. Faster we went. We screamed with laughter. A roundabout loomed ahead: we sped up. I shouted at him to slow; he sped up more: I screamed at him to slow; he ignored me. I looked at him: he was asleep. I looked at John. John looked at me, sobriety washed over us. We closed our eyes. We prepared for death. The car mounted the roundabout with a smash and a tearing of metal. We crashed through a billboard and some scaffolding and hit something solid. The car crumpled, we fell in heaps. Glass everywhere. We fell out the car. Bits of us were bleeding but we could all stand up. We looked at the car; it was much shorter than it was when we had got into it. It looked shredded.

"It's my dad's car," said the South African.

We commiserated. The police arrived. The South African sat on the grass and wept. We patted his shoulder. The police took him away in the back of a car. The police took us back to our ship in the back of a van. We were deposited at the dock gate, our dreams of greater adventure unrequited.

From left to right: John, the unknown South African driver and the author in Durban, South Africa late one night, shortly before the car accident.

★　★　★

Film nights were a ritual; I always enjoyed them. We usually had one film a week at sea. We would take delivery of the big metal boxes of films at the seaman's mission, exchanging our boxes of films that we had already watched. Each box would usually contain nine reels of film in cardboard sleeves, each film being three reels. It was the cadet's job to show the film for the officers. The crew had their own showings on other nights. The films were a mix of the fair and the dire, with an occasional good one. Most were ancient, some were foreign, some were utterly senseless and unintelligible. We usually started with the best and worked our way down towards the Italian-dubbed musical, or whatever was deemed to be the likely worst of the bunch.

Sometimes, in the tropics, we would show the film out on the boat deck abaft the funnel – smoking on tankers was only allowed on deck aft of the funnel. We would rig up a double sheet as the screen, stretching it as tight as we could, then set up the projector on a table. It was impossible to get every wrinkle out of the sheet and it would sway with the movement of the ship and distort the image. The projector would sway in turn, so the picture leaned first one way then the other, compressing and stretching on the moveable sheet.

Films on deck were only watchable if the weather was good, the sea was calm and the wind was right. If the breeze was too strong then the makeshift screen flapped wildly and the film became impossible to watch. If the wind was from astern then the soot and fumes from the funnel would drift down onto us, until the smell and the mess drove us inside. If the swell of the sea was too large then the excessive screen movement rendered the picture simply unwatchable.

More often than not we would show the film in the bar in two showings – one from 4.30 to 6.30 p.m., and one from 8.30 to 10.30 p.m. Film nights were good for us cadets because one of us was allowed to finish work at 4.00 p.m., to get everything set up. We took turns: one of us did the early showing and the other two went to the late showing. Setting up the film meant hand-winding the reels back to the beginning and then threading the film through the ancient projector, testing, focusing, setting up the speaker and putting out the chairs. Finishing at 4.00 p.m. gave ten minutes to get showered and changed, and 20 minutes to get everything ready. I could shower in two minutes, even if covered in grime, scrubbing myself fiercely with a stiff bristle brush under the tepid flow of water.

The first film show was for the eight-to-twelve watch-keepers, the third officer and the fourth engineer, the twelve-to-four watch-keepers, the second officer and the third engineer and any day-workers who had been given an early finish for some reason. The second showing was for the four-to-eight watch-keepers, the captain and chief engineer and the majority of day-workers. The sparks and the chief steward came into whichever one they wanted. I preferred the first showing as it was mainly younger junior officers and was more fun, more raucous.

When I was the projectionist, I would get the film started at 4.30 p.m. on the dot, regardless of whether or not everyone had arrived. The first ten minutes of every film was broken up with the latecomers barging in, swearing and complaining because we hadn't waited, demanding we start again and cursing when we wouldn't, clattering around behind the bar to get their drink and then taking a deliberate slow walk in front of the screen to their seat, to the accompaniment of hoots of protest from the rest of us. For the inside showings, which was most of them, we had a purpose-built pull-down screen, which gave a better surface for the image than the sheet. Sometimes it jammed though, and we had to tack the sheet up. There was a constant buzz of conversation throughout the film, interspersed by everyone telling each other to keep quiet. The hiss and crack of beer cans being opened was continual. We shouted and jeered at poor films and often threw things at the screen, empty beer cans and cigarette packets and anything else that came to hand. Every 40 minutes or so, the reel would end and flap wildly around the projector arm until the machine was switched off and the new reel threaded. This signalled a general mobilisation for the bar and toilets.

Minor disasters were a function of film nights. The film would break or jam and burn; the projector bulb would blow; the reel would come off if it hadn't been clipped on properly and it would bowl around the room, scattering film everywhere; the screen would fall down.

It was common to end up with the soundtrack a couple of seconds out of synch with the image, which was maddening – we would shake the projector and beat the speaker in our frustration.

The unforgivable crime was to get the reels mixed up. They were commonly in the wrong cardboard sleeves, with reel three being in the sleeve marked 'reel two'. The people in the first showing often mixed them up deliberately to assassinate the enjoyment of the second showing. The film would usually start properly with the right reel; we could always tell because it had the credits in the early part. In a long and confusing film however – particularly one that was fractured with many subplots – it wasn't unknown for the third reel to be shown second, provoking howls of rage when the film came to an unexpected end. The flow of the film was continually being broken anyway and people were drinking more as it progressed, so it shouldn't have caused much surprise when this happened. But it always did. Vitriol was hurled at the hapless cadet, who was cursed as a fool who had ruined the evening. The second reel was then shown anyway, to a continual current of grumbling and swearing.

I once showed the Second World War epic, *The Battle of the Bulge*. It was a four-reeler, one of those films full of soldiers and fighting where every scene looked like the one before. The showing went smoothly and when it finished everyone was remarking how good the film was. I dismantled and boxed the projector and while I was doing this I found another reel, still in its sleeve. I said nothing, fearing a roasting from the audience. No one noticed; the audience was tired by that time.

We arrived in Yokahama on a cold November early morning and anchored in the roads. The officers were bad-tempered after a testing trip through the Inland Sea on Honshu Island – the busiest waterway in the world, crammed with every craft imaginable and fraught with every conceivable aspect of bad maritime manners.

I was on the bridge as we came into Yokohama Bay, manning the engine telegraph, swinging the big brass handle to the Old Man's instructions, from 'Full Ahead', through 'Slow Ahead', to 'Dead Slow'. LJ sent me down to the main-deck to meet the pilot, who leapt from his launch onto the white wooden pilot-ladder that hung over the side, clambering up and over the rail.

The bridge was crowded: the Old Man – always there when going in and out of port; the chief officer, LJ – because he was the officer of the watch; Ben the senior cadet/fourth officer – who was LJ's shadow; the AB – who was on the wheel, because auto-steering was dispensed with when manoeuvring; the second AB of the watch – to take turn at the wheel and to be there for anything that needed doing; the pilot; and me – general dogsbody.

The *Vexilla* crept slowly through the other ships at anchor in the pre-dawn. When we reached our anchorage-spot, the engines were nudged 'Slow Astern', and when the churning wash from the propeller was level with the bridge, the call was given to the third mate on the fo'c'sle to let go the anchor. The chain paid out evenly as we slid astern, paying out six cables (a cable is 15 fathoms or 90 feet). For a big sea-going vessel, it's the weight of the chain that keeps the ship fixed, not the anchor itself. The anchor just locks the chain with the sea-bed. John was up on the fo'c'sle, assisting the third mate and the bosun to drop anchor. Barry was left to have a lie in, lucky sod.

Yokohama had a good reputation and was cheap in the early 1970s: the exchange rate was 800 yen to the pound. The officers filled our minds with fabulous stories about Japan. We craved a run ashore and bickered about how we would work the watches.

We each subbed 25,000 yen. We were going to be in port for two nights in Yokohama, then off to Kobe and Nagoya. LJ called us up to the bridge for a lecture. He leaned against the bridge wing and stared us all down: "Do you lads know Tony Morrell?"

We looked at each other vacantly, then shrugged: "Not me, sir."

"Nor me, sir," I lied.

"Me neither, sir."

We had all heard of Tony Morrell. Tony was a senior cadet, now languishing in Kobe gaol, six months into a 12-year sentence. He had, reportedly, agreed to deliver a package for someone from Singapore. The delivery was to a bar in Kobe. The police were waiting at the delivery. The package was drugs. Tony was threatened with life imprisonment. He said knew nothing about drugs. He was beaten. He said he knew nothing: he was only doing someone a favour. He was given 12 years. He was 19 years old. Stories seeped out about what a hard time the Japanese guards were giving him.

I knew Tony, vaguely. He was a lanky lad from Dublin with a big heart. Tony had paid a visit to the Valvata in in Maracaibo the previous year. His ship was alongside the same jetty and he came across to visit Paul, who he had known since they both went to sea at 16. Paul, Rolo and Tony sank a few beers in the bar, while I listened and learnt. I remember that Tony Morrell made a point of including me in the conversation, while the other two made a point of excluding me. He was softly spoken and dry, and smiled a lot. At the time I wished I had him for senior cadet.

"Morrell was a fool," pronounced LJ. "He's inside now and he'll be lucky to get out. Don't any of you ever, ever, try anything as stupid as he did, to earn some quick money." LJ then went on to tell us his version of the Tony Morrell drug run, which had ended so badly for Tony. It seemed a stretched version of what we had already been told. "The Japs hate *gaijins*."

"What's a '*gaijin*'?"

"'*Gaijin*' means 'round-eye': 'Westerner': 'outsider'. The Japs may be grinning bastards, but they're mostly bastards and they hate us all. Don't forget that." LJ wore Second World War ribbons and had served in the Far East during the hostilities; he had his sensitivities. "When you go ashore, whoever is going to be going [all of us, we thought simultaneously], make sure you act politely, don't argue, keep quiet, don't talk back to a Jap policeman or any Jap official or any Jap in uniform. Got it?"

"Yes, sir."

"Yes, sir."

"Yes, sir."

Joey the second mate sauntered up and stood beside LJ, looking grave and nodding at the wisdom being dispensed. He shuffled out of LJ's vision and made daft grimaces, trying to get us to laugh. We kept straight faces; sniggering would have meant no shore-leave. Joey knew that. LJ sent us away and stood talking to Joey. They looked like Laurel and Hardy. I liked LJ. The others didn't.

Most seamen saw Yokohama as a good place for a run ashore in the early 1970s. It was cheap, it was different, it was exotic, there were lots of bars, it was crime-free, the people were polite – almost servile – the girls were pretty and delicate and fawned over men.

Barry did a 16-hour stint to let me and John have a decent run ashore in Yokohama. We went down the gangplank at 5.00 p.m., in jackets and ties, dressed to gain entry to anywhere. The intention was to have a wander around the streets before hitting the bars, although we pretty much started and finished in a narrow street of small bars and clubs on the dock edge of Yokohama. We went in several – they were all very similar: warm against the cold outside, hot even; they had low lights and were cleaner than any other bars in the East; the music was low and the tables small. We sat at the bar and drank Kirin from frosted glasses. 'Kirin' is a Japanese beer that looks and tastes like American beer, although in actual fact it was established by a Scotsman in Nagasaki. 'Kirin' means 'giraffe' – we speculated that this was because it comes in long-necked bottles.

The girls encouraged us to feed the juke-box with 100-yen coins. The Japanese music was mostly unintelligible to us: scratchy instruments overlaid with a shrieking and wailing that had no discernable melodic content to our western ears. We tried pot-luck on a few but they were all bad. We gave the girls coins to choose songs but they all seemed much the same.

We found some western songs, which were a clunky middle-of-the-road collection: Dean Martin's *Little Old Wine Drinker Me*; *Danny Boy*; the Beatles' *Revolution*; assorted Frank Sinatra; *The Carnival is Over* by The Seekers; Diana Ross' *Blue Moon*. It struck me later that they were mostly maudlin, probably selected for us to slur along with. John became hooked on *Blue Moon* and played it over and over. After several beers, he became maudlin for his Alsatian dog that had died the previous year and started weeping. The girls were worried; I told them he was crazy. They tried to brighten us up by encouraging us to sing along, which we did: me howling away with Dean – a pair of little old wine drinkers. John bravely warbled his way through *Blue Moon*, wiping tears with his fists. When we left, our bill was huge because we had been buying drinks for the girls and didn't realise how expensive they were. John started to argue but the big bouncer from the room behind the bar became intimidating and we paid up and left.

Later, with our small amount of remaining funds, we ate noodles in a street stall. The noodles were peppered with vegetables and nameless meat. We hunched on wooden stalls next to a brazier and afterwards spent a thousand yen each in an arcade, playing *Go* – a mindless but addictive Japanese flick-ball game with no objective: you just pour coins in and stare through the glass while catapulting steel balls round and round. Inane, but good fun if you are drunk with dulled motor reflexes.

People either smiled at us or ignored us. We had no *gaijin* trouble.

At 2.00 a.m., we walked back to the ship. Taxis spurned us; perhaps they thought we looked evil. Our gait was the untimed co-ordination of a pair who had drunk too much: while walking along together we would diverge for no reason, then converge and bang into each other, causing us to diverge again. It seemed normal and didn't break our pace and we got back to the dock gate within an hour.

Barry was taking ullages with the Chinese sailor as we clattered up the gangway. Joey leaned on the rails watching them. We barracked and boasted of our evening, then headed to the ships bar for a night-cap.

The noise from the bar rolled towards us in a wave as we approached. It was packed: everyone off-duty was in there, in full swing. The Old Man was sitting straight and large and serious on his stool, large gin in front of him, large hand wrapped round it. LJ – uncharacteristically up late – sitting next to him, not drunk but looking relaxed, his forehead crinkled in sympathy as he listened to the fourth engineer telling him a tale of woe. The chief engineer and the second were at the end of the bar; the chief loud and raucous, jabbing his finger at the second, a dour Welshman, his head hanging, his mouth slack, his eyes vacant. Sparks seemed happy, not talking, just sitting on his stool grinning and smoking. The third mate was playing a loud game of darts with a couple of fivers and the chief steward. The engineer cadets served behind the bar, squabbling. The music bashed out of the big Sony box. As we walked in – as we actually walked through the doorway – *Blue Moon* struck up. I glanced at John, thinking the song would set him off again, wailing about his dead Alsatian, although he seemed to have got past that.

We nuzzled in to the group around the bar and signalled to the engineer cadets for two cans of beer. They passed us two cold Tigers. We looked at each other, we cracked open our cans, we looked around at all our fine comrades – at three in the morning in November in the Yokohama docks, and toasted.

6

Sailing By

My trip on the SS *Vexilla* was nearly nine months long: a tramp around the Far East and across the Indian Ocean – a tramp around Conrad country. I went to the ports and places that for me were an adventure just by their names – places I had read about and had wanted to go to before I ever even came to the East: Djakarta; Singapore; Port Klang; Penang; Bangkok; Sarawak; Manila; Tabangao; Cebu; Hong Kong; Keelung; Kaoshung; Yokohama; Kobe; Osaka; Nagoya; Sapporo; Pusan; and back again, then back again. We sailed through the Malacca Straits and the Singapore Straits and across the Gulf of Thailand and through the Sunda Straits and the Balabac Straits and the Mindoro Straits and the Luzon Straits and the Korea Strait.

We sailed across the Sulu Sea and the Sea of Japan and the South China Sea and the Celebes Sea and the Java Sea and along the edge of the Pacific Ocean and across the Indian Ocean. Nine months hard.

I arrived home for 40 days leave. I was burnt brown, toughened, eyes wide open. I had worked day upon day upon day of hard, hard labour, cramming in my studies between it all, living alongside the casual brutality and routine violence, the drinking, the carnality, the times when I was stunned and blurred by lack of sleep.

It changed me, but did not change me into a brutish person, because alongside all of that was the joy and the wonder; all the beautiful things. These things changed me more: the never-ending blue so-deep water; the flying fish skittering across the surface of the sea; the nights when I slept on the boat deck because it was too hot inside, lying on my back watching shooting stars streak across the velvet diamond-studded night sky; the nights when

I leant on the rails and watched the dark sea fold back from the ship like molten black toffee; the mornings when everything was yellow, a creeping of yellow light, lemon-yellow cloud, banana-yellow skies, shattered yellowed sea; the evenings when the sunsets were explosions of red and orange, vivid and stark, like a punch; the bright hot days in the centre of the watery earth, no ships in sight, just the *Vexilla* and sometimes some dolphins to help us on our way, light breeze on my bare back as I spliced rope with the casab on the main deck. Of all these things, most of all I loved being on a yellow sea under the yellow sky in the early morning.

I felt I was an alien, now I was home, as far removed from all around me as if I had two heads. I was 17-and-a-half years old.

It was good to see my mother and father and they professed to be glad to have me home, but it was awkward for me and I suspect the same for them. I was uncomfortable with my speech, my manners had no fluency and there didn't seem to be a place where I fitted. Sometimes I went to the pub with my father; I was always proud to be with him. Peter was working in a bank by now and had his own life mapped out. He hadn't set out to be a banker but a car accident had blocked his plans to join the RAF. We went to pubs together; we both drank too much. He pumped me for tales. I obliged but they lacked context and seemed too far-fetched as we stood together in an English pub with our pints of Ushers bitter. He scoffed at some. He couldn't connect.

I met up with John on a couple of occasions. I was then living in Ruislip, West London; my father had been posted to RAF Northolt while I was away on the *Vexilla*. John lived in North London, in Watford. We met in town and got drunk in the West End and rehashed the recent past. We drank in the Kings Road and went to clubs in Soho. We both told each other how great it was to be home. I couldn't wait to get back to sea.

The early spring days dragged by. I watched television in the evenings if I wasn't going out, lying there inert, smoking, watching the fare of the day: *The Saint*; *The Avengers*; *Danger Man*; *The Invaders*; *Softly, Softly*. In the day I explored corners of London: I wandered the Maritime Museum, the Imperial War Museum, the National Gallery; I drank in the Blind Beggar in Mile End Road and found the alleys where Jack the Ripper did his exercise; went in the Whispering Gallery in St Pauls and wandered the silver vaults. Sometimes I walked the 14 miles home to Ruislip: past Paddington, White City, Ealing, Greenford, eating up the miles. Occasionally I would get drunk somewhere in London and catch the late tube back, only to fall asleep and be woken up and ejected from the train by a guard at the end of the line, to walk home in the early hours.

The shipping company made contact after I had been home for a fortnight and reminded me that I needed to send in the correspondence coursework that I had been given to complete at sea. This gave me direction for the following two weeks and I filled my days with mathematics and navigation and naval architecture and meteorology and much more, finishing off the work I should have already done.

I waited for the postman each morning. I waited for my orders. I drove my mother mad.

Then the letter came. In a white envelope, B4 size, medium-weight, first-class mail, my name and address typed on the front, the company logo franked in blue ink. I carried it through to the kitchen, made tea, sat at the table, slit open the letter with a knife, ritualistically.

Inside were my joining instructions, one rail warrant, one ticket to fly BOAC from Heathrow to Dubai in ten days, to join the *Horomaya* in Ras al Khaymah.

I looked up Ras al Khaymah: it was south of the Strait of Hormuz, just inside the entrance to the Persian Gulf.

I telephoned the personnel office to see what I could find out. The *Horomaya* was a white oil tanker; fairly old, built in 1956. She was expected to load a full cargo for India. I would be flying out with one other person – another cadet: Jimmy.

I met Jimmy at the check-in desk at Heathrow and we exchanged stories as we went through the procedure that finally decanted us onto the early morning BOAC flight to Dubai. It was good to see Jimmy again. He had been on one of the gas carriers plying from northern Europe to Morocco and hadn't enjoyed it much. The other cadets were not his type and he had got on badly with the officers: the experience seemed to have knocked some of the joy out of him.

On the flight out we drunk beer and smoked duty-free Rothmans cigarettes and played cards. There was a film, although we were too far back in the aircraft to see the screen properly so we carried on a mini-party with a couple of oil workers across the aisle. The air hostess ferried us a regular supply of beer: we all had a fine time.

Dubai airport was an ex-RAF base that had been handed over to the locals: wide hangers shimmered in the desert heat; the wind sock hung limply; a scattering of low, white-painted buildings and a military control tower. There was still a squadron of Meteors based there, although the RAF presence was muted. The arrivals reception was quiet and kept fresh by big wooden ceiling-fans pushing the air around, as Middle Eastern men in white flowing robes sat on the cool floors and talked amongst themselves. There was no one to meet us so we sat outside under the shade of the overhanging awning and waited. The roads were not that busy but the drivers made up for it by using their horns continually, talking to each other in code by the sound of it.

After an hour, the agent arrived. He was a small, fat Egyptian in a white suit, driving a big white limousine, seemingly unworried by his tardy arrival. He had planned to drive us to Ras al Khaymah that day and put us on a launch to the *Horomaya*, which would pick up us as it steamed west. That morning however, the ship had been reported floating in the Indian Ocean following an engine breakdown and wouldn't be arriving for a couple of days. We were to be put up in the Ambassador, one of the few Western hotels in Dubai. He checked us in, subbed us each 50 pounds in *dirhams* for expenses, told us to sign for everything in the hotel, and advised he would pick us up in two or three days.

The dark-red-painted hotel stood by itself on the edge of an empty white-sand beach. There were roads behind it, although nothing on either side. There was a bar though, and a pool, and a fine restaurant and the hotel was on its own and it was on the beach, so we were happy.

The place was deathly quiet: we seemed to be the only guests. We spent lunchtimes and afternoons by the pool by ourselves, drinking icy lager from frosted glasses.

In the mornings we took long walks along the deserted beach. On the second morning we saw a young European girl watching us from the road as we walked along the sea edge, picking up shells and drift. She came down to see us and we stopped and chatted and found out that she lived here with her parents. She said there was nothing to do and she was bored stiff. She was English and about 15. She walked with us and we all plodded along the sand for an hour, before turning back and retracing our steps. During the walk, we told seafaring tales of derring-do to impress her: she was attracted to Jimmy. She ignored me.

When we arrived back opposite the hotel, a huge, fierce English woman with a red face came pounding across the sands towards us, screeching. She grabbed hold of the girl by the arm then told us our behaviour was disgusting and we should be ashamed of ourselves for trying to entice away an innocent girl. The girl looked cowered as she was dragged away. We stood there looking ashamed of our evilness. The woman hurled abuse over her shoulder as she stalked back to her car, dragging her daughter behind her. There are few sights more unnerving that an outraged Englishwoman abroad.

On the morning of the fourth day, we set out from Ras Al Khaymah on a fast launch across the clear blue waters of the Persian Gulf to rendezvous with the *Horomaya*. We came across her half an hour later as she lay rocking in the gentle swell, an 18,000-ton white oil ship with a wooden pilot-ladder slung over the side for us to scale. The ship was light in the water and it was a long climb up the hull. We were both fit and strong, although clambering up a swaying rope-ladder is never easy. The Egyptian agent was having a real struggle ahead of us. He was fat and over 50 and he wheezed and groaned and stopped continually while we all held on, swinging gently back and forward, the launch far below. Jimmy and I looked at each other, sharing the same concern that the agent would have a heart attack and fall off to crash down onto us; we wished we had gone first. Two sailors swung out a small derrick and lowered a net to take our bags, which they hauled up to land on the deck. The bags arrived before we did. Eventually, the agent arrived at the top, mounted the rails and flopped on the deck where he sat for a few minutes to recover.

The H-class *Horomaya* was quite a bit smaller than the two V-class ships I had sailed on, although it was essentially the same three-castle layout – as were most tankers built in the 1950s: a raised fore-deck, then the fo'c'sle, the midships accommodation and stores block at the midpoint of the ship, and finally the bigger accommodation block at the after end, sweepingly known as 'aft', where the galley, the crew quarters, the engineers quarters, most of the stores and the entrance into the engine room were.

The ship seemed well cared for and had been freshly painted. We carried our bags across the gleaming forest green deck to midships, to seek out our cabin. There were in fact two double cabins for cadets and we were the only ones, which gave us a cabin each. That was a good start. We dropped off our kit then went up to see the Old Man and sign on.

The Old Man was an odd looking Geordie – jug ears, long neck, huge mouth, multi-directional teeth, big hands and big feet: a short man but gangly at the same time. He had a foghorn of a voice: "Howay, why-aye, lads! 'Bout time ta! Bluddy wog agen', buggerin' ev'ythin' oop. Naa mind. Yoos canna cumta better ship than the *Horomaya*, man." He glowered at the 'bloody wog agent', who was sitting oblivious on the day bed, still sweating and looking pale and exhausted, clutching a frosted can of Tennants lager. "Look at 'im! Fat bastard!"

"Yes, sir," I said.

"Aye, sir," said Jimmy.

"Reet, yoos two. Apes? Aye, course y'are. Gimme yoos discharge books." We handed them over, together with our seaman's ID cards. "I donna want them bluddy things, man!" He tossed the cards back to us impatiently. "Just yoos discharge books."

He entered our details in the big buff-coloured log-book and then pointed to a place for us to each sign. "Here, sign here, both of yoos." he jabbed at the page.

We signed. Committed. No going back, not that there was, once we climbed aboard the aircraft to Dubai anyway.

"Reet, that's done. Yoos trapped. Now, lissen t'me. I'm Cap'n Carrow and I'm either a bastard with a capital B, or yoos'll love me. I conna care less which it is, man. Work hard, do all yoos course work and keep in the mate's good books and everythin'll be greet. If yoos dinna do that, it'll be bluddy hell on earth, Geddit?"

"Aye, aye, sir," we said in unison.

"Reet, now booger off and see the mate!" He turned his back on us and shouted at the agent. "An joss what the bluddy-hell is gannin' on, Abdul? I've been hangin' around here fa' bluddy ages, man!"

We left and went down a deck to find the chief mate. The chief mate was quiet in comparison with the Old Man. He looked quite old to us – probably mid-40s, a hard-looking man with iron-grey hair and a granite jaw. He looked weary although he greeted us with some warmth. "First cadets we've had on here for a while. The crew will be pleased." We smiled politely. "In fact, first time I've seen them happy for a while, when they heard two cadets were joining." We could imagine. Always nice to have someone firmly at the bottom of the chain.

The chief mate gave us a briefing. We would be on day-work at sea and on watch with the officers in port, and also when arriving and departing. I would be on the four-to-eight – the chief mate's watch – and Jimmy would be on the twelve-to-four, with the second mate.

We were warned to tread carefully with the crew: "They're a bad bunch and nothing but trouble. The bosun is good and so are a couple of the senior ABs but the rest of the deck crew are nothing but trouble. Bone-idle too."

"What sort of trouble are they, sir?" asked Jimmy.

"Well, we have a split crew on deck," the mate replied. "Half of them are young lads and the other half are older. Each group has its problems. You'll soon see," he added mysteriously.

We were told to unpack, then have some lunch, and then turn to, seeing the bosun for work. Our first job: holystoning the boat deck – my favourite. So nice to learn new skills.

The crew weren't so much a bad crew – they were just badly run. The bosun was a good seaman but not really tough enough to run a white crew of a deep-sea ship where everyone was away from home for at least nine months. The chief mate looked a hard man, but in truth he just wanted a quite life and he let the ship run on a casual basis. Between the chief mate and the bosun they let things slide, which suited the crew because they could then work at an

The SS Horomaya *at sea (www.fotoflite.com).*

easier pace. There was no real trouble as such and no need for Jimmy and me to 'watch our step'. There was just a lot frustration for the chief mate, who couldn't get things done as he wanted – but that's what happens if you let things slide.

White crew or Chinese crew? This was an on-going debate among officers aboard ship. The *Horamaya* had a white crew. A lot of the officers preferred Chinese crews because they didn't give as much trouble, generally speaking. Others thought there was nothing better than a true-blue British crew, because they could be relied upon more when the chips were down. At that stage of my life I didn't have a preference; I was happy with either crewing system; they were just different.

The crew of the *Horomaya* were not efficient, because of the division between them and because of the lack of discipline that had been allowed to take hold. Essentially, the division was because there were two groups: the 'old' ones and the 'young' ones. This division affected both the deck crew and the engine-room crew, although we deck cadets were only concerned with the deck crew – of which there were four grades: able seaman (AB); efficient deck hand (EDH); deck hand uncertified (DHU); and deck boys. Deck boys were first-trippers under the age of 18.

Of the deck crew for the *Horomya*, the old ones were experienced ABs who were mostly in their 40s, some in their 50s. They had been to sea for decades and were good seaman who knew most of what there was to know. The young ones were in their late-teens and 20s, ABs and EDHs, mostly competent seaman although clearly less experienced. The old ones thought the young ones were idle lads who didn't know what they were doing and needed to be kept in order, whereas the young ones thought the old ones were over-the-hill fools who couldn't work properly and didn't know what was going on. It was, I suppose, pretty much the same relationship that existed in all walks of life and had existed for time immemorial.

Now, that might have been a resolvable situation, if that were all: but there was another dimension. The older ones drank; the younger ones took drugs. We referred to the old ones as the 'alchies' and the young ones as the 'junkies'.

In the morning, the crew would turn to for work, or at least the junkies would. The alchies would be unable to get up because they were still suffering from the night before, after drinking into the early morning hours. At mid-morning smoko, the alchies were starting to surface, although they remained unfit to work, hanging around listlessly, glugging cold water and drinking tea. The junkies were then enjoying their first spliff of the day. By late morning, the more robust alchies were back at work and holding their own with the junkies. After lunch, all the alchies were back at work, even though some remained a bit delicate. The first junkies had dropped out after a narcotic lunch and the rest started in the afternoon, although were only operating at half-speed. Come mid-afternoon smoko, all the alchies were working at full-rate and the last of the junkies had left the stage, too spaced out to continue working.

The alchies bought their beer quite legally from the ship's bond. They crew was supposed to be limited to buying beer only – no spirits – although, in practice, they managed to get whenever they wanted to drink by a combination of bribing the stewards, stocking up on local hooch when the ship was in port, and the odd bit of opportunity theft. For the most part however, beer was the drink of the day: they drunk it by the crate, day in, day out. Their appetite for drinking was prodigious. There was no real restriction on the amount of beer they could buy – only a poorly-enforced rule that no one should have the equivalent of more than four cans a day on average. However, the junkies didn't drink much and were quite happy to buy beer for the alchies' use, selling it to them at a slight premium, which then paid for their marijuana and occasional pills.

The junkies had catholic tastes in drugs and would try anything – organic or chemical – that they believed would give them a buzz. The *Horomaya* had come from India, which offered good scope for marijuana and had allowed them to stock up well. In the East they would venture into obscure parts of town to buy whatever amphetamines and barbiturates could be obtained. Their conversations were peppered with talk of uppers and downers, reds and blues, bennies and bombers, browns and dexies, jelly beans and purple hearts, sprays and cleaners, sniffs and dunks. They carried out controlled experiments with shoe polish, varnish and various cleaning agents. There were always a couple of junkies hanging around the paint store, where they could be seen sucking in fumes from the big drums of red lead, zinc chromate and other oil-based paints. The real delight for the junkies on a white oil tanker was the cargo itself. For an instant high, they would unscrew the ullage cap of a tank full of JP4 or some high-grade propellant fuel, insert their face over the ullage pipe and draw in a huge deep lungful. That would cause them to flop backwards, saying things to each other like: "Wow, man. Try a hit of three-starboard tank. That's real high-grade stuff in there, man. Too much, man… too much." And then they would float off around the deck. Junkie heaven.

So, what we had was a crew that kept going throughout the day in a fractured way; never at full strength, although always with enough people to continue the job, albeit at an overall sedentary pace.

Once we saw the working pattern of the crew, we became a bit despondent because we thought that a lot of extra work would fall on us two new cadets. Jimmy growled about it and was set to rebel. However, things didn't work out like that, and we settled into a slightly slower pace of life than usual – certainly slower that I had been used to.

The crew of the *Horomaya* were mostly a docile bunch and didn't have the suppressed menace and violence of the only previous white crew I had sailed with. The alchies became riled on occasions and fought among themselves, but that was rare. The junkies never caused trouble.

There was only one exception: one singularly different individual; one person who walked out of step with the others. He was grouped as one of the alchies, even though his drinking was only occasional, thankfully. He was McAllister.

McAllister was unchanged from when I had known him on the *Valvata*: genial, soft-spoken, polite and reserved when sober – which was most of the time – although a monster when drunk. People said he was lucky to get another ship after his escapade on the *Valvata*, although his sober charm had probably carried him through, as it had done for many years. He knew his faults and tried not to drink. In the evenings, he sat in the crew's mess and talked and played cards with the alchie brigade, absorbing their increasing erratic behaviour as they became more and more drunk, until it was too much for him to bear and he went to bed. In the months I was aboard the *Horomaya*, McAllister only fell off the wagon once: it was another sight to remember.

We had been aboard about six weeks, during which we undertook the standard slavish labour, when the chief mate decided our knowledge of navigation and bridge-work was woefully inadequate and we should spend a week on the bridge under an officer of the watch. We were pleased about this, because it meant a respite from our usual fare.

I was put with Max, the third mate, on the eight-to-twelve watch. Max was good fun. He had transferred over from Palm Line, where he had served his cadetship going back and forth between the UK and Europe to West Africa. Max had a wild edge and we whiled away the night-watches with many a fine story of his escapades along the West African coast, during which he appeared to have shagged the entire female population.

Usually, as we approached and left port, we cadets would spend time on the bridge – although this was mostly dogsbody work: meeting the pilot, manning the engine telegraph, putting up and taking down flags, and all the general jobs that a well-trained monkey could do; well, I suppose we were apes after all.

The bridge at sea was altogether a different place the when going in and out of port: none of the frantic activity we were used to, just calm and measured progress as the ship cleaved its way through the water. We were mostly in sight of the coast during my week, and under Max's tutelage I plotted the ships course by taking compass bearings, kept radar watch, kept watch for other craft – large and small – making sure we kept a wide berth. Traffic was moderate in the South China Sea and we could expect to meet several other deep-sea ships each watch – as well as a constant host of small fishing vessels, usually open wooden dugouts with outboards, which stayed within a couple of miles of the shore. At night they were lit up with naphtha lamps.

I wrote up the log-book at the end of the watch, using the flowery language that the task required. In addition to being a commercial oil tanker, we were also a weather ship, which meant that we also had to keep a special weather log every six hours: observations on cloud type, wind speed and direction, visibility, the state of the sea, air and sea temperatures, air pressure and barometric graph trends.

In the morning watch, the lookout was given maintenance tasks near to hand and Max and I kept lookout and did all the chart work. The steering was on autopilot.

I enjoyed the night watch, because I could either talk with Max or loaf on the bridge wing, leaning on the dodger and staring out at the night. The bridge was kept dark to ensure we didn't lose our night vision; the lamp in the chartroom was kept down low. On the night watches I learnt to keep a lookout for other ships by looking 5 degrees above the horizon – not at it, because our light vision is in the periphery of our eyes.

On some nights, the marine bioluminescence, which the old sailors called 'phosphorescence', caused bright green and white flickering lights to tumble along the side of the ship in the turning wake; it could be hypnotic.

The watch sailor would be hunched against the corner of the bridge wing at night, keeping lookout and slyly smoking when the third mate was in the chart room. If a ship passed by close at night – close being within a couple of miles – Max would tell me to connect the Aldis lamp and engage in a Morse-code conversation. There were usually a lot of British ships in the South China Sea and we would often find ourselves conversing with ships of the P&O Line, Blue Funnel Line, Ben Line, China Navigation, Bank Line, Jardine Matherson and others. The messaging was always much the same, ship after ship:

'What ship and where bound?'

'Sinkiang for Singapore. What about you?'

'Vexilla for Kobe.'

'Where from?'

'Hong Kong. Where you from?'

'Djakarta.'

'What cargo are you carrying?'

'General and machinery. What about you?'

'White oil.'

'What beer do you have?'

'Heineken.'

'We've got Tiger.'

'Happy sailing.'

'You too.'

And we passed in the night.

The Old Man usually came up to the bridge just before the watch commenced, to chat to the chief mate, see the watch was properly changed, study the chart and write up his night orders. If we were going to be sailing by a narrow passage or passing close to shoals or some busy headland, then he would ask to be called on the approaches, otherwise, his written orders would usually say the same thing: 'Plot position every 30 minutes, keep at least 5 miles off and land or shoal, watch for drift. Call me if the weather turns or if in any doubt...'

Working in white tropical uniform day after day, bereft of grime, was a novel experience, and an enjoyable one. The only bad aspect was having to wash and iron our whites a lot more. On day-work, we only wore whites for meals and in the bar: a set of whites would last several days. On bridge-work we had to change into fresh whites every day. Unlike the officers, we cadets had no steward to do our laundry.

Laundry was called '*dhobie*': an Indian word. Jimmy and I were hopeless *dhobie*-men and we both caught *dhobie*-rash, which is a painful red itch caused by not rinsing out the soap powder properly and then sweating in the clothes. The washing machine we used was a square noisy tub with a big centre paddle. We threw all our dirty clothes in, filled it with cold water, poured in a generous helping of soap powder then went off to the bar. The machine was known as a 'tanglematic' for the good reason that everything became meshed into a string of hard knots by the end of the wash. We would drag it out of the machine at the end, flop the whole mess of clothes into the shower for a rinse, wind it through a mangle, and iron the sorry result. We looked much smarter than we deserved.

After a couple of months we received orders to sail east across the Pacific, through the Panama Canal to Curacao and then across to West Africa. Max was delighted to receive the orders and was looking forward to seeing his old West African stomping grounds of Sierra Leone, the Ivory Coast, Ghana, Togoland and Nigeria. The Pacific crossing was back-to-back, long and balmy days; both of us on day-work, chipping, painting, holystoning, repairing ropes and wires, getting browner, getting stronger.

We crossed the Pacific without cargo, just water ballast in several of the tanks. We started tank-cleaning a couple of days out, although this was a white oil ship and so the cleaning process was a much easier task: it was easier because the product was cleaner and there was no sludge, although it was more dangerous due to the gas content being much more lethal.

We watched all the films then watched the best of them again. The days merged into each other, broken by Saturday-study and Sunday. On Saturdays, we were corralled into the ship's office and forced to grind through our wretched correspondence courses. Captain Carrow would come in sometimes, when he was bored, and berate us in his strangled English, looking over our shoulders and telling us how mediocre our standard of work was compared to when he was our age.

And then there was Sunday. Sunday was a special day. At least, Sunday afternoon was special: Sunday morning at sea was inspection day. Our cabins had to be spotless, cleaned and gleaming, with everything in its place. We set to after breakfast, scrubbing and washing and wiping and cleaning and tidying. The inspection party set off at 10.30 a.m.; it was comprised of the Old Man, chief mate, chief engineer and chief steward, touring every cabin, every alleyway; every public space.

The cadets' cabins warranted special attention: the Old Man would come in, shrieking before he even got to the doorway: "A' why-aye, man! Whut the bluddy hell is gannin' on here?"

"Good morning, sir."

"Whut a bluddy shite-house! Chief Mate! Order two bales of straw for this dirty bastatt!"

"Will do, Cap'n."

"Chief Steward! I dinna want this animal in the saloon agin. Jos' bring a big trough in here for the filthy bastatt to eat from!"

"Aye, aye, sir."

"Chief Engineer! Get the air-con turned off in here! The porthole needs to be opened ta drive oot the bluddy stink!"

"Yes, Cap'n."

The Old Man would then wink theatrically and move off, the others trailing in his wake.

I would hear the same show repeated in Jimmy's cabin as the team passed down the alleyway. Nothing varied, week on week.

Sunday afternoons at sea were a luxury: time off. Sometimes, provided the mate was satisfied the ships stability could warrant it, the swimming pool was filled up. Sea water was used; fresh water was too precious. It wasn't much by swimming-pool standards: 30 foot by 20 foot and 8 foot deep, and the water sloshed over the sides if the ship was rolling. The pool was situated just aft of the funnel, so it was noisy, the water vibrated and occasionally gouts of soot would fall in, but it was great fun to jump in and out of, and fight each other in the water.

Afterwards, I would lie in the sun on the monkey island, which is the deck on top of the bridge housing, and grill myself until well-done, reading a book. Jimmy had pale skin and burnt easily, so generally stayed out of the sun if he could, but I loved it and would go as brown as an Asian.

The ship's library didn't have that many books and they were hardly ever changed, so I ended up working my way through books I would never normally have opened. I started off by going through the adventure novels and thrillers, working my way to the low-end westerns and science fiction, interspersing with histories of the great and the infamous – of Hannibal and Napoleon and Scott and Hitler and Wolfe – accounts of engineers who built great railroads and bridges, scientific journals, diaries on discoveries, wars, archaeology, nature, wildlife, books on hypnotism and card tricks and pubs and woodworking and gardens and food and mountain climbing and much more. There was also a paperback library, full of books left behind. All in all, there was enough to read, as long as you were content to have a broad expression. I read a lot, when I could; Sundays and other days.

Jimmy was surprisingly tame, I didn't know whether to be disappointed, surprised or impressed. The trip on the *Vexilla* with John and Barry had been pretty wild and I suppose I had been expecting more of the same, or even more, when sailing with Jimmy. I envisaged him capering and fooling about, to either everyone's rage or amusement, but he was altogether more serious. He had his turns and would often have me be rolling around the deck, unable to speak with laughter. But a lot of the time he aired his views on life in a serious way:

his support for the IRA, his passion for Glasgow Celtic, his socialism. He seemed strangely moral; more so than me anyway, which was no great feat. He would even give me occasional lectures on how to conduct myself in life, which I thought was a bit rich, although he was always very astute in picking out my weaknesses.

Jimmy got on well with the crew and they all liked him. Captain Carrow thought he was an oaf and the mate thought he was deliberately exaggerating his accent so as to make himself unintelligible, which might not have been far from the truth, although most of the other officers liked him.

He was certainly a different person that the clown from P1 23. I said this to him once and he replied by saying: "Get off your horse, Hally. Ah'm no' here for ye bloody amusement." I thought about that for a while and concluded: 'How true.' He was close to his family, although his father had had a stroke or suffered an accident of some sort – I'm not sure which: I just knew he couldn't work. It made Jimmy sad talking about it. He had a younger sister and I used to goad him by saying I was going to come up to Glasgow and shag her. His sister sounded bright and attractive and I used to quiz him about her for hours: I asked him how he would feel about having me for a brother-in-law, which would always be guaranteed to bring the conversation to an end.

Jimmy had some wild friends in Glasgow; some of whom I had met during the term-break in P1 23, when we went up to Scotland for a few days. I remember them all as being fearsome drinkers and hilarious companions. Jimmy would regale me with tales of Glasgow nights.

We arrived at Balboa, at the Pacific end of the Panama Canal, and trundled through, assisted by the Panama mules. In days gone by, real mules were used to drag the ships through the locks, although today's mules are little engines on rails, diesel-driven. Ropes were shackled to the mules, run through the rollers and secured to the ship; the little mules, small but strong, then towed us steadily through the canal locks. It was an interesting experience: Jimmy and I were posted on deck to watch for any veering off that might necessitate dragging a pudding fender into place to protect the ships plating from damage. This resulted in a quiet and gentle trip through for us for the eight hours it took to traverse the canal, mostly just watching the Central American world go by, between locks and smokos and minor crises.

We reached Cristobal, on the Atlantic side, cast off the pilot and set course across the Caribbean for Curacao. Curacao was part of the Dutch Antilles and was famous among seaman for two things: the biggest oil refinery in the Caribbean – the Shell refinery – and the biggest brothel in the Caribbean: the *Campo Alegre*. *Campo Alegre* translates to 'Camp Happiness'. Most people went to the *Campo* just to say they had been there and because they had a lively bar which made everyone welcome, even those who were not participating in the main activity.

The crew queued up outside the chief steward's office for king-sized subs for the *Campo* when we arrived. There was a regular bus from the docks and most of the off-duty crew clattered down the gangway in a swarm, clutching fistfuls of *guilders*, as soon as the ship was granted customs and immigration clearance.

The author in tropical white uniform on the deck of the Horomaya.

I was on the eight-to-twelve watch that night and went up to see the *Campo* with Max after we got off at midnight. The *Campo* was huge and clean, lots of brightly painted cabins scattered around a big central area with a bar and restaurant. It was packed out with British and Dutch sailors and a few Germans. We sat at the bar and drunk Amstel, girls twittering around us: gorgeous Latin ladies, mostly from Venezuela. They had poor English skills but made up for it with South American smoulder. After about an hour, Max announced that he was going shagging and I was left at the bar with a group of Dutch junior officers from the ship that was tied up astern of the *Horomaya*. They seemed a nice enough crowd, although I noticed the bosun keeping a wary eye on me from across the floor. It was a long night; at 2.00 a.m, I went down to the chocolate box capital, Willemstad, with the Dutch officers, to be introduced to the late night-life. I don't remember going back to the ship, but the next morning I felt ghastly and ruined and moved around the deck like one of the living dead.

We loaded a full cargo in 30 hours and set off, heading for West Africa, with brief outward stops at a couple of Caribbean islands before we hit the Atlantic.

☆　☆　☆

The Atlantic crossing was fairly uneventful. The junkies were getting excited about West Africa because there was apparently a lot of good weed to be had. The alchies were looking forward to it too; heaven to them was sitting in Tema Harbour, sun-reddened and staggering drunk on cheap local beer, telling each other the same old stories they had told each other the previous time they were ashore.

Our orders gave us a busy pattern of ports, unloading our cargo as we went along. We would start at Freetown in Sierra Leone then move down the coast, stopping at various places as we went. Each stay in port would be for between 12 and 24 hours. The next stop would be Abijan in the Ivory Coast, then east to Tema and Takoradi in Ghana, Lome in Togoland, Cotonou in Benin, southeast to Bonny in Nigeria, then down to Pointe Noire in the Republic of Congo. It all sounded enticing to me. I was particularly keen to see Tema, because I was charmed by the enchanting song *Tema Harbour*; and also Pointe Noire, as I had recently read Conrad's *Heart of Darkness* and wanted to view the rolling Congo River.

I had a fever attack in Freetown. The Old Man told me, with a happy face as I remember, that I had malaria and I could look forward to it being with me for the rest of my life, suffering periodic attacks. I was still expected to work though, and I lurched around the deck, sweat pouring off me in rivulets, my head hurting so much I couldn't see, my every joint aching. Eventually, I became too weak to carry the ullage tape and collapsed outside the ship's office. The third mate and the duty AB carried me to my cabin and lay me on my bunk and I was given the rest of the watch off. The next morning I got up and lay in the shower and wept with pain, misery and self-pity, before going out on deck. The chief mate looked at me with concern and sent me back to my cabin. I woke up three days later, as we were leaving Takoradi. I had the strength of a five-year-old and took a further two days to fully recover, but my head was better and I was as hungry as a horse. I was annoyed I had missed Tema. I never had another fever attack.

We left one of the ABs behind in Takoradi – one of the junkie-set who was known as 'Leech'. Leech was a pale, skinny man of about 25, with shoulder-length ginger hair, a nervous twitch and a permanently spaced-out expression. In fact, he looked exactly like everyone thought a drug-crazed hippy should look, although I always found him a friendly man who could be quite charming in between his bouts of sticking his head into a tank of jet fuel fumes or stuffing himself with pills, after which he moved into another world. It remained a mystery as to what actually happened to him. The ship was delayed for several hours and the captain and chief mate looked very grim. Jimmy and I made sure we wore our grim faces too.

There were various stories circulating that he had been thrown in prison, had been kidnapped, had been murdered, had signed on a Norwegian freighter or had gone into the bush to join a tribe that grew weed. I subscribed to the belief that he had been killed in a fight in a bar near the docks and dumped in the harbour with weights tied to him. I based this on the good authority of Jimmy, who had been told this by the second mate, who had been told this by the chief mate. It was only after a few days that this story lost its credibility when I found out that the chief mate's source was the bosun, who in turn had been told by one of the AB alchies, who had been told by one of the dock workers, who he had met in a bar when he was drunk out of his skull.

Usually, when a sailor went adrift and missed his ship (a fairly frequent occurrence), he eventually turned up and was then sent on to join the ship at the next port of call: he had to pay his travel expenses for the privilege. We were therefore expecting Leech to turn up before we left Pointe Noire, but he never did and was never heard of again, as far as I know. Perhaps he is actually at the bottom of Takoradi Harbour.

Leech's disappearance aside, the junkies had a good run during the West African sojourn. Weed was plentiful and the pace of life was… West African: the sun always shone and the *Horomaya* was an easy ship to work – it didn't make any great demands.

The alchies had an equally good time. The ports that were in ex-French African colonies had a certain refinement not usually present in the ex-British West African colonies, which tended to be grim with few redeeming virtues. However, there was reasonable beer at good prices in most places, as well as good wine in the Francophile countries. These aspects, coupled with the sun and slow pace of life, made the West African coast admired by the alchie crowd. They would set off ashore when the sun went down, clustered together in a noisy bunch, clattering down the gangway in good spirits, the earliest returning from midnight onwards.

The midnight returns were classic Jolly-Jack-ashore scenarios: singing, weaving from side-to-side, sometimes slightly bloodied, broke, happy. At the top of the gangway they would shout greetings to the deck watch, throw their arms around each other, sing louder, urinate over the side, fall down, vomit. It was all very entertaining for those of us finishing the eight-to-twelve watch.

Those who returned the next morning, alone or in ones and twos, presented an altogether different picture: they looked dreadful, like zombies. There was no noise, no jollity, no trace of merriment. One foot was slowly and painfully planted in front of the other while looking straight ahead, clothes torn, blotches of blood, patches of vomit, terrible deathlike faces. Sometimes a woman would be in tow, usually an awful creature in the same state as the sailor who had brought her back: she had to be turned back at the gangway by the duty cadet, to her crushing dismay and to the sailor's utter indifference.

One of the memorable highlights of the West African trip was the loud thump as McAllister fell off the wagon. He was a midnight returnee in Cotonou: he crawled up the gangway on all fours, muttering and swearing to himself, after ostensibly having gone ashore for a 'breath of fresh air' in the late afternoon at the end of his twelve-to-four watch.

I was handing over to Jimmy at the time. We moved into the shadows under the manifolds when we saw Mac crawling up the gangway. When he reached the top, Mac hauled himself to his feet and stood there swaying and glaring around for someone to abuse. No one was there. "Arrgghh!" he screamed at the top of his voice, trying to draw someone out. "Arrgghh! You're all bastards!" He then fell backwards onto the gangway, slid down head-first for a couple of yards and rolled under the rope rails and out over the side.

Gangway nets are slung under gangways for that very purpose, to catch those who are not sure of foot. Mac fell squarely into the net and lay there entangled, arms and legs hanging through the holes. He lay still for a moment or two; then started screeching and thrashing about, which only caused him to become more and more enmeshed. When five minutes had passed, we deemed it safe to go and inspect the catch. Poor old Mac, trussed up like a beast for slaughter: he glared at us in mad fury.

"What you doin' there, Mac?" asked Jimmy.

"Bugger off!"

"Sleeping outside tonight, Mac? Is your cabin too hot?" I enquired.

"You're a pair of bastards! Get me oot of here!"

"No chance, Mac. You sleep it off."

"Bastards!"

We walked off, chortling. The second mate came up and stood looking down at Mac, wrapped up in his net: "Well Mac. At least you're back for your midnight watch, I'll grant you that."

It was a good result really. Mac would have needed to be restrained if he hadn't become knotted in the gangway net. He was left there overnight to sleep it off. When I went down for breakfast the next morning, he was still in the net, sleeping like a baby.

My runs ashore in West Africa had become limited. I had worked throughout the whole stay in Freetown to let Jimmy get ashore, with the plan of me spending time off the ship in Tema and Contonou. However, I was then flattened by the fever I picked up, and was out for the count in Abijan, Tema and Takoradi. I then had to work the full stays in Lome, Cotonou and Bonny, to make up for my laziness in the previous three ports; I didn't mind working Bonny because we were offshore, tied to a buoy.

My only real time-off came in Pointe Noire in the Republic of Congo. I went ashore alone and wandered the streets, which were surprisingly clean, and had a pidgin-English-French conversation with a grizzled French trader in a bar. He had stayed on after independence. He told me tales of how wonderful life was in the good old days: it all sounded a bit exaggerated to me and I felt it was a case of someone looking over his shoulder at youth departed. I vowed never to become like that and kept reminding myself: 'These are the good old days.'

I wandered the market to look at the fly-blown food and all the junk laid out on sheets of coloured cloth and then had lunch in a quiet old colonial-style hotel, sitting on the terrace, cooled by a wooden fan clacking over my head. I felt a bit like Stanley searching for Livingstone. Sadly, I discovered that the Congo River itself, which I had wanted to see, was 100 miles to the south.

Jimmy and I bought parrots in Freetown, the fourth engineer and one of the alchies bought sooty mangabey monkeys. The vendors swarmed onboard from their fleet of wooden bum boats when we anchored in the roads, clutching animals and all sorts of exotics to sell. Our parrots were West African greys; I named mine 'Maurice'. He cost me 200 Rothmans. Maurice was noisy and vicious: he sat on the end of my bunk, where I had him restrained by a line tied to his leg; he squawked and bobbed and flapped his wings and defecated over my sheets and lunged at anyone who went near. I bought him in the morning and was fed up with his aggression by the afternoon, by which time I was starting to come down with the fever. The mate wanted a parrot too but there were no more for sale. He took a fancy to Maurice and I gladly sold him on, inflating the price to 200 Rothmans and a case of beer.

When we approached the end of the coastal run and were moored in in Pointe Noire, the Old Man announced that parrots could stay aboard after we left Africa although the monkeys had to go. The sooty mangabeys and had become very unpopular by that time: they were spiteful, vicious thieves that lived on the poop deck. Several sailors had been bitten. They ran up and down the deck, tethered by chains that slid along one of the deck-head pipes, leaping on the capstan and the railings, defecating everywhere, screaming incessantly. Food was flung at them because most people were too unnerved to go too near.

The fourth engineer muzzled his monkey and took it ashore in Point Noire to sell to a Frenchman for a loss. The alchie, an AB named Jardine, decided he would keep his monkey aboard the *Horomaya* and hide it from everyone. This probably serves to illustrate how uneven Jardine's mind was; he genuinely thought he could successfully keep a filthy, shrieking dangerous primate as a secret guest.

The Old Man got wind of the stowaway shortly after we had dropped off the pilot on leaving Pointe Noire and he sent the chief mate aft to find out what was going on. Jardine took fright when he heard the mate was on his way and he flung the monkey over the side. The crew were outraged at Jardine for his heartlessness and he took a beating, which put him in his bunk for the next two days.

Jimmy kept his parrot for several weeks before selling it on to the deck storekeeper.

Although fraternising with the crew was discouraged, we ignored this rule when it suited us. Jimmy used to spend a lot of time talking to a fireman and a deck boy, both of whom also came from Glasgow. I used to tell him that I could understand the monkeys and the parrots better than I could the three of them, when they started talking together in rapid-fire Glasgow street slang.

By this stage of my life I was a keen drinker – mostly beer – although I had not made any foray into drugs. This changed when I became friendly with one of the junkies – a friend of Leech's called Gus. Leech and Gus had always kept each other's company and he was upset when Leech failed to turn up before the ship sailed out of Takoradi. Gus was of a similar mould to Leech: shoulder-length hair and a pale, vacant expression. He was permanently grubby and had a strongly unpleasant smell.

I actually found Gus quite interesting. Despite his appearance, he was engaging beneath the surface and we had many long talks as we squatted in the sun and painted. He was the black sheep of the family; one of five well-educated sons, although the only one who hadn't conformed to his father's expectations in life. He was quite sanguine about this.

We steamed south after leaving Pointe Noire, heading for the Persian Gulf via the Cape of Good Hope: these were busy days as we put the ship in order following three weeks of abuse on the African coast. The bosun wanted me and Jimmy to help with the stowing of the ropes in the rope-locker, which meant that one of us went down in the locker and the other fed the rope down. I had expected to work with Jimmy, although the bosun decided that we should each work with one of the sailors, so Jimmy went forward with one of the ABs and I went aft with Gus. I was down in the locker coiling the 8-inch mooring ropes that Gus fed down the hatch. It was easy to start with, but by the time the fourth rope was in place, my arms and shoulders were heavy and aching. The bosun came to tell us to stand down as we were finishing the eighth and final rope. I clambered out of the rope locker and we both fell on the deck with exhaustion; I could hardly move my arms. The bosun gave us each a cold beer and we sat on the bits and watched the highway of the wake stretching out behind us while we recovered. Gus went off to the crew mess and returned with a couple more beers, then he brought out an enormous cannabis joint.

It seemed rude to refuse his offer to share, so we finished the monster together. Life slowly loosened for me and all problems and worries disappeared. Gus went inside and returned with more cans of beer, which were warm. He rolled a second joint.

I had an fleeting out-of-body experience and saw myself for what I was, as clearly as if I were sitting nearby as an observer: nearly 6 foot tall now, skinny, stringy muscles, burnt dark brown, blue shorts, bare-legged, paint-spattered deck shoes with no laces, faded blue work shirt, sleeves cut off at the shoulders, unshaven, hair over my ears and down to my collar, grinning foolishly at Gus and sucking on the weed. Gus said: "You're not like a real officer."

I put on a mock serious face and barked: "What did you say?"

Gus thought he had upset me, he stammered: "Wh-what? I meant, I meant, what I meant was…"

I laughed and said: "I'm not a real officer, Gus. I probably never will be." I felt the weed gripping my brain. We both started to laugh maniacally.

I could feel myself sliding into a dissolute place; into a dark pit that I felt I might not escape. I was not yet 18 but I drunk like a fish, worked like a beast, lived on the edge of violence and debauchery and now I was addling my mind with drugs. I opened the next can of beer with the spike that hung around my neck, took a swill and started choking with laughter. Gus came over and started pounding me on the back, asking me what was wrong. I was laughing and coughing too much to explain and had to carry on choking for a few seconds before I could reply. Finally: "It's the ultimate decadence, Gus," I spluttered.

"Whaddya mean, 'ultimate decadence'? What ultimate decadence?" He asked.

"I can't go any lower, Gus. I'm at rock bottom."

"I'm confused." Gus was confused.

"I'm drinking warm beer. How low can a man get?"

We hooted at my wit. The pit beckoned but I didn't look in: I just sat with Gus and chuckled at nothing and talked nonsense and drank warm beer and smoked good weed as the sun went down and the *Horomaya* steamed south to the Cape of Good Hope.

Age 18

I had my 18th birthday in the Indian Ocean, west of the Chagos Archipelago, en route to Bombay with a cargo of naphtha... Old enough to vote now.

7

All the Girls in the World

When it came to girls and sex, my weeks of shore-leave were a constant reminder that most people ashore had absolutely no idea of what life at sea was all about: no conception, nothing beyond bad cliché. It was beyond me to explain this to them; so I never bothered. The commonly held view was that girls who consorted with sailors, who worked in bars and clubs frequented by sailors, who sought relationships with sailors, or even if they happened to come into contact with sailors on more than an occasional basis, were automatically cast as being of dubious value: they were, in short, believed to be 'bad' girls. The term 'bad' was not intended to indicate dishonesty, although dishonesty was thought to be one of the many vices they probably possessed; it was more to indicate that this was a girl that they wouldn't consider taking into their own society. Such girls were believed to be, among other things: coarse, predatory, morally bankrupt, diseased and probably dishonest to boot.

Most people who went to sea, me included, thought otherwise. The 'bad' girls I met were just girls, they weren't bad: most were poor, most were uneducated – although usually good at languages – a lot were desperate, a lot had no choice as to where life had landed them. They made their living, one way or another, by contriving methods to part a sailor from his excess cash. Short of outright theft, any methods were acceptable. Everyone in the game knew what their respective role was and everyone accepted that wholeheartedly. To people who went to sea for a living, these girls were no worse (and often a lot better) than many of the girls in England who went downtown in packs on a Saturday night, looking to snare a likely lad.

'Bad' girls could be tremendous fun; they could be hugely entertaining and highly intelligent. But would they be considered the sort of girl to take back home? Sadly, the answer was a resounding 'No'. From time to time people did it – but it was not common.

In my teens, before I went away to sea, my experience with the opposite sex was limited. I was, in fact, a hopeless case: bashful and clueless, my tongue clogged in my mouth whenever I attempted to hold a conversation with any girl who was closer to me in age than she was to my mother. My attempts at being witty were met with looks of pity. When I dared to try and be charming, the payback was bewildered derision. When I tried to be suave, girls would snigger. When I acted offhand, I would simply end up on my own, standing there like some madman with my eyebrow-raising and mysterious smile. I was socially inept and I lived in fear of being forced into an encounter that would humiliate me. I was a tall and good looking lad and I attracted girls in the first place because of this, although I would generally drive them off in record time because I would say something so grossly foolish that I invariably ended up alone, the words of their shallow excuses ringing in my red ears.

Like all young men in their mid-teens, I would put on a good front with my peers though: a blend of indifference and confidence, interspersed with knowing comments about sex and everything that led up to it. It was vital to put forward that you knew what the whole game was about, even if you were still struggling to become a fringe bit-player – as I was when I went to sea.

I did try and I was desperate to succeed: there had been some meaningful groping with Doreen from Exeter and some heated struggling with Julia, a pretty girl at my last school. Julia took a shine to me because I was outside the mainstream and she believed I had some hidden strength and power; qualities that attract most girls. In my case however, any such qualities were particularly well hidden. Julia eventually discovered this and moved on to someone else; I feigned indifference.

There was also Carole and Beverly – both in my class at school in Singapore. Carole was the most beautiful girl I had ever seen: blonde hair, blue eyes, lips like moist cushions. Carole liked me – really liked me – and I liked her back. She was pursued by all the strutting athletes of the school and went out with most of them, but always came back to spend time with me. Not that we ever got beyond hand-holding and the occasional peck. My inability to really capture her tore at me; watching her move to her latest beau was like having a stake shoved through my heart. Eventually, I became fed up and disgusted with my mascot status and told her she had better make her mind up whether she wanted to go out with me or not. Bad move. We hardly ever spoke again.

Beverly was different: more of a minx, bordering on being 'bad'. She was petite and gorgeous and looked the picture of eye-fluttering innocence, although swore like a navvy and loved to talk about the detail of sex in a way that had me squirming with embarrassment. We went to the cinema a couple of times together, and once we met after school and went back to her house to roll clumsily around her bedroom floor, but in my heart I knew I had as much chance with Beverly as I did with Caroline: absolutely none.

Those apart, I had had a number of minor encounters, but otherwise was an innocent. Some people awarded me greater status in this area than I ever deserved, but when I left home at 16, I was as green as could be in the matter of the opposite sex.

My time at the School of Navigation in Plymouth gave me a kick-start, because I was closeted with John and Jimmy and Barry and others who knew how to act towards girls, knew how to speak to girls, knew how to pick up girls, knew how to charm girls. I aped their behaviour as best I could within the confines of my own personality, and began to grow in confidence and ability. I soon discovered that I was only really effective when I was drunk, although this proved to my advantage in my new world, where I usually became drunk whenever I went out: the requirement thus aided my chances, rather than hindered them.

When I first starting meeting 'bad' girls in the East, I couldn't believe how they acted towards me. I made jokes – they laughed; I told stories – they listened attentively; I complained about my hard day – they commiserated; I spoke of going to some dangerous place – they told me how brave I was; I bought them a drink – they told me how generous I was: if I was hurt, they comforted me; if I was agitated, they calmed me down; if I was tired, they soothed me. They made a point of telling me I was as handsome as a film star, that I was tall and strong and funny and rich and clever and fantastic company.

For a while, I thought that I had undergone some magical personality transformation, until the truth started to dawn: 'bad' girls acted in the same manner towards anyone who came into their orbit. They would have acted the same towards a monkey on a stick if it had money in its grubby little paw.

★   ★   ★

he 'bad' girls I met for the most part were bar-girls. Their job was to ensure the bar had an ambiance that brought customers in and kept them there. Customers, or the best customers, were men off the ships – preferably European, preferably young. The girls were uniformly young; most of them were poor and weakly educated, but by no means all of them. Some were absolutely stunning; most were good looking: the joke at the end of a run ashore was that even the ugly ones were good looking. Bar-girls usually finished working in bars by the time they reached their mid-20s. Some carried on until their late-20s or early-30s, but it was a struggle: front-line girls in the best bars had to be the best-looking ones.

Bar-girls were paid a pittance – if anything – for being in the bar and they made most of their money from commission on the drinks they were bought and any from tips they could get. Their drinks were small shots of coloured water, which cost the bar a few cents but cost the customer a few dollars. The uplift in money was split between the bar owner and the girl; the major part went to the bar owner. Some of the girls told us that only received a few cents for every drink that they were bought, but we usually took this to be an exaggeration: an attempt to extort a big tip by appealing to our sense of pity.

In the Far East there were bars of this sort in most ports – the bigger the port the bigger the bar area. The Ermita district in Manila was probably the most renowned: a long, sprawling, noisy mess of streets, bar after bar after bar and a few restaurants dotted between them. If a bar was empty then the resident girls would hang out the door and coo and call to passers by. Wanchai in Hong Kong was another well-known bar area, although the growing sophistication of the colony was causing the Wanchai bar area to shrink when I went to sea. When in Hong Kong, I preferred the Kowloon side, where there were fewer bars but they were more fun. All the big Japanese ports had bar districts too, but these were a mix that were also given over to local trade, with the sailors bars scattered in clumps among them. The same was true for Keelung and Kaoshung in Taiwan. Singapore's famed Anson Road bars were slowly closing as the city-state grew in prosperity and morality.

Most bar-girls spoke English of a sort, or at least spoke enough English to get by. They all flattered, most could be funny, and they could all dance. They all lived in hope of getting a rich Western boyfriend. Some whored on the side but these tended to be the minority. They were always pleased to see us arrive and always sorry to see us go.

Everyone recounted their runs ashore in the mainstream ports, because the names alone had a certain glamour and because this was where most ships went: Singapore, Hong Hong, Manila, Bangkok, Kobe, Pusan, Yokohama, Jakarta, Keelung, Kaoshung, Davao, Saigon, Penang. All these places had their respective bar areas, even though these were often chock-full of multi-purpose joints for sailors, the military, tourists and locals.

The 'best' bars, the real-McCoy-sailors'-bars, the bars that were only used by sailors, were in the little ports – the backwaters – the ports where we had to go upriver and tie up to a small jetty where there wasn't much except some cargo sheds, oil tanks and a few buildings... And a couple of bars.

These bars existed solely for the sailors that came in with the ships. The girls' lives revolved around the sailors. Places like Surabaya and Illigan had bars that would have closed down if the ships stopped coming in. They also tended to be a bit wilder than those in the big port bar districts and I seemed to get into more scrapes in the smaller places than I did in the major sea-ports.

In Makassar, a Dutchman whacked me in the face with a bottle for taking his girl: I hadn't done anything; he had stopped buying her drinks and she came over to my table to see if I was any more generous. As I was deliberating this, I saw a blur of green approaching me from the side and then his bottle of Heineken connected with the side of my face and knocked me off my chair. His attack caused a massive fight because a large complement from my ship was in the bar: they rose up and charged the Dutchman and his party. I saw little of the fight, lying stunned and bleeding on the floor, but afterwards I was told that we had won. I was lucky his bottle was full and hadn't shattered in my face. We celebrated by strutting among the admiring girls, who cooed at us victors. I was particularly admired because my face was bloodied; I played up heroically.

Later, the group of damaged Dutchmen came back into the bar to make peace and we ended up as a mob of friends, raucously chugging Heineken together and telling tales of other nights in other bars where similar antics had taken place; the girls were left out on the fringe, watching us curiously like we were lunatics.

One of the most memorable nights out I had in a Far East bar was in Bislig, in Mindanao: the second-largest of the 7,000 islands that makes up the Philippines. Mindanao had a problem with Muslim separatists, who shot government officials from time to time and occasionally blew something up, to get increased press coverage. The Mindanao problem had been around for decades. During the Japanese occupation, the separatists stopped killing government officials and started killing Japanese. At the end of the Pacific War, the Japanese were driven out, so they reverted to their old practice of killing government officials again.

When we arrived in Bislig, there had been a flare-up of hostilities after the separatists had discovered they received more media attention if they killed a foreign worker or a tourist. The government had sent in more troops and the shipping agent warned us not to go ashore: he was worried that we would be considered to be both foreign workers and tourists and would therefore be targeted as a sort of two-for-one offer. We thought this was nonsense and asked the Old Man if we could go ashore. He said he was quite happy as long as we had a guard; he gave the agent the task of providing one.

A canvas-top Jeepney drove up to the gangway and whoop-whooped its multi-tone horn. The shore-party – half a dozen of us – climbed in the back and sat on the bench seats that ran along either side. Our guard sat in the passenger seat: he had an M1 carbine across his legs and a Remington pump-action shotgun was propped up between his knees. He turned round and grinned at us – big piano-key teeth – then banged the dashboard and shouted at the driver in Tagalog. The Jeepney roared off into the early evening and we bumped down the rough road towards Bislig town centre.

We cruised down the main street. There were boardwalks either side, like a Wild West town. The guard asked us to pick a bar. We chose the Pink Pelican, which sounded decadent and looked good with its pink neon sign and batwing doors. The guard walked towards the bar, M1 carbine hanging on its strap over his shoulder, the Remington pump gun held port across his chest. He booted the batwing doors open like Wyatt Earp, and shouted in Tagalog at the people inside. A huddle of Filipino men slouched out reluctantly, glaring at us. The guard beckoned us inside, then took a chair and sat outside the batwing doors, facing the street, keeping us safe from whatever horrors of the night lurked out there.

The startled girls inside looked at our arrival as if Christmas had arrived. They shrieked with delight and rushed towards us. They were all small and light brown and smooth-skinned, with big eyes and big teeth and were as delicately tough as only Filipino girls can be. They made a tremendous racket, chattering and squealing as they grabbed at us.

The bar owner was so pleased to have some genuine high-spending customers instead of the frugal locals, that he declared a party night, which meant that the girls were allowed to join in by drinking real drinks, rather than coloured water. Their drinks cost us twice as much as our own beer but we still thought that was fair enough. We all grouped around a cluster of tables next to the bar, everyone shouting at each other and yelling with laughter.

The barman turned the music up and we grabbed partners and capered around the room to the blast of the Bee Gees, between rounds of San Miguel. I was with a girl who was sure-footed and as quick as a whip; I felt pretty nifty myself and I let myself imagine that we must have looked a dapper couple, like Fred Astaire and Ginger Rogers. The others all looked oafish, but not me, I was on top of the world.

There was a small stage at one end and from time to time the music would be turned off and one of the girls would mount the stage and bray tunelessly at us. We cheered, despite the awfulness of the acts.

There was a gathering crowd outside who were curious to look in the door and see us all at play and every now and then the guard would shout at them and wave his Remington threateningly. Small boys lay on the boardwalk and looked under the batwing doors. In between the music from the juke-box and the impromptu stage acts, we could hear a crackle of small-arms-fire from outside the town; it sounded quite close. The evening went on into the morning and we had a fabulous time.

Later, in the early hours, bumping back down the road towards our ship in the Jeepney, tracer-fire arced across the sky like angels going home, and we drank our bottles of San Miguel and clutched our precious memories close.

'Boat-girls' were a different set of ladies. They lived and worked on the small wooden boats that came out to ships at anchor. Some were official craft – the water tanker, the food-stores boat, the engine-room-stores lighter – although most were unofficial vendors waiting for the Q flag to be hauled down to indicate that the ship had health clearance, at which time they would swarm onboard. A ship at anchor in the roads of Hong Kong or Bangkok or Singapore or any of the big Far East ports would be a honey pot to the flies.

The Old Man sometimes gave orders not to let any girls onboard, but that was a losing battle. The crew would lower a monkey-ladder over the poop when no officers were there and the girls needed no time at all to be up the ladder and over the rail. They didn't sneak aboard; they rushed up the ladder, like a river of lemmings in reverse.

There were girls selling fruit and cold drinks: melons and rambutans and lychees and citrus and Coca Cola. They would take local currency, US dollars, pounds sterling, Deutschmarks, Japanese yen, Australian dollars or any major currency. They were as quick as machines in calculating exchange rates, which they always tipped in their favour.

Boat-girls were not shy: once aboard they would tour the ship, banging on the cabin doors and marching in, thrusting their wares at you and asking for a good reason if you didn't want to buy. It didn't matter what state you were in or if you were busy or even half-dressed. If you were asleep they would put the light on and wake you up. They would pester and badger and argue and try to charm until, in the end, most people would buy a cold drink or a piece of fruit just to get rid of them.

There were also the girls who sold all manner of souvenirs: carvings, bright and garish pennants, statues of ancient Chinese people, tee-shirts, semi-precious stones, old coins, birds in cages, grass snakes, small monkeys. They tended to be less aggressive and didn't go round all the cabins; instead they set up stalls on the poop deck or at the end of the flying bridge, waylaying everyone who went by, hectoring, goading, boasting, begging, bargaining.

And of course, inevitably, there were the boat-girls who sold themselves. The sailors would leer over the rails when their boat came by, sizing up the cargo. The girls leered up at the rails, doing likewise. The sort of girl who would be found motoring around the anchorage, selling herself for a 'short time' with the sailors was usually someone who was on a downward slope. She had probably been a bar-girl when she was a few years younger, who had done some soft whoring on the side, going with a customer who was good company and who she liked and was attracted to, beefing up her tip by sleeping with him.

These 'boat whores' were usually in a collective of half a dozen or so, with a male minder. They screamed up at the crew leaning over the side, as they approached:

"Hey, Johnny! You want jiggy-jig? You want short-time? Thirty dollar? You want?" They would thrust and grind their pelvises and shriek with laughter: "Come on, Johnny! You want me, yeh! Me plenty good jiggy-jig! Me clean girl! Thirty dollar, short time, jiggy-jig!"

The crew would banter back at them: "I give you five dollar, all-night jiggy-jig."

Cue outrage from the girls: "You cheap, Johnny! You cheap! All night 60 dollar! Short time 30 dollar!"

More goading from the crew: "How long short time? Four hour?"

"No! No! No! Short time only one hour! One hour: 30 dollar!"

"You cost too much! Twenty dollar for jiggy-jig for old woman like you!"

Real anger now from the girls: "You bastard, Johnny! Me not old! You old! Me young girl! You bastard, Johnny, you bastard! You old-man bastard!"

Roars of laughter from the crew: "Come on, old woman: come on ship and earn your 20 dollar!"

"You bastard, Johnny! You cheap! We go Japan ship! We no like British ship!"

After the banter died down, one of the crew would throw a monkey-ladder over the stern and the girls would clamber onboard, squealing and shouting, and going below to the crew quarters to ply their trade.

Brothels were invariably located near the docks, near the bars. I went in brothels on a number of occasions – not to partake, I hasten to add: I went when I was ashore with someone who wanted to visit, or with a group where someone felt the need. You don't leave your friends and shipmates when you go ashore, even if the place where you had to go was strange, or repulsive, or dangerous, or all of these. You could never walk away and leave someone to go into the dark alone. This binding to my fellow shipmates, even when I wanted to be anywhere else except where I was being led, caused me to visit brothels, cock-fights, street fights, drug dens, sex shows: all manner of strange and dark places that I would not have gone to if I were on my own.

I didn't find brothels particularly repulsive, although sometimes they could be dangerous. An American GI threatened to break my arms one evening in the lounge of a brothel off Geylang Road, Singapore, because he thought I was staring at him. He was spaced out. I sat without moving and waited for his friends to drag him away, which they did, although I held my bottle of Tiger ready to lay across his head if he came for me. Mainly though, I just found brothels tremendously sad.

A typical brothel in one of the ports in the Far East at that time was unobtrusive from the outside, comprising of a stand-alone building with a balcony that wasn't used, louver windows cracked open, and dim lights inside. The taxi drivers always knew where these places were. Sometimes one of the crew who had been to the port before might know of somewhere, but generally it was left to the taxi driver, who would receive a house commission for ferrying the party there. In the case of the super-brothels, such as the *Campo Alegre*, no guide was needed.

The other occasions when no one was needed to take us there, were when we were in one of the small river ports, where everything was at the end of the jetty: the bar, sometimes two, perhaps a shop and a brothel. In the really quiet places, where ships only came in once a week or less, the brothel was part of the bar, either upstairs or out the back.

To get into the typical brothel of the Far East, we had to hammer on the door or ring the bell. The door would be opened almost immediately by a smiling man in his 40s. He had level and unwavering eyes, like all hired muscle everywhere. He would size up the party and usually let us in. We were always in boisterous mood, which was acceptable, as was mild drunkenness; excessive drunkenness was not.

Jimmy and I had drinking with one of the fivers in Anson Road one evening. At midnight, the fiver became desperate for sex after being rejected by a bar-girl: it was the mark of abject failure to be refused by a bar-girl and we ribbed him mercilessly. We agreed to find him somewhere to sate his needs and gave instructions to a taxi driver to find us a 'good place, with good girls for short time.' The taxi driver drove us to his favoured place, which was across Singapore Island in Serangoon. We beat on the door, but as it opened – as the door was actually being opened – the fiver started vomiting. The man jumped back, as partly digested noodles propelled by Anchor beer came rushing out, splattering on the man's flip-flopped feet. He looked at us, he looked at the fiver, he looked at his feet, he glared at the taxi driver; he shut the door. The taxi driver muttered angrily to himself all the way back to Bugis Street and we felt compelled to give him a large tip to make up for his loss of commission.

Once inside a brothel, we would be led into a large lounge with sofas scattered around the walls. No music, dim lighting, tiled floor, little or no decoration – just a ceiling fan whirring and clattering above our heads and the cheep-cheep sound of night insects coming through the louvered windows. The man would depart and the *mama-san* would arrive. She fussed around and brought us cold beer and asked who was wanting what. Once she had identified the participants, the rest of us were ignored while she agreed terms, which was always money upfront and paid to the *mama-san*, never to the girl.

Essentially, the choice was 'short time', which was an hour, or 'all night' which lasted until early light and could be anything between two and six hours, depending upon when we arrived. We invariably arrived after midnight. No on ever wanted more than a short time.

The *mama-san* asked the players more specifically as to the type of girl wanted. Brothels in Singapore were generally acknowledged to be the best. The country and its citizens continually boasted of the success of its multi-cultural society, long before 'multi-cultural' became a buzz-word in the Western world. The Singapore brothels proudly shared this totem, and as such, always had a good range of girls: two or three sorts of Chinese; Malays; Indians; a Tamil; and a couple of Eurasians.

The *mama-san* then ordered the beauty parade. Although she might have nodded wisely when someone expressed a preference for a small Chinese or an experienced Indian or whatever else had been asked for, she still brought out a diverse stable to choose from. The girls would come into the room and stand in a line – smiling, posing, tilting their heads, and doing their damnedest.

This was always the part that I found so palpably sad: it was heart-cracking to see them all standing there. I wanted to throw all my money at them and run. They stood in their plain, everyday clothes, nothing particularly exciting or revealing: simple dresses, perhaps jeans and a top, bare feet or plastic sandals. Their expressions were etched on: plastic masks would have been as genuine. God knows what was going on behind the façade, what nest of worms.

It was rare to see any girl in any brothel who would be considered beautiful. They were mostly a bit plain, a bit old, a bit fat, a bit used, with bad skin or in a bad shape, distorted by too much childbirth or fatigue or bad health. They all looked trapped. Not trapped by way of imprisonment; trapped by circumstance and trapped by necessity. They never looked ashamed – they did there best to deliver as bad actresses.

To me, they all looked grim and old – even when I was drunk, when everything usually looked better (and I was drunk on every single occasion I ever set foot in a Far East brothel). I couldn't imagine the circumstances when I would actually want to go with one of the girls, however low I sank.

Whomever had come to use the place – the sparks or one of the junior engineers, or sometimes the third mate – would make his selection, and the girl would simper as if she had just won first prize in the lottery. Then off they would go, arm-in-arm.

While he was off 'performing', those of us left behind in the lounge would carry on drinking as if nothing was going on. A girl would reappear periodically to bring us more beer and we treated the whole event as just being at yet another bar.

At the less salubrious establishments, we were sometimes reminded where we were because we could hear the grunts and squeals and slap-slap sounds coming through the paper-thin walls. This would culminate in cries of fake ecstasy from the girl, then silence, at which point we would whoop and cheer and clap.

The partaker would eventually return wearing a half-embarrassed-half-victorious smirk, the *mama-san* would come in beaming and try to entice another customer, and then we would have another beer while we waited for our taxi.

I made a wretched fool of myself at a whore-house in Singapore – I think it was somewhere in Katong, off the East Coast Road. I was ashore from the *Horomaya* with the second engineer – a big, course Welshman – and one of the fifth engineers who was a timid first-tripper. The second was taking the fiver to lose his virginity.

We sat in the lounge on rattan furniture while the parade started. The second chose a monstrous Indian woman to celebrate the fiver's sexual christening. She looked cock-a-hoop: it was probably the first time someone had chosen her in an age. The fiver had actually preferred a homely-looking Malay who was standing quietly at the end of the row, but the Indian was having none of it. She grabbed him by the arm and dragged the hapless man off to her den. He looked back over his shoulder at me, his face a picture of bewildered terror. I waved at him, merrily, giving him a thumbs-up sign and what I felt was a reassuring smile. The second chose a chunky, grinning Chinese woman. The *mama-san* looked at me and cocked an eyebrow to see if I was going to partake, but I shook my head. She clapped her hands and the remaining girls filed out in a troop and I was left there on my own.

I sat in the chair and drank my cold Tiger and smoked and waited. I watched the cockroaches scuttling across the floor and watched the chit-chats – small geckos – navigate the walls and ceiling, chasing flies. I could hear a distant rhythmic slapping of flesh and wondered what was happening to the poor fiver. I finished my bottle of Tiger and placed it on the tiled floor with a deliberately noisy double-click, to signal I wanted another.

The girl who arrived a couple of minutes later took my breath away. She was about my age, Chinese, possibly part-Eurasian, hair like silk, delicate features, charming smile, slim, elegant, poised, straight-backed, a complete picture of oriental beauty.

It was one in the morning. I was drunk. I wanted to rescue her.

I asked her to sit down. Her name was Mai. I told her she was beautiful. She smiled and giggled. I asked if I could speak to her for a while. She smiled and told me to wait. I waited, conjuring an image of us fleeing the clutches that trapped her in the place: me having delivered her from evil; saved before she moved from waitress to sex worker. Mai returned with the *mama-san*, who was looking pleased: "You want Mai? Thirty dollar short time."

"No, only talk," I replied.

Mama-san looked at Mai, then back at me. She smiled understandingly: "OK. You talk. Thirty dollar for short-time talk."

I said: "*Mama-san*: I only want to talk. Talk here. Nothing more."

Mama-san showed signs of exasperation: "Thirty dollar for jiggy-jig. Thirty dollar for talk. You want Mai, you pay thirty dollar."

It was clear that I would have to pay thirty dollars, regardless. For the noble ends I had in mind, it seemed a price worth paying. I handed over three red ten-dollar bills. *Mama-san* nodded with satisfaction, said something to Mai in Cantonese and left the room. Mai took me by the arm and led me down a narrow corridor that was so poorly lit it was almost in darkness. She opened a door at the end and we went into a small room.

And it was a small room: single bed; bedside table; sink; three-drawer chest of drawers; clothes hanging on hooks on the wall; and street light filtering in from a small, high window. She closed the door, pulled a cord, and a single bare bulb lit up the room. The place was grubby; muscular cockroaches scurried under the bed. Mai turned and took me by both hands. She smiled: "You want jiggy-jig with me? That's good!"

I protested: "No, no. I just want to talk to you: be friends."

She looked baffled. She dropped my hands. "You no want jiggy-jig?"

"I just want to talk to you."

She started to look annoyed. "You don't like me?"

"I do like you, but I just want to talk to you."

Mai tilted her head back and peered at me down her nose for a moment. Disdain crept in: "Something wrong with you, yes? You sick? You no can jiggy-jig?"

I was a bit outraged and rushed to defend my manliness: "There is nothing wrong with me! I just want to talk to you, that's all."

Mai said: "Hah!" She sat down heavily on the bed. Her mouth twisted: it became ugly. I could feel my plans begin to slip away. I endeavoured to be earnest but I had drunk too much and I just pontificated, foolishly and to no effect. The situation continued to slide over the next 45 minutes while we sat on opposite ends of the bed and I tried to speak to her about her life and her job. My idea of her escaping seemed ever more ridiculous as she made it clear that she was no simple serving girl, and was in fact a quite willing member of the stable.

There was no real conversation as such. Mai mostly stared at the wall and ignored me or otherwise she grunted in monosyllabic reply to my questions. She did have occasional high-pitched eruptions, in which she told me I was stupid and didn't understand anything. I didn't discover anything about her, apart from the fact that she was shrewish and nasty. Beauty is only skin-deep. I was relieved when there was a banging at the door, followed by a man's voice saying: "Time finish now. You come out now."

I went back out into the lounge, Mai walking behind. She snapped bad-temperedly in Cantonese at the waiting *mama-san*, who looked at me sharply. The second and the fiver were sitting on the sofa.

The fiver was looking crushed. The second leered at me and said: "Well, Mr. Goody-two-shoes. I see you waited until the nice girls arrived, after we got saddled with the old cows."

I smiled weakly.

Wives at sea were like a different species to the girls we encountered ashore. The first thing that became apparent to me was that they adopted the rank of their husbands. The captain's wife would be treated with the greatest deference, unlike the wife of a fiver, who would just be regarded as great fun, if she was a fun-type person. This adoption of rank was, however, only in terms of looking up. For instance, the second mate would be ordered about by the chief mate, and in turn the second mate would dish out orders to the third mate and the cadets. The second mate's wife would be seen as being nominally 'above' the third mate and the cadets in terms of status, and nominally 'below' the chief mate and captain. However, while she would be looked up to by those below, she would never be looked down on by anyone superior to her husband.

Wives were great loafers. They loafed in the sun by the pool when it had been filled up at sea; otherwise they loafed in the sun in bikinis on the boat deck or on the monkey island. In cooler weather they mostly loafed in their cabins. They spent a lot of time in the bar, usually in the company of their husbands, although sometimes not – particularly when he had to sleep during the social hours because of the watch he was keeping.

Most wives spent a lot of time reading. Some had hobbies, some kept diaries. In the main, the majority of wives were kept on a fairly tight leash by their husbands, who had no illusions whatsoever about the level of morality of many people at sea.

A wife who was too independent of her husband and spent time drinking with the rest when her husband was in bed was not well thought of, for two reasons. First, it was generally assumed she was bored, which was probably true, and was therefore after a thrill of some sort. Too much drink and lack of female company make an interesting cocktail: a wife showing a loose side would be homed in on soon enough. Everyone could see it coming and everyone knew there would be trouble. No one wanted the trouble, but the potential pursuer, or pursuers, would be powerless to resist. Second, a wife on the prowl, away from her husband who was tucked up in bed, would be tolerated, although there would be resentment if she horned in on too many work-related conversations. The general feeling was that if someone brought their wife to sea, then they had an obligation to look after them, entertain them, and keep them from disrupting the wheel of life onboard.

Some wives were good value: amusing, clever, adding spice to the social life and blunting the harder edges of their husbands. This was greatly appreciated by most onboard, particularly by those at the bottom of the pile, the cadets. These were the better wives to have onboard: they organised games and quests and contests; they weaved a better social fabric through our lives, giving us more to do than just sit at the bar and drink and tell each other tales. They brought out the best in us.

One of the fivers had his wife with him onboard. He had been on for a couple of months when she flew out and joined him in Singapore. He was a non-descript man, small in stature and personality: the sort that joined the conversation in with a low-level laugh, although was always an onlooker and not a participant. On the odd occasions I found myself talking with him, he didn't have much to say; he just answered questions I asked, or acknowledged points I made, never adding to the stew of the conversation. His wife Tina arrived like a carnival hitting a sleepy town: she was a blast. She shrieked with laughter, she mocked everyone from the captain down – she mocked herself. She leapt on the bar-top and danced when loud music came on, and she told risqué jokes. She had a degree, her father was a vicar, she spoke four languages, she was as sharp as a whip, and she could out-argue anyone with a tongue. She understood how steam turbines worked and how aeroplanes flew. No one could beat her at chess or table tennis. She could explain Napoleon's tactics at the Battle of Austerlitz. She understood the philosophy of Herbert Spencer (I thought I was the only person alive who understood him). She was so charming that she inflated everyone she spoke to. We all felt better after a conversation with Tina. She was short and blonde and pretty and smiled – smiled all the time. She was slightly dumpy but all the nicer for it. I fell in love with her; everyone onboard fell in love with her. Everyone wanted to talk to her, and to be with her. She lifted her husband up. He became fabulous company: he was charming, he was witty, he was clever. We all wanted his company too. Tina was the very best of wives at sea.

Others were invasive and insensitive to the problems they caused and the tensions they created. The wives of the middle-ranking officers were often the worst and would sometimes try and act with too much authority, often to be brought down with a thump by a crude joke at their expense, and left stranded in abject humiliation that was difficult to recover from.

On the *Vexilla*, the second mate's wife was exactly the wrong sort of wife to come to sea. No one was equal to her; they were either superior or inferior. The superior-inferior line was a direct correlation with her husband's rank. It was very simple: her husband had two gold stripes, so three- and four-stripers were superior, whereas one-stripers and no-stripe cadets were inferior. There was a bit of blurring at the edges with other two-stripers, such as the third engineer and the radio officer, although she generally treated these as marginal inferiors because her husband was a deck officer and not a grubby engineer or a radio man.

The superior people were granted her clear and rapt attention. She manoeuvred to be near them, and she looked straight at them with eyes wide open and with a smile that showed her teeth. She laughed at their jokes, however poor they might be. The inferior people were given a thin, begrudging smile (no teeth), and were never looked at for long: just a one-second glance to allow her to absorb their low status. She never laughed at their jokes, however funny they might be.

The more superior a person was, the more toadying her attitude, and vice-versa to those below her. I was an extremely inferior person in her reckoning: more like a dog than a human.

One evening, she was sitting at the end of the bar next to the chief engineer (four gold stripes), finishing her second gin and tonic. The fourth engineer was behind the bar, sporting a much inferior one gold stripe. With languid grace, she extended her arm full-length towards the fourth: her hand holding the empty glass, she rattled the glass and the ice clinked. The fourth engineer looked at her; she rewarded him with a lipless smile, nodded her head towards the glass, then turned to the chief engineer, giving him the full piano smile. The room went quiet. There was a hiss. She turned her head to look at the fourth's cigarette end in her glass. The fourth grinned at her. We all laughed. She burst into tears and ran out the bar.

A small minority of wives were deliberate in the disruption they left in their wake. They made prolonged eye contact and gave meaningful sideways looks; they wore too little and laced their language with suggestion. They nudged against and brushed along people they liked; they made small quivery moves with their lips and used all the subtle body movements that can drive a man to a wild place. These were the wives that caused the greatest problems, hammering wedges between friendships, making the husband a figure of fun, bringing out the lustful worst in all of us.

A well-known chief engineer called Clements had such a wife. The chief was a brutish man, usually drunk before the sun was down. When sober, he liked to bully and humiliate his engineers in equal measure, and in the early stages of drunkenness he became even more unpleasant – as deliberately nasty as it was possible to be. As he drank more though, he became maudlin and altogether a much nicer person. His wife Greta was in her late-40s. She looked as if she had been a good-looking woman in her younger days. In fact, she was still good looking, although she had to work at it. She was childless, and she didn't seem to have any interests or hobbies, or any friends from what I could make out. She was Greta to all the officers, though we cadets had to call her 'Mrs Clements'. She watched the chief like a hawk until he entered his maudlin stage, the point at which he would mostly stare into the middle-distance and become largely oblivious to what was going on around him.

Greta would then pick her victim for the evening from among the officers in the bar. She would first speak in a low voice to bring him in; then change to a breathless voice to keep him close. The tip of her tongue would appear and slide slowly across to moisten her upper lip while she took full eye contact. Sometimes she would slowly stroke her nipple with the edge of her thumb. As the evening wore on, she would engage more and more with the officer she had chosen, holding his hand for emphasis, throwing her head back to laugh and then dropping it forward onto his chest in a supplicant gesture. The officer would be getting more and more worked up, wondering how to take the situation: whether he should take advantage of it or not. This was the wife of the second-most-senior officer on the ship: her husband was sitting four yards away; the rest of the bar was watching…

And then it ended. She would get up with a sudden start, take the chief by the arm and heave him to his feet and go. The jilted officer would stare after her for a few moments in disbelief, before turning with a guilty look to meet our smirking faces. This was Greta's habit several times a week.

And, bringing up the rear, exactly where they shouldn't be, were all the girls we left behind. I suppose I was lucky in this regard, because I didn't have a girl to leave behind at that stage of my life. At home on leave, my confidence was growing, although I was still prone to make a fool of myself when pursuing a 'real' girl. My stunted chat-up lines were poor offerings, usually borrowed from someone else, though having been stripped of all timing and context and style prior to delivery.

I used the crutch of demon drink, which banished my shyness and unfolded my tongue and conferred me with a talent to amuse that lasted the evening. I remained a real whizz with bar-girls in the Far East, drunk or sober. I could laugh and joke with them with easy fluency and although they never forgot their job of extracting as much cash from me as possible, I could tell I was good company to them – certainly better than the many who treated them as meat rather than people, and made it clear their only attraction was that they took their clothes off easier than most girls. With careful drinking I could replicate my Far East persona when I was home on leave.

But neither of these talents of mine – the easy charm with bar-girls cum part-time whores, or the frenetic alcohol-inspired one-night courtships in English pubs – conspired to put me in the position of having a girl left behind, waiting for me to return. I had usually forgotten the last girl I was with by the time I reached the airport to join the next ship.

Occasionally I received a letter out of the blue from someone I had been out with, who had tracked me down, but they were rare instances and had little meaning. As I sat on the poop and smoked and read the letters, I could barely connect with the life I had left behind: the minutia and the sentiments in the letters were so unreal to me that they might as well have been written by a Martian.

I took heart from receiving these odd letters from time to time though, marking the page for a phone call when I returned home. I did feel a bit sorry for the authors; they must have been fairly sad and lonely if they were reduced to pursuing me across the other side of the world. I suppose they must have seen something in me, although I cannot think what it could have been: in my teenage years I was lacking in any form of commitment. Any girl who saw promise in me must have been looking very deep.

The only girl at home in those early years at sea was my mother, who wrote me a two-page letter religiously every fortnight, every year I was at sea. They were always the same: blue self-seal airline letters. These told me the comings and goings at home: who was doing what, who was going where, who was achieving, who was dying; they kept me connected. I always wrote back too, although with a sanitised picture of life on the ocean wave. I wanted to shield and protect my parents from the life I was discovering and the moral corruption I was experiencing. This led me to write and recount tales in hurrah-for-adventure language, terribly over-British, using script that could have been plucked out of a Victorian boys' annual. I didn't write every fortnight, but I always wrote.

People at sea rarely talked about the girl they had waiting for them at home – the girlfriend, the wife. Men at sea don't generally talk in that direction. When there was truly a girl who was waiting back home, most people onboard ship kept her in a private place and avoided sharing her in conversation with others. Men at sea usually occupied themselves telling each other hilarious stories that involve drink, other women (although never the one left at home), and random acts of foolishness. Perhaps we should have been talking about the girls we left behind in a serious way, but no one ever did – not even in our homesick stages.

8

Return of the Tramp

My first voyage on the *Valvata* with Starling around Europe, across to America and the Caribbean, and then back to Europe again, lasted three months. The second trip on the *Vexilla*, with John and Barry, took me away for nine months, mostly in the Far East with diversions to India and Southern Africa. The third trip on the *Horomaya* with Jimmy was another nine-month affair, during which we ranged over large parts of the world: the Middle East, the Mediterranean, the Caribbean, West Africa, and the Far East.

Although I dwell on the sordid – the drink, the depravity, the violence, the back-breaking work – I do this probably because it sits in my mind more and it tells well. All these extreme times though were also braced by events of enlightenment: by times we had that made the soul sing.

On a ship, a stage is a strong wooden plank about 10 feet long and 12 inches wide, just wide enough for a man to comfortably sit on. There are wooden handles 1 foot in from either end, extending out for 6 inches. One-inch manila ropes are wound round the stages by the handles and the rope is tied to something sturdy at deck level. The stage itself is then put over the side of the ship. Two people sit on the stage and slacken the ropes at either end to lower it down the ship-side until it sits, swaying, adjacent to the section of the hull that is to be maintained. Paint brushes and paint pots, scrapers and wire brushes are then lowered down to the two workers on the stage, who scrape off the old paint, scour away the rust with the wire brushes then slap on the a smart new coat.

Working on a stage requires skill and balance. If the two ends are not lowered in harmony, all the working gear – and the workers – will start to slide off into the water. When working, each person has to move carefully with one eye on himself, and one eye on the overall balance of the platform.

During our spell on the South African coast, I spent two days working on a stage with John in Durban Harbour while we anchored awaiting port clearance. We were barefoot and only dressed in shorts, balancing against the gentle roll of the ship, slapping on fresh paint, the sun beating on our backs, small groups of hammerhead sharks circling 20 feet below us in the dark green sea. Barry adjusted the ropes on deck and watched over us, lowering bottles of water and the occasional can of beer to keep us going. I painted and reflected on life, planned and looked ahead at what the world held for me, and cooked gently in the sun. All the bad things in my world disappeared.

For sheer frightening exhilaration, hanging in a bosun's chair 80 feet above a rolling deck is difficult to challenge. A bosun's chair is a step of wood, 2 feet long, 9 inches wide, 1 inch thick. There are large holes in the four corners with a rope threaded though each and joined together at the top. The 'chair' is then hung by the point where the ropes converge, which is about 3 feet above the wooden step. You sit on this thin piece of wood and the whole apparatus is heaved into the air by a long line that runs through a block positioned way up the mast. Up you go, clinging on, backside perched on the tiny seat, hands gripping the rope, the chair swinging and gyrating as you go higher and higher. When you reach the point where you are going to work (usually a section of the mast), you grab hold of it and tie the chair on with a line that you have been clutching.

Your mind screams: "Don't look down!", but you have to, because you have to lower another line so the tiny figures on the deck can tie on your paint pot and brush for you to haul up. When I glanced down from such a height, from such a precarious position, the world rocked and heaved and I felt weak and supplicant: I felt death tapping on my shoulder and I gripped the ropes until my fingers hurt.

I had never liked heights and a trip on the bosun's chair was always difficult for me. Jimmy loved it, singing and swinging and acting the fool. I tried to look as if I was enjoying my turn, but everyone knew I hated the travel, which made great sport for those on the deck in making sure my hauling up was done with particular gusto to enhance the swing. I clung on with a sickly expression and willed myself not to faint and plummet to the steel deck.

But when I was up at the top and safely tethered to the mast, above any noise from the tiny figures on the deck, clear of all the dirt and argument and strain of closed humanity, all my fears fled and I would sit and gently swing in harmony with the motion, painting my section. I felt as if I was high up with the gods; the ship below a painted splash upon a painted ocean.

Painting ships rails sounds fairly tedious and mindless. Ships rails – the metal railings on the lower decks, as opposed to the smart teak taff-rails around the upper bridge deck and boat decks – are made of galvanised metal, not steel. Fools, fireman and first-trippers sit on rails; second-trippers paint them. Due to the galvanised structure, ships rails do not extrude gobs of dirty rust; they gently weep grubby brown tears. The scraping and scouring is therefore altogether a more gentle process. The painting of the primer is also a much finer undertaking. Bare steel requires heavy red lead primer to be lathered on before the undercoat. Red lead paint is thick and cloying and unpleasant on the skin. Galvanised rails are primed with a yellow zinc chromate primate, light and delicate. In the mind games I played with myself, I equated the difference of the preparation and painting of a steel bulkhead against the painting of ships rails, as being the same as the difference between slapping paint on a garage door and a the painting of a landscape on a canvas easel. I regarded rail painting as having a certain amount of artistry. I never shared these thoughts with the others of course; I would have been laughed to my bunk.

The real joy of rail painting though, was that it was generally only carried out when the weather was fine and always, by obvious necessity, done with the painter facing the sea. All the great oceans are vast and sometimes seem as empty as the end of the world, but when you are squatting in the sun, not burdened with any great amount of manual labour, there is much to see. The wash of the bow wave trailing down the side of the ship in its ever-changing pattern of tumbling wave and foaming swirls could become hypnotic, dragging my eyes aft, releasing them, then dragging them back again. A single dolphin would appear, sometimes just rolling over in the blue water, sometimes leaping high. When the dolphin were leaping, it usually meant there were several in the vicinity. On occasions I saw great fleets of dolphin, all leaping in harmony, rushing towards the ship, closing fast, only to swing round the stern in formation when they were 20 yards off. When the sea was calm and flat, schools of flying fish skipped across the surface, flapping and skittering until they plunged under again.

Ships mostly take the shortest route between two points, which means that even in the midst of the vastest sea you would be likely to be in a shipping lane that was at most 20 or 30 miles wide. Ships would pass, sometimes a distant smudge on the edge of the horizon, sometimes so close you could hear the thump of machinery and the wash of the water being pushed aside.

There was no real excuse for a close encounter in the middle of the ocean. When two ships are approaching from opposite directions and are destined to meet head on, Rule 18 of the Collision Regulations applies: *When two power-driven vessels are meeting end on or nearly end on, so as to involve risk of collision, each shall alter her course to starboard, so that each may pass on the port side of the other.* In practice in open waters, each ship will wait until the closing distance is between 4 and 5 miles, which is about eight to ten minutes from collision, and then nudge the head of the ship 4 or 5 degrees to starboard, allowing both ships to slide safely past each other by a few hundred yards. Sometime the officer of the watch, seeking a thrill, will wait longer before altering course, bringing the vessels closer together. I was on bridge-watch once with a slightly unhinged second mate, who regarded these situations as tests of nerve. He would never alter course until after the other ship had started to open. Sometimes of course, the officer on the bridge of one ship will be working in the chartroom, oblivious to what is happening and the onus will be on the other alone to avoid collision. On rare occasions, both officers of the watch are oblivious, with the result that the ensuing incident makes the front page in the *Lloyds List* newspaper.

It was good to pass close by another ship in mid-ocean. When it happened, those working on deck would leave their tools and walk to the side and wave to those lining the opposite rails across the narrow stretch of water.

I found great pleasure in rope and canvas work. From time to time we would be seconded to the deck storekeeper. 'Stores' would endeavour to impart some seaman's skills into us. The rope-work involved splicing ropes together from the big 8-inch mooring lines to manila working ropes for stages. We used fids to prise the strands apart: fids are large, rounded, wooden spikes that are worked into the strands until the gap was big enough to pass another strand through. This allows a weaving together of two ropes, or of two parts of the same rope. Generally speaking, two ropes that are spliced together will be stronger than two ropes that are tied together – although neither is as strong as a single unbroken rope.

Rope-work usually took place out in the sun on a clear deck. Sometimes just one of us would be sitting there among the working clutter, although more often there were several of us working together. Working with ropes was clean, physically easy and visibly satisfying, as well as being quite social as we could chat to each other while getting on with the job. Rope-work was coveted by the sailors, who would glare at us with envy and irritation when we were out on deck with our ropes festooned all over the place. The glares were particularly intense when they were trooping off to do something much less pleasant, such as cement washing the water tanks or some other hideous task that was usually the preserve of the cadets. As a general rule of thumb, the sailors were always delighted for us cadets to take over the ghastly shipboard jobs, though judged it unfair if we were ever given any task that had a passing association with enjoyment.

Wire-splicing was like rope-working, although with effort and was mostly carried out in one of the deck stores. Steel wire is dangerous: a taut wire that snaps under load can cut a man in half. Thick wires are hung over the bow and stern of a ship when in port. These are known as 'fire wires' and are hung there in case a tug needs to tow a burning ship away from the dock. Fire wires need to have large eyes spliced in either end: one end is hung down to water level and the other is placed over a pair of mooring bits on the deck. The 3-foot-long eye has to be as strong as possible and we always used a lock splice, which is virtually unbreakable. Unlike rope-splicing, when hands and fingers are used, wire-splicing is more difficult. The wire is set in a vice and steel marlin spikes are used to prise open the lay of the strands, with pliers then gripping and pulling through each strand to be woven into the eye. New rolls of wire are packed down into tight coils that are restrained from springing apart by being tied in sections; it is only ever the length of wire to be used that is eased out of the coil. Anyone working with wire needs to be alert to the fact that the whole tightly-coiled length, if not kept retrained, could spring open like a giant man-trap, trapping and removing fingers, or worse.

Allied to working with ropes and wires is canvas-work. Canvas covers soon rot and need replacing at regular intervals. I think the main reason I enjoyed canvas-work is that it made me feel that I was on some old-time sailing ship. There was something about sitting in the open air on the foredeck – canvas spread over my knees, stitching away with a big fat needle which I pushed through the canvas using a leather palm attachment – that carried me back in time. The thread was hempen line that I had run through a block of beeswax beforehand to make it water-resistant. Unlike the more social work of splicing, canvas stitching requires careful concentration to keep the line of stitches true. I used to think my stitching was neat and well-aligned, although Stores would peer at it and sneer, telling me that my work wandered all over the place as if done by a blind man and I should be ashamed of such poor sewing skills. I felt that was unfair, especially as the finished product is always turned inside out anyway so no one actually sees the quality of stitch. We made covers for the lifeboats, covers for the ventilators, covers for the compass binnacle and covers for sundry exposed items where the goal was to keep out the worst of the weather. After making covers for everything in sight, we made new canvas surrounds for the cork lifebuoys; this was a few years before cork lifebuoys were superseded by modern plastic ones.

All this skilled work though – real seaman's work as I saw it – was, in truth, a minor portion of the great slog of labour that we undertook. Most of the time we were chipping and painting, or scrubbing and scraping, or digging out the filthy tanks. In port, we would either be loading or unloading and both involved swinging the big heavy wheels on the deck valves to open and control the flow in and out of the tanks, until our muscles screamed. The seamanship work however, was always welcome. It made me a better seaman: I became more dexterous, I became more organised, more single-minded, it improved my concentration, I learned greater patience, I took greater pride in what I did, my judgement improved. I became a better person.

It is easy to shape a young man if you have his clear and undivided attention and can organise his every waking hour: that is the position that we were in. We arrived as schoolboys, perhaps with some petty bravado and some minor experiences, but we were boys. We were clay to be moulded, to have our boyishness squeezed from us. First there was the beasting, in which we were taken down and reduced to the lowest level. There was no glamour, no glory: there was only the hardest type of physical labour, the dirtiest work that the lowest sailor would have shied away from. There was continual hounding and berating and hard, hard work – constantly – in hard, hot conditions. It was drilled into us, over and over, that we had to be able to do every job – however foul – to the best, to the best of our ability, and in the best way in which the job could be done. Until then, we would remain the lowest form of marine life. Even a lazy person – even a great shirker – experiencing that pressure to work day-in-day-out becomes someone who not only knows how to work, but who starts to view others who can't work as well and as hard as lesser people. This was the major and overriding thing I learned through it all: I learned how to work and how to cope with work, and how to cope with all manner of hardship and humiliation, and how to hide any pain and shame, and how to never slack or shirk or let down the person I was with.

About three months into the *Vexilla* trip with John and Barry, there reached a point during a particularly bad session of tank cleaning when I suddenly knew the work just couldn't get any worse: things just couldn't get any harder; couldn't get any dirtier; couldn't be any more unpleasant. I was bone-tired; my mind was dulled by lack of sleep, having catnapped for four days and having just worked a punishing 24 hours to finish the cleaning before we reached port. I was filthy beyond description; clogged with oily muck in every pore and every orifice to the extent I thought I would never be clean again. My muscles shook from exertion; my arms and legs were burned and covered with rashes from the oil sludge. My head was thumping with pain, I was hungry and parched and I couldn't concentrate. I started to stumble; I felt sick from the pockets of gas. I vomited in the bottom of the tank. The Chinese sailors laughed at me, thinking I was drunk. I could hardly climb the 60 feet up to the surface. I felt I would fall back into the darkness. When I eventually flopped onto the deck, escaping the stifling, sweltering, steaming tank, the tropical night into which I emerged made me feel as if I had walked into a freezer. I almost crawled down the deck to the midships block and heaved myself up the gangway and into the accommodation, where I ate a handful of salt tablets, drank a litre of water, and then descended into the centre-castle to peel off my boiler suit and scrub myself with grubby kerosene. Later, as I sat on the floor of the shower under tepid water, accompanied by three cans of cold Tiger beer, it was at that time I knew – I knew – that it could never get any worse.

From that point on, life became easier because I knew I could cope: we all knew we could cope. We could cope with whatever we were asked to do. Our faces didn't fall, our heads didn't dip: we did whatever we were asked to do and we laughed and it became easier. We had journeyed a long way down into the ravine and now we were on our way up. In the manual of *How to Train a Deck Officer* (if there ever was one), this would have been the critical defining moment that the trainer was working towards: the change of direction whereby every difficulty becomes something to be coped with and not something to be wary of. That crossing of that line made my next trip on the *Horomaya* with Jimmy so much easier to bear.

This new-found coping didn't suddenly carry us into a better class of work of course, No fear. We carried on with more of the same, day after day, month after month, which made us strong. We were not body-beautiful posers as you find on the beach, nor were we sleek in a gym-toned, diet-driven way in quest of the perfect shape. We just became tough and resilient: we were strong and we had stamina and we could work hard all day in the hot sun, then stay up most of the night and then recover quickly to do the same again, and again and again.

It became clear at a very early stage – about day two on the *Valvata* for me – that the days of swanning around in a smart gold-braided uniform were going to be well into the future. Until we became confirmed copers, until we slogged through our studies, until we learned all the nuances of life at sea, we were labour fodder of the lowest order. We were like slaves – we were the lowest form of marine life. And we started to love it.

There is a strange and unfathomable nobility about being able to work harder than anyone else around you – about being more bruised than anyone else, about always being the one to go into the dirtiest place, about being the last out – which eventually starts to elevate you above the rest. In that missing manual of *How to Train a Deck Officer*, there comes a time for the trainer to remove the person from that environment before he becomes too enamoured with the nobility, and to then to send him back to school, to Phase 3 of the process: back to the school for tramps.

Plymouth was familiar but different. John and I caught the train together from Paddington to Plymouth one Sunday morning. We arrived in style: mildly drunk, having bought a case of beer to accompany us on the journey. The place looked smaller, or perhaps it was just more manageable because it was no longer daunting to us.

Our class was P3 23 – Phase Three, 23rd intake. They put us all in a hostel near the railway station, which was handy as we only had a hundred yards to walk with our kit after arriving at the station. Phase 3 returnees, fresh from 18 months at sea, were always kept at arm's length from the main population of the School of Maritime Studies, to avoid contamination of attitude. In our case, particular vigilance was to be applied. P3 23 had already been to sea before Phase 1 even started – a mistake by the college not to be repeated – and we were thought too long on the leash to be kept in close proximity with the mainstream intakes. P3 22 was part-incorporated into the main college block, as would be P3 24. However, P3 23 was to be treated differently and kept apart – like lepers we thought: we were half insulted and half pleased.

Throughout Sunday, people trickled in: old colleagues to be greeted with cheers and hooting. Everyone seemed to be back, apart from the Irish Shipping boys who had only done a year at sea and had already been back to college and gone again. Starling and Bell and Phil were there when John and I arrived and had taken a four-person cabin on the ground floor. They didn't seem keen to invite me to be the fourth, which I was relieved about because I would have refused. Jimmy trailed in, then Barry and Tim, Dick and Des, Smoothie Jack and Roy, Charlie and Bob and all the others in ones and twos. Raz and Persian Monty, on trusted release from Iran, arrived in the late evening, by which time we had mostly wandered down to the Pennycomequick pub to drink and swap stories of our times since we were last at the college.

We were young lions, no longer cubs. There is a wealth of difference between a 16-year-old and an 18-year-old in any event; even more so if the intervening time has been spent in a harsh environment. We were men, although we acted like boys a lot of the time. We were strong and experienced and fully formed. There was no one who couldn't work a 20-hour day; no one who couldn't drink until they fell down or saw the others fall down around them. No one was a stranger to bullying, to violence, to cruelty, to sights of abject poverty. There were no virgins. No one slouched: our upright posture was courtesy of Chiefy Rozer's daily drill during our first spell. Our eyes were level in gaze and we had no fear, no trepidation whatsoever of the coming six months. We were here for some keenly anticipated R&R and we would do the studying in between our hedonism.

We looked part-wild. Our hair was long, over our ears and collars. Most of us were still burned by the sun. John had a shark tattoo, Tim had an earring, most of us were scuffed and slightly scarred – there were a couple of Zapata moustaches and a few beards. It was a cold January and spatters of hard rain drove into the pavements, but we wore open-neck shirts and no jackets and laughed as we walked down to the Pennycomequick in the icy winter gloom.

Our hostel opposite the railway station was called Standard House and I ended up bunking with Jimmy and Smoothie Jack in one of the top-floor rooms. It was a compact four-bunk cabin, although we had more space than expected as there were only three of us. We each had a locker that contained one locking drawer, although I don't think anyone ever locked theirs – none of us had anything of worth anyway. Virtually all of our allotted space was taken up with things that we needed rather than items of indulgence.

In the week, we would wear our blues uniform, unless we were sailing or doing seamanship. Our working gear was blue shirts and trousers, with woollen jerseys and oilskins and we all carried clasp-knives with folding marlin spikes – some of us also had slim-bladed Green River knives in soft leather sheaves. As regards our civvies, we were not creatures of fashion. We all had multifarious shirts and trousers and jackets that were adaptable for going down the pub, getting into a club, or kicking a ball around the Hoe. Most of us had a serviceable suit for looking smart on a Saturday night. A few, notably Smoothie Jack, had several sets of very smart clothes, but people like Jack were the exception. There was a table in our cabin with four chairs and we filled the surface with our books and files and assorted study materials.

The warden for Standard House was Captain Daventry, who I remembered as the no-nonsense navigation lecturer from Phase 1. He had been given the task because he was felt to be the best man to keep the newly-returned intake 23 in check. I groaned when I heard who it was, although we soon learned that he shut his door early in the evening and ignored most of what went on, unless the antics and noise started getting out of hand.

We all ate in a communal wooden hut that had been built in the grounds. Meals were taken using a canteen arrangement, rather than the table-server system of the other hostels. At meal times, we lined up with our tin trays and tried to chat-up the cooks into giving us extra helpings. The quality and range of food was good, although it wouldn't have mattered much if it was average, just as long as it wasn't awful. We had all had the fussiness knocked out of us during our time at sea: if the food was hot and well-cooked then everyone was happy; we just ate what we were given.

It was easy enough to get in through one of the ground-floor cabins once the door was locked after the curfew hour, by tapping on the window until someone eventually slid the sash window up and allowed you to climb in. I was pleased that I had taken a top-floor cabin.

The classroom work in Phase 3 was intense; the standard far more advanced than Phase 1 and the expectations were higher. The day was much the same as before, although there were no daily inspections, no drill – just the warden's walkabout on Saturday morning. Breakfast was at 08.00. Lectures began at 09.00 and continued until 17.00 with compulsory late classes after the evening meal. We were usually finished and free by 19.45 each night. Saturday afternoon was spent sailing at the boat centre. There were 22 of us in Phase 3, which meant that we pulled duty cadet every three weeks. That apart, the nights and all day Sunday were ours.

It took a week or so to get back into the groove of studying. We had all completed a fairly gruelling set of correspondence courses at sea anyway, so our minds were still alight. The structure of work continued as unrelenting cramming with little opportunity for independent thought: we weren't there to reflect or discourse or consider or discover, we weren't there to interpret or re-interpret or argue. We were there to learn what the higher powers had decided was necessary to learn; we had to assimilate information and prove that we had effectively memorised it all by being able to regurgitate everything in its pure form. That was the nature if what we did, for 50 hours a week.

No one was expected to drop out from Phase 3: that happened on Phase 1 and quite often after the first trip to sea on Phase 2. We had one person who did leave though – Tim – who arrived back at college to say that he had had enough and he wasn't going to do the whole three-and-a-half years. I only knew Tim in passing on Phase 1, as he had been in the 'A' stream of supposedly brighter Cadets (I had been with the standard block). None of us could quite understand why Tim had bothered to come back to Plymouth at all: he put in minimum effort and was deliberately obtuse to the lecturers. He made out that he was biding his time while waiting for something to turn up, although he was from a seafaring background and I suspected the delay was something to do with family pressure. However, he did leave towards the end of the first term and became a nightclub DJ in Torquay. A crowd of us travelled down to see him one Saturday night – John, Jimmy, Barry, Dick, Des, Charlie, Smoothie Jack and me. Tim put on a good show and shouted out a lot of dedications for us ex-colleagues who were cavorting around the floor. Tim joined us for drinks at the end of the night, although it was clear he no longer belonged. Some of us slept on the beach around a fire we built; Tim went back to his digs.

Standard House, the cadet hostel where the author stayed during the second phase at the School of Navigation. The place is now sadly semi-derelict.

✻   ✻   ✻

In addition to the studies, we had to undergo a wealth of practical training during Phase 3. This fell into three areas: ancillary certificates; sail training; and survival training. Of the three, survival training was the most challenging. Our initial survival training day took place on a bitterly cold day in the English Channel in February. We sailed out of Plymouth harbour on the *Tectona*, a wooden sail training ship from between the wars, which was our deep-sea sailing ship. Captain Polata was in command, with Daventry as chief mate. The wind was blowing a force 6 from the west and rain pelted us in icy sheets as we huddled on the deck awaiting orders; we were not looking forward to what was going to happen.

When we were well out into the Channel, Polata heaved to and we set about manhandling the huge 20-man inflatable yellow dinghy towards the rails. The raft was circular with a rubber bottom and it had inflated walls about 2 feet high. There was a rubber covering on a frame that gave 4 feet of headroom – sufficient for the occupants to sit up. There was a doorway about 2 feet wide that could be sealed by a rubber flap.

The survival exercise was to drop the dinghy into the water, let it drift away a hundred yards or so, and then, on a signal from Polata, all 24 members of P3 23 would leap off the boat and swim to it. When we reached the raft, we would climb in and then stay there for several hours to experience to full delights of being in a rubber dinghy on the open seas. We were fully clothed in heavy, blue serge shirts, trousers and deck shoes, and we wore big orange Board of Trade lifejackets. The three non-swimmers were looking nervous: they were supposed to be marshalled and helped along by designated stronger swimmers. I was not one of the stronger swimmers.

We flung the dinghy over the side into the sea, taking care to tie the line to the rail beforehand. The dinghy landed upside-down. We all looked at it. We all looked at Polata. The two strong swimmers were ordered into the sea to heave the dinghy over. In they went, dropping the 6 feet into the sea. They shrieked with the cold as they surfaced, bellowing like two angry walruses. We laughed and shouted helpful advice as they clambered across the bottom of the dinghy, took a firm hold of the grab-lines then heaved themselves backwards across the base. The big yellow dinghy rolled right over on top of them and they came to the surface, spluttering and spitting and swearing as they trod water. We all clapped and cheered.

"Let go the line!" shouted Polata.

Someone slipped the hitch and we stood by the rails and watched the dinghy start to drift away. As it came out from the lee of the *Tectona*, the wind and sea took hold and started to force it downwind at a fast rate. At 50 yards we shuffled to the rails and tensed. "Wait for it, wait for it…" said Polata.

A few other lecturers had come along for the spectacle and they leant on the conning enclosure with Daventry and Polata, taking and joking with each other, looking forward to seeing P23 get their desserts.

A hundred yards…. "Wait for it…" 'Come on,' we thought: 'That's a long swim.' One-hundred-and-fifty yards… "Wait for it…" 'You bastard, Polata,' we thought collectively.

Approaching two-hundred yards, I remember thinking: 'This is beyond a joke, it's too far.'

"Jump! Now! Go! Jump! Jump and swim!"

We leapt over the side of the *Tectona* like lemmings, taking care to aim for clear space so as not to land on top of someone already in the water, holding fast to the collars of our lifejackets to avoid breaking our necks. The brutal cold bludgeoned the breath out of me as I went in and under. I bobbed quickly up again and I roared as I surfaced. Everyone else was roaring around me. It was like being in a colony of sea-lions. I sucked in great gouts of air until my breathing stabilised. Barry was in the water next to me, Starling was on my other side.

"Jesus! It's bloody freezing!" Barry screeched. "Let's get out of here!"

The whole pack of us set off in a dense scrum, churning through the waves, heading towards the fast moving dinghy. The dinghy may have been moving fast but we were like Olympians, the cold and panic of becoming entombed in the icy depths lending speed to our efforts. We closed on our yellow target in a tight bunch. I was vaguely aware of Polata's screams from behind; it was only afterwards we realised that the non-swimmers had been left to drift down the Channel.

The half-dozen fastest swimmers reached the dinghy first and flopped through the open doorway and onto the rubber floor. Then the rest of us arrived in a clump; 15 people struggling to get out of the water at the same time into a 2-foot-wide opening. There was a lot of pushing and shouting and swearing: anyone who was too close to the doorway without managing to get in was used as a platform by the others. Eventually we were all in; the remaining few being heaved onboard by those inside. Most of us sat around the edges in a circle, looking towards the middle, miserable. We were bone-cold and exhausted from our frantic chasing of the life-raft. We sat in the 6 inches of water that we had slopped in. There was a noise approaching: Polata had started up the *Tectona*'s engine and motored in pursuit of the three panicking non-swimmers who were drifting down the Channel in their lifejackets. He picked them up and brought them over to us. The three were deposited in the water in front of the doorway, with Polata shouting accusations at those who had been tasked with looking after them and who had shirked their duty. They were hauled aboard: the two Persians (Raz and Monty), together with Jock, a Scot who was with the Reardon Smith shipping line. All three looked dazed and fearful. There was no more room around the circular walls of the raft, so they sat glumly in a deep puddle in the middle, in the gaze of the rest of us. The *Tectona* chugged off, Polata shouting that he would be back in three hours, once we had assimilated what is was like to be in a survival life-raft.

As I had discovered on my first trip on the *Valvata*, I did not suffer from seasickness. Following time spent at sea, everyone in the raft had developed a fairly resilient stomach to the standard shipboard motion and no one was expecting to be ill. However, the difference between an inflatable dinghy and a solid-hulled boat is that the waves move the boat, so it rocks, whereas in the dinghy, every movement of the water ripples across the rubber bottom and you are floating on each individual wavelet, feeling every flick and motion of the water.

Starling was the first to go, lunging for the doorway and heaving into the water. He was closely followed by Phil and Roy. They slumped back, white-faced and weak. The rest of us hooted. After a few minutes pause, there was another rush: four people this time. Only three could lean out at any one time, so the fourth spewed over the backs of the others. The laughter was more muted, more groaning disgust than laughing. Over the next hour the motion got to most people in the raft. Those sitting over the far side couldn't make it to the doorway and were sick where they sat. This soon became the order of the day, with people simply vomiting into their laps. Someone was sick on Raz, right into his face. He sat there cold and wet and sick and miserable, bits of vomit snagged in his beard as he vomited back weakly.

I carried on chuckling for a while, confident in my power to withstand being sick, although I could start to sense the other occupants turning against me, so thought it best to keep quiet. After an hour the water in which we were sitting had a foam top of vomit, looking like the head on a pint of Guinness. The smell was appalling. The sound was of intermittent retching and groaning. There were only five of us who had not been sick and I could feel the bloodshot eyes of the affected looking at me with hatred, willing me to start heaving, to join in the misery. It certainly was miserable, and became more so as the second hour stretched into the third. The intensity of the vomiting became less. People mostly lay slumped in the water, occasionally twitching their throats and expelling a dry rasp of bile.

Eventually we heard the thump-thump of *Tectona's* Gardner engine getting closer. Several of us jumped out the doorway into the sea at that stage, where we clung to the outside grab-lines, revelling in the fresh air. Others joined us in the water as the *Tectona* slowed to take us onboard. Only a few of the very sick remained inside, lying in their carpet of vomit, too weak to move. Polata and Daventry and the others all leaned over the side, grinning like Cheshire Cats. A rope-ladder was slung over the side and we clambered onboard where we were met with bacon rolls and hot tea, which eventually put even the sickest back on form.

The *Tectona* was the official sail training ship for the School of Maritime Studies. She had been built in India in 1929 by a well-to-do major who had her rigged as a cutter. She was a sturdy craft, built of solid teak and displacing 65 tons. The teak build gave the name to *Tectona* – the botanical name for teak being *tectona grandis*. She wore a complicated rig of six sails, flying 2,000 square feet of canvas off two masts and a long bowsprit when fully rigged. Technically, the style of rig was that of a gaff ketch. The hull was paint – dark blue with a white topping – and the decks, hatches and deck furniture were all oiled or varnished teak. Below decks there was a mess-room, a good number of bunks and a decent size master's cabin. The *Tectona* was well known around Plymouth; she was a gorgeous boat.

On our *Tectona* sailing days, we would all be given turns at the various tasks: steering; lookout; washing down the decks; greasing the windlass; repairing ropes; cooking; and a myriad of other sailing ship tasks. There were a lot of us and we all knew what we were doing so the trips were always relaxing. There always seemed plenty of time to loaf, although in truth, it was probably only 20 minutes here and there. We would climb the side-rigging to the high mast and sit on the cross-spars; the bravest would shin up to the top of the mast to sit on the truck. My favourite retreat was lying in the net under the bowsprit on a warm spring day, the bow wave hissing beneath me, clumps of cloud ambling across the blue sky as I lay there and looked up at the heavens.

Captain Polata was always the skipper. Although he gave the appearance of a flustered man, he was a first-rate seaman. We had our adventures: once, we went aground off Fowey. Polata stamped around and swore when it happened, although under his command we then received an object lesson in kedging a big boat, which could have been imprinted as a textbook guide. First, we launched the wooden dinghy and rowed round to the bow; four of us were in there with Captain Daventry. When we were under the bow, the anchor was slowly lowered on its big hawser until it was below the surface of the water. We wrapped a thick line around the hawser to keep it close to the dinghy and then rowed out to deep water, while the crew on the *Tectona* slowly paid out the hawser. When we reached the deep water, about 100 feet away, we stopped and slowly lowered the anchor down while the crew onboard the *Tectona* continued to slacken out the hawser. Once the anchor was on the bottom, the weight came off the hawser and we let slip our rope and rowed out the way. The *Tectona's* windlass was then engaged and it started heaving on the anchor, which slowly, slowly heaved the big boat off the sea-bed. Perfect.

We spent one weekend undergoing a different type of survival training, which involved being dropped off somewhere in Dartmoor at night with a two-day supply of food and water, a map and compass, and a sealed envelope in which we were told our objective. The idea was that we had to first discover where we were, then hike to the objective, taking care to avoid the live army firing range, the occasional marsh bogs and any other humankind. The exercise didn't seem to have much relevance to shipboard survival, although we were told it was a test of aptitude under stress and initiative testing – which we accepted, because we didn't have a choice.

We were dumped in the various dark locations in groups of three. I was with Bell and Smoothie Jack. As the Land Rover drove off into the gloom, we pitched our tent as best we could, the only light source being our torches, and climbed into our sleeping bags for a snooze for a few hours. The early-spring morning was chilly. We yawned and stretched and moaned, then boiled tea and ate cheese and took stock of where we might be. We had no idea. Everywhere looked bleak: craggy hills rolled away, and there were no signs of life. We picked out the biggest of the hills and narrowed it down to one of four places: it looked to be about 10 miles away and we calculated that we then had a slog to our objective of between 8 and 14 miles, depending upon which hill it turned out to be. We packed up and set off. Our counter plan, which we felt showed great initiative, was to hang around if we crossed a road or track that showed signs of recent vehicular use and then hitch a lift from whatever came along.

We didn't come across a road, but we did come across an unexploded mortar, which made us realise that we had strayed into the army live-fire range. We beat a hasty retreat, although we at least had a reasonable idea of where we now were. We cut a wide circle around the range, which added 4 miles or so to the trek. The ground became marshy at one stage and Bell slipped under to his waist, his backpack keeping him up. He stayed as still as he could while we reached over and dragged him out. Looking back, the venture was perilous and ill-conceived by the school: letting groups of untended people wander – lost – around the moors. I heard they cancelled the moors trips a couple of years later after some cadets from P3 25 nearly died when the weather took an unexpected turn for the worse.

We slept the second night among hill sheep and the following morning was even colder. We made our destination late in the afternoon without any further incident. We were deposited on the coach by the Land Rover that was collecting all the walkers. Everyone was pleased that the jaunt was over, experiences were exchanged, and we eventually arrived back at Standard House – dog-tired – just before midnight. Just time enough to get a decent night's sleep before Monday morning heralded the start of another week.

The duties of the duty cadet were much the same as they had been when we were in Plymouth for Phase 1, although we were all generally more relaxed and confident. The duty cadet – or 'DC' – would start at 19.30 and would position himself (in uniform) at the small desk in the hallway by the telephone. The television lounge was out of bounds to the DC although most would lurk in the doorway if there was an interesting programme showing. Fire rounds were undertaken every hour, looking in each room (which were always known as 'cabins') to make sure all was well. A lot of us smoked – probably the majority – and fire rounds became more important after the pubs closed and everyone came trickling back, usually the worse for wear. The DC had to make sure someone didn't fall asleep holding a half-smoked cigarette. We kept a log-book to record telephone calls, fire rounds, visitors and anything noteworthy. The DC had instructions to lock the door at 23.00 on Sunday through to Thursday, and at midnight on Friday and Saturday.

The DC list was pinned to the noticeboard, showing our duty days for the whole term ahead. Pulling a Friday or Saturday duty was bad news, because these were the nights we went wild, or wilder, and because the duty lasted until midnight – an hour longer than during the week. The warden didn't mind if we changed our days among ourselves, although trying to get out of a Friday or Saturday was not a case of a straight swap and usually demanded a high-premium by whoever was taking it on. The only chance of swapping a Saturday night was if you could find someone who was flat broke and then pay them a reasonable sum.

The DC was also supposed to ensure people were recorded as being in or out. This was a supplementary log-book where everyone signed in and signed out again as they came and went. The warden would generally pay a brief visit to the desk a few minutes before the curfew hour, to makes sure everyone was back who didn't have a late pass and to generally inspect the state of the returnees. Girls were never allowed into the hostel – that was a dismissal offence and no one ever broached it as far as I was aware. A late pass could be applied for during the week if there was good reason, and could be applied for on Friday and Saturday with little reason. Late passes allowed us to be out until midnight on weekdays and one o'clock on Friday and Saturday: they had to be obtained beforehand – someone couldn't just phone up just before midnight and ask for one. The DC disliked late passes because he had to either stay up or set his alarm to get up to let them in.

The signing-out log underwent massive fraud, although it was a point of procedure among us that the DC of the night was never asked to doing anything irregular. This meant that if Jimmy and Barry were going to be out until the early morning hours, I would sign them back in again before the curfew hour. It would be fine for me to blatantly do this in front of the DC, as long as he didn't do it himself. The absconders would then tap on the windows of the ground floor cabins to be let in when they returned. This was such a common practice that few people actually bothered applying for late passes. It was inconvenient for the ground-floor cabins, who had to cope with cadets climbing through the windows in the early hours. After a few weeks of this, most left their windows slightly open so the returnees could open them themselves without waking the occupants; although a couple of cadets stumbling drunkenly through the cabin in the dark was usually enough to wake everyone anyway.

When we attended Phase 3, it was the year of the power cuts. I never really understood the underlying reasons at the time and only knew that it was due to striking miners and subsequent shortage of coal. The effect, however, was that we would be without power for prolonged periods – sometimes a day or more. The newspapers and television (between cuts) were banging on about it being some sort of low-point of British civilization, although, like most young people, we accepted it in our stride and got on with life.

On two occasions when I pulled DC there were power cuts. I sat alone in the hostel with a candle on my desk whilst everyone else went out, either to more distant parts of the city that weren't suffering the cuts, or more likely to local pubs where they would sit and drink beer by candlelight. I loved the solitude; sometimes I would blow the candle out and sit in the dark and on others I would wander around the empty hostel with my flickering candle on a saucer, my shadow dancing on the walls.

The power cut periods were memorable: sitting in pubs in the semi-darkness; no music, no jangle of fruit machines – just the stuttering candles on the tables and the glow of cigarette ends and the buzz of conversation, which became more muted than usual. It certainly wasn't a crisis for us.

✶   ✶   ✶

John's behaviour became more aggressive during Phase 3. He had always liked to fight, for no other reason than he liked to fight. Now that he had become bigger and stronger and more experienced, this hobby of his became more pronounced. As a rule, he was usually satisfied to simply goad people, to mock them and call them names, seeking to embarrass them, to highlight their faults. This caused them to become distressed and angry, which was a source of huge amusement to John. If they then lost their temper and lashed out, it was so much the better because he could give them a good thumping. John could have just as much fun goading his friends as he could perfect strangers; there was no shortage of flare-ups in Standard House.

When out in the evening with John, it was common for him to decide to stir up a scrap; I was uncomfortable with this and saw little joy in either getting a good pasting or having to stick it to someone else. However, the problem for me was that when I was with John, I couldn't walk away just because he was so foolish as to generate a menacing situation.

On several occasions, when John was bored or drunk or both, he would start to deliberately barge into people, knocking over their drinks, knocking them over sometimes. Mostly people ignored him, or pretended not to notice, but sometimes they would challenge, which would start a pushing match with a few punches thrown.

Sometimes it turned into something a bit more serious.

We went to a dance one evening at the main college to which the School of Maritime Studies was affiliated. The dance was held in one of the main college halls; it was very crowded, very loud, and full of head-banging students with shoulder-length hair. We stood out starkly with our cropped heads. As the music got wilder, the head-banging became more extreme, with people thrashing about on the dance floor, heads dipping violently as if they were being electrocuted. Cue John, walking through the floor, kicking head-bangers as he went. Head-bangers fell, dead legs, mouths howling soundlessly under the blasting sound of rock. I trailed behind – John's Praetorian guard – smiling at the fallen, feeling sorry for them, watching his back.

On one occasion, in a shabby nightclub in the Barbican, an enormous man came up to John. He looked down at John: he was the size of a bear. John looked up. I looked across, thinking: 'This is going to be painful for both of us.' The bear said: "Did I see you push my friend?", indicating a smallish man sitting nearby.

John said: "If I did it must have been an accident."

"Do you want to push me?"

"No thanks."

The bear shoved John with a paw the size of a dinner plate. John fell against a table.

"Sod off, both of you, before I get annoyed."

We slunk away.

It didn't stop John of course. Violence and the scent of violence were an important stimulus he needed. An evening out with John was never boring: it always had an edge.

There was a cadet at the college called Crockett who caused a stir. As he was a second-year engineer cadet, he was someone we didn't come into contact with – the only reason we knew of him was because his father was reputably a fabulously wealthy casino owner. It was rumoured that Crockett Junior has been despatched to sea because he was a black sheep of sorts. I had seen him a few times and he looked fairly ordinary.

In the middle of the first term there was a fire in the main college block. The alarm went off mid-morning, when we were in the middle of a navigation lecture. We welcomed the interruption and filed out to stand in the courtyard. We were counted while the powers set about discovering what was happening. We stood and smoked and chatted for 20 minutes, after which we were herded back in. Apparently, there had been a small fire in one of the cadet cabins, supposedly set off by an electrical fault.

Two weeks later there was another fire: a waste bin outside kitchens – full of cardboard and food wrappings – was set ablaze just before midnight. The fire spread to some other cardboard and wood that was on the ground nearby and caused a decent blaze. We were unaware of this over in Standard House as it was half a mile from the main college block, although the next morning everyone was awash with the story. We all studied the blackened walls: there was an arsonist at work.

There were two more fires over the following month; both at night, both small but with potential. The second was in the tower where there were several hundred cadets living in close quarters, eight to a cabin. There was a lot a concern building up; people had visions of a towering inferno, roasting hundreds of people trapped on the upper floors.

They caught Crockett in early April. He stacked up bundles of paper and cardboard then piled on several mattresses in one of the cabins on the second floor. This was during the early afternoon lessons when everyone was attending lectures. There was a canister of petrol standing nearby: he was going for the big one. Crockett was caught by a couple of cadets who had come back to pick some books up. They dragged him down to the chief warden's office, none too gently. He went that evening: a black Rolls Royce picked him up. He left all his gear behind; we all jeered as it drove him out the gates and back to London to start his fires elsewhere.

★   ★   ★

Girlfriends came and went. I was starting to shrug off my mantle of shyness, which was huge relief to me. My inability to have a sober conversation with girls had made me feel as if I were handicapped. We decided to get a flat for extra-curricular activities. Having a flat was strictly forbidden, but it was a secret everyone knew about. There were half a dozen of us involved in hiring the place: a dingy hovel not far from Standard House, near the Pennycomequick pub.

The flat was dark, damp, poorly decorated and cheaply furnished. There were two bedrooms, a sitting room and a kitchen. We had extra keys cut so that we had one each. We devised a sort of booking system so that if we were taking a girlfriend back, we would inform the others to make sure that the place wasn't overflowing.

From a poor start the place deteriorated fast. It was a dismal dump when we took it over, though we managed to make it ever more smelly, cluttered and disordered, as each week passed. No one ever cleaned the place, the rubbish was never taken out; empty bottles littered the surfaces. The sheets on the beds were rarely changed and they accrued an alarming collection of stains. An inquiry was held when some ghastly smears appeared on the sheets of one bed that looked suspiciously like someone had defecated in it. No one owned up and the soiled sheets were flung into a pile of rubbish behind the Pennycomequick.

We only ever saw the place by night, usually arriving after midnight, half-drunk, with a girlfriend, usually also drunk. We were so ashamed of our hovel that we rarely turned on the lights, not wanting the girls to see the disgusting state of the place in case it scared them off. The idea was to head for one of the bedrooms as quickly as decency allowed and then get out before morning. The booking system was fallible and it was common to arrive after closing time, thinking you had the whole shabby palace to yourself, only to find it full of bodies.

I had two girlfriends on Phase 3. The first was Donna, who worked in a bookshop and was considerably older than me. I was 18; she was 25. She was large and ungainly, although I found her fun at first and she saw me as a good catch. She was a bad judge of character. I took her back to the flat a couple of times: she made it plain that she didn't enjoy the experience. As the term went by, she became less fun and spent a lot of effort trying to infuse me with more domestic grace, which I wasn't ready for. I announced the parting of our ways. She was miffed and took to stalking me for a couple of weeks, which I ignored. She gave up the chase after I came out of the Jamie Pub and across the road to where she was lurking one evening and asked to borrow a fiver because I had run out of cash.

The second was Julie. Even though time has passed and I now strive to be kind, I can't. By any measure, Julie was not a pretty girl. I met her one evening following an over-indulgence of Double Diamond beer. True to form in my inebriated state, my charm slid out from under its rock and coiled around Julie, who I was finding rather attractive. Beware the Double Diamond. We met the next night. She was grim: small, skinny and hunched with a lantern jaw and beady eyes. I rushed her to an out-of-the-way pub behind the Barbican, where I was sure no one I knew would go. To my horror, an engineer cadet who I knew slightly came in with his girlfriend, who was gorgeous. He looked at me, then he looked at Julie. He smirked. I shuddered and drank beer quickly.

I ended up going out with Julie, on and off, for most of the second term. Although looks were not her strong suit, she had a good heart and I mostly enjoyed her company. John and Jimmy and the others had a good chuckle at my expense and I defended her as best I could.

I was not running my life with any sort of exclusivity at that time. In between Donna and Julie, and even during the time I was going with them, I met other girls during nights at the Top Rank and down the dark dives around the Barbican. Most of the others had regular girlfriends who they went out with three or four times a week, while I suffered sporadic relationships interspersed with events that just happened. I woke up one Sunday morning in the flat with a complete stranger. I couldn't remember who she was or where we had met or what we had done. She looked rough. I just felt ill: my head was thumping, I was racked by nausea, I felt embarrassed, foolish, and I wished I was somewhere else. I hated myself.

There were periods of escape from the college. We had one weekend leave per term and a two-week break between the two terms. A few cadets had cars by now, although I could neither drive nor afford one. My main group remained John, Barry and Jimmy, who were all in the same non-driver mode. Dick and Des both had cars: Dick's was a nifty MGB and Des had a Triumph Herald. They drove us around to some extent, although a long journey was generally made by the power of the thumb – hitchhiking. We always hitchhiked in uniform, which was a near guarantee of someone stopping to pick us up. John used to cheat sometimes by wearing his uniform cap and raincoat, although this tactic usually annoyed the driver when the coat fell open as John embarked, to reveal a Micky Mouse tee-shirt or something similar. I tended to stay in full uniform when on the road.

On the first weekend leave, John and I hitchhiked to London where we stretched out our time as long as we could, arriving late on Friday, catnapping Friday and Saturday nights, taking in the sights of the time. When we arrived on Friday we headed for Chelsea Drugstore in the Kings Road: the Chelsea Drugstore was the in pub of the day. John wanted to start a fight with man who looked tough enough to bite the glass necks of beer bottles; I talked him out of it.

On the Friday, we trawled the pubs and clubs around Frith Street and Greek Street in Soho: these were rough and vibrant streets at the time, long before they smartened up and became part of the gay iconography. Street prostitutes cooed at us, and dark-eyed Maltese in light-blue suits watched our progress as we approached. In a near-black club in Greek Street, where we nursed overpriced drinks, a man ran in screaming with his suit jacket slashed to ribbons and one ear pouring blood. We ate noodles in a Chinese stall in the small hours and then took an early morning tube to John's parents' house, where we slept until the afternoon.

In the fortnight between the terms I went to Glasgow with Jimmy and had some eye-opening experiences with his friends. They were universally funny, decent, kind-hearted, religious and violent at the same time. We saw the Scottish Cup Final – Celtic verses Hibernian. I lost contact with the others in the surging crowd and spent most of the game staring at the back of someone else's head. Someone stole my watch but I never felt it go. Celtic won 4-0. I met Jimmy and his friends in a bar outside the ground after the match.

On my weekend leave during the second term, I went home to see my parents, who I had been neglecting. The hitchhike home started badly. A middle-aged man picked me up: he didn't say much, though he did tell me he was going to Salisbury, which was more than half way. I had always hitchhiked as one of a pair, which was the best way to travel because one could doze while the other talked to the driver so as to give him the company he had stopped for. On my own however, I had to do the talking. Hitchhiking in uniform was generally easy and we never had to wait for long; everyone trusts someone in uniform. I wasn't really watching where we were going as I talked to the middle-aged man. I did most of the talking and he just made a remark or asked a question from time to time to move the talk along. Then I noticed that we were on a narrow lane with thick bushes overhanging either side. We had turned off the main A38 between Plymouth and Exeter, but I hadn't noticed. I asked him where we were. He told me it was a shortcut. I stopped talking. The road became narrower. I asked where we were. He told me not to worry. We came to a crossroads. I told him to stop. He said there was no need. I shouted in his face to stop the car now! He looked at me and smiled. I grabbed his arm and told him to stop the car or I would stop it for him. He stopped. I jumped out with my bag. He stepped out and came round the car. He was 50; he was fat. I could outrun him or outfight him. I dropped my bag. He swore at me and got back in the car and drove away.

I walked down deserted lanes for an hour before a couple picked me up and took me back to the A38. I was a wiser hitchhiker after that. It was 2.00 a.m. before I arrived at my parents' house.

The exam timetable appeared on the noticeboard at Standard House, announcing a three-week final push of gruelling work to shape up for the seven days of examinations. Most of us were adrift in one subject or another. Navigation theory had finally slid into focus for me, although I was finding naval architecture as baffling as ever as I endeavoured to memorise and reproduce cross-sectional drawings of various parts of different ships.

Against common sense, our outside activities became even more intense in the final straight towards the examinations. In truth, and it was a truth that most of us had rumbled, the Phase 3 examinations were not as important as the lecturers made them sound. Phase 1 exams were important, because if someone was found too intellectually wanting it was early enough in the process to cull them and send them on their way. Training a cadet is expensive (even though I felt the shipping company more than recouped its pound of flesh) and after two and a half years of a three-and-a-half-year training period, it was unlikely that someone would be sent down for a poor Phase 3 result. The real test came, of course, at the end of Phase 4 and the subsequent return to college, after which we actually sat the Board of Trade exams: that was the real thing. Armed with this knowledge that Phase 3 exams were important – but not that important – we each took a view as to how well we needed to cope to avoid utter disgrace with whichever shipping company we were contracted to. There was a danger that Phase 4 at sea could be made a particularly unpleasant experience if the shipping company detected that someone was just along for the ride. In the tanker company I worked for, there were several hell-ships operating in hellish parts of the world where the bad and the mad were exiled. I didn't want to finish my time slaving on a bitumen carrier on the North African coast, roasting in the sun and broiling in the sludge tanks, ruled over by a drunken oafish chief mate who was bitter about being passed over for promotion (for being drunken and oafish) and who took out his spite on the cadets.

I guesstimated that I would cruise towards mid-table again, between eighth and twelfth in the year: I actually ended up slightly better at sixth.

In the final week, we had the cadets' summer ball, where we wore dress uniform – best blues and black tie – and turned up with our ladies of the day, or ladies of the night in some cases. I was torn between taking Julie and finding someone else for the ball. After a few practical struggles to find a good-looking partner and a minor moral one in thinking I should really be taking Julie, I indeed asked Julie. She surprised me by not wanting to come at first, mostly because I had told her the previous evening that I would be unlikely to see her again after leaving to go on Phase 4. She relented though after a mixture of flattery and begging and we turned up on the last Saturday of the last term to the Holiday Inn function room for a fairly superior hop, a rousing speech by the head warden, and a scattering of incidents – mostly drink-fuelled – to enliven the evening. The ball went on until 1.00 a.m., after which we continued the party in ever-decreasing numbers in various late-night clubs.

The final night in Plymouth was marred, which was a shame. We went out in a big group. Some of P3 23 had already departed after the weekend of the summer ball and everyone was leaving in dribs and drabs. We all had to be out by the Friday, the official last day of term. Our group was about 15-strong in the beginning and we started toasting ourselves at the Unity – the bright and noisy pub we all knew well, going back to Phase-1 days. It was a good time: we rehashed the year and talked of where we were likely to be going next. A few had their shipping orders already, though not me; I was still due nearly three weeks leave and didn't expect to hear anything just yet. As the evening wore on, it followed the usual pattern: we drifted to a series of other pubs, we became more raucous, and people gradually fell by the wayside. I stayed to the bitter end: in the last pub until closing time, then into the Top Rank (studiously ensuring I stood without swaying, adopting a sober and serious face that fooled absolutely no one), then to a late-late club – somewhere I had never been before: dark and smoky, slightly menacing and expensive. Small gaggles of whores, groups of drunken men, and several sober men sat quietly at tables and watched everyone else.

Then it was the end. It was 2.00 a.m. I sat under the stars on the edge of the civic square fountain with John. We sipped from drinks we had lifted from a table as we walked out of the club. We were broke. I had absolutely nothing in my pockets – not a penny. My bank account was overdrawn and it was ten days until I would be paid. All I possessed in monetary terms was the train warrant to get me home, where I would sit like a beast in its lair, waiting for orders or payday – whichever came first. I had six cigarettes. John was equally broke and we discussed our sad state of affairs.

John said had a brilliant idea. We were sitting on the edge of the large rectangular pool, into which the fountain dribbled.

"What is it?" I was expecting one of his jokes.

"Look," he said, pointing to the water.

I looked. "What?"

"Look! There! Money!"

I stared harder. All I could see was the inky-black water, streetlights reflecting off the shimmering surface. I looked at John: "Yeah."

There was a splash, water showered over me. John had jumped into the pool. The water came up to his knees. He reached down with both hands then stood up again, water streaming off his arms. "Look!"

I looked. John was holding two fistfuls of coins. Like every civic pool and fountain anywhere, the one in Plymouth attracted people to throw in coins and make a wish. My understanding of the mythology was that throwing a coin in a fountain originated in Italy in Roman times and was to buy a safe return from Neptune for someone who was about to set off across the seas. Our 20th century wish was not that dissimilar: we wanted to buy a safe return to a bar. I jumped in with him and we waded around the pool, hunched over, heaving out handfuls of coppers and filling our pockets. The cold water was as shocking and invigorating as a slap in the face. We whooped as we continued our pillaging.

"Cops!" John suddenly shouted.

Two policemen were running across Royal Parade towards us, big and getting bigger. We looked at each other. We said, in harmony: "Let's get out of here!"

We leapt out of the pool and headed up towards Plymouth Hoe at a sprint. John yelled: "Split up!"

I peeled off to the left and ran towards the courts and up Princess Street. I thought if I could make it to the Barbican I had more chance of escape in the narrow streets and alleyways. John continued south, uphill towards the seafront of Plymouth Hoe. Fear lent wings to my feet, my lungs were screaming and I cursed myself for smoking. The booty I had reaped from the pool was in my side pockets: it weighed me down and swung viciously against my legs. I didn't want to stop and unload the illicit cargo because of the delay that would cause and because the clatter of money on the road would attract or accelerate the efforts of the policemen. I hared along as fast as I could, keeping tight into the side of the road, fleeing the lights, eventually making the darker buildings of the Barbican. When I neared the fishing docks, I dared to look behind; it was quiet and there was no one in sight. I ran behind the Three Crowns and leant against the wall to recover my breath. I then took off my jacket and tie, loaded my coins into the jacket pockets, stashed it behind a low wall and laid some planking on top. I rolled up my sleeves, pulled my shirt outside my trousers, picked up an empty beer bottle and started to walk back to the hostel in a staged drunken stagger. I was stone-cold sober after the cold paddle, the dash through the streets and the injection of adrenaline. My changed appearance may not have fooled any eagle-eyed member of the constabulary for long but it was the best I could do. I would recover the jacket and my new found wealth in the morning.

John fared worse than me. The police decided to stick together and only go for one of us – John. As he laboured uphill, silhouetted against much brighter lights, they gave chase and bagged him after a few hundred yards. As they slowly caught up, one of the pursuers reached for John's jacket – John pulled it away and continued his fruitless flight. They caught him after another 20 yards and decided the pulling back of the jacket constituted resisting arrest. They weren't interested in the coins; the resist was a more significant and rewarding collar. They even left him with his coins.

John was glum the next day, having spent the rest of the night in the cells. He was being charged with resisting arrest. We walked down to the Barbican and recovered my jacket

*The Three Crowns
Pub in the Barbican,
Plymouth, another
haunt of the author.*

from behind the Three Crowns then went for lunch, using our earnings from the fountain to suppress a mighty pair of hangovers with coffee and bacon sandwiches. We were due to get the train back after lunch, although John decided to delay for a day while he found a lawyer and took some advice. In the event, John stayed for a while to get his mess sorted out while I was rushed back to sea earlier than I was expecting.

As the London train clattered out of the station that afternoon, I sat alone in a carriage facing the rear, my kitbag and case hogging the overhead baggage net. I watched the houses falling away, and then saw the red-brick Standard House sitting on the hill – my home for the last six months; font of so many memories, finally dropping out of sight as the train picked up speed and made for the east.

Age 19

I flew out to Italy not long after my 19th birthday. I was flying alone. My Globetrotter suitcase was packed with less than half the gear I had taken on my first trip. The plane dipped down over the Gulf of Trieste and I saw the ships anchored in the sea-roads below, sparkling like gems on the gleaming surface of the mirrored sea. I wondered if mine was down there among them.

9

My Father's Dream

My orders arrived a week after I returned from Plymouth. The instructions were to join the *Hima* in Trieste. I was given a three-day notice period. The letter contained the usual rail warrant and flight ticket, though I was annoyed about the curtailed leave and short notice: first, because I still needed to buy some replacement kit; and second, because I felt I deserved to be treated with a crumb of respect; not just dragged from college and heaved straight back to sea, like a slave.

I was flat broke apart from the remaining coins I had stolen from the fountain and I called the company to beg an advance on my next month's salary. My blues uniform had taken a terminal beating during Phase 3, where I had worn it every day, so I went to Miller Rayner – the naval tailors in Fenchurch Street – and picked up a new one, together with sundry other replacements for worn-out kit. Luckily I was stock-size and didn't have to wait for any alterations. I then had myself punctured for cholera, which was the only inoculation I required. I was due my medical at the company headquarters, though they waived that so as not to interfere with my speedy despatch. I thought: 'Nice of them to care.' That exhausted my newly-acquired funds and I spent the small part of my remaining leave at home, idling and recharging.

I caught the late-morning *Alitalia* flight from Heathrow to Trieste. No one else was flying out to join the *Hima* and so I was travelling alone, or at least I was a seaman alone among a wedge of tourists and businessmen.

By my reckoning, I had sea time of about eight months to serve, after which I would be eligible to sit the examinations for my second mate's certificate. I expected to serve all the remaining sea time on the *Hima*, unless I was promoted to uncertificated third mate, in which case I could expect to be transferred. There was a still a shortage of junior deck officers and a lot of senior cadets were being made up to uncert' third mate. This meant that they finished their cadetship in style, with decent pay and more leave entitlement. There was a slight disadvantage in that they had to serve beyond the normal maximum of three-and-a-half years, although only usually by a couple of months.

Trieste is a northern Italian city port and has seen many masters over the centuries; so many that it would be impossible for the town burghers to put up commemorative plaques for all of them. Although it was a settlement before recorded history, Trieste rose to prominance as an Illyrian province, before coming under the Romans where it was known as Tergeste. It was Julius Caesar who granted Tergeste colony status. After the fall of Rome, the city went on to become controlled successively by the Byzantines, the Lombards and the Franks, before being settled in as part of the Habsburg Empire for several hundred years. Napoleon Bonaparte briefly took control of Trieste, as did the Austro-Hungarian Empire, the Germans and the Yugoslavs. In the 1940s it enjoyed a brief stint as an independent city state, finally finishing up as part of Italy. The city has had a colourful existence and taken a battering over the past two millennia from numerous parties.

Trieste airport looked as if it had taken a battering too: shabby and grubby and dented, full of redundant areas and broken machines. No one was there to meet me so I went to the desk marked '*Informazioni*', where there was an envelope with my name on it. It contained two vouchers: one for a taxi and one for the Hotel Milano.

I arrived at the hotel following a hurtle through the streets of Trieste, my taxi piloted by a driver who seemed unhinged. I gripped the door handle in fear for most of the journey while he jabbered at me. The Hotel Milano was smart in an austere way; there was a second envelope at the hotel check-in desk containing a letter from the agent telling me I would be collected at ten o'clock the next morning. Inside the envelope was yet another envelope; this one containing 50,000 *lira* for meal expenses (which was about £25). The envelope business must have been doing well in Trieste. I was pleased that the hotel was in the centre of town, not too far from the docks, as this allowed me to punctuate the evening with a tour of the local bars, making full use of my *lira*.

The *Hima* was a white oil tanker identical in build and function to the *Horomaya*. The H-class ships were the workhorses of the fleet and were generally the most popular tankers to serve on because they were relatively small at 18,000 tons, which meant they could get upriver and into the smaller and more interesting places. This was the time when 200,000-ton supertankers were first making their appearance. These behemoths rarely touched land and spent their days travelling from one mooring buoy to another and were generally unpopular among seafarers.

There was a lot advantage for me in that I was completely familiar with the workings of the *Hima*. The chief mate was extremely pleased that I was an H-class veteran with three voyages under my belt. There were three other cadets onboard: two first-trippers, one second-trip lad and one senior. I was replacing the senior, who was being sent to another ship as uncertificated third mate. It was a huge relief to me that there were junior cadets onboard, as they would get the real drudgery, while I would spend my time at sea on the bridge in clean uniform, understudying one of the officers and learning the practicalities of

The Hima *alongside a jetty.*

navigation on a day-to-day basis. If there had been no juniors, then I would have had to take the temperatures every day and would no doubt have been dragooned into all sorts of others tasks: my bridge time would have been cut in half.

The ships orders after leaving Trieste were to part-discharge in Split on the Yugoslavian coast, then sail south through the Adriatic to pass through the Messina Straits between Italy and Sicily, and head across the Tyrrhenian Sea to unload the final few tanks of cargo when we reached Cagliari, the ancient city port that nestled at the southern end of Sardinia. We would then steam west through the straits of Gibraltar and across the Atlantic to the Caribbean to load up again in Curacao for north-European ports.

For the first time since I went to sea, I actually started to feel like an officer. My days on ships so far had been little short of hard labour, whereas now I spent my time in crisp, starched, white uniform, on the bridge for eight hours a day – two four-hour watches.

I was initially placed on the twelve-to-four watch with the second mate, with the intention that I would be moved to the other watches periodically.

The twelve-to-four watch suited me. The afternoons were quiet because the Old Man and the chief mate were both snoozing. The Old Man always paid a visit to the bridge after lunch and hung around chatting to the second mate for 15 minutes or so, before taking to his bunk, after which we were undisturbed.

In coastal waters, the convention was to fix the position of the ship on the chart at least every 30 minutes by taking cross-bearings of prominent headlands, lighthouses and other landmarks; at night we took bearings of lighthouses, buoys, radio masts and whatever else we could distinguish by lights. The second mate would do the fix on the half-hour and hour, whereas I would fix an interim position on the quarter-hour.

After a few weeks, once I was trusted, I would do all the positioning and the second mate would carry out a spot-check every now and again to make sure the ship was where it was supposed to be. The second mate made it his mission to get me to do as much of his work as possible, while he loafed or caught up on his backlog of chart corrections. When the Old Man made his appearance, he would scurry about with greater industry, barking orders to me and the lookout, scanning the horizon with his binoculars, frowning over the chart, and generally making a meal of everything. The Old Man wasn't fooled though and raised his eyebrows to me on a couple of occasions.

The bridge carried two radar sets. Both were the Marconi Raymark 16 type, which was the best-seller of the day. Although the radar set could show where we were quite accurately – by using the cursor to take a bearing and using the radar distance finder to measure the distance from the land – most captains had first gone to sea in the 1940s and 1950s and insisted on using cross-compass bearings to fix the position of the ship. We were only allowed to use the radar as a check and to alert us to approaching ships. When we were out of sight of land, the radar was switched to stand-by, and sometimes turned off altogether. I liked the radar and enjoyed staring down at the hypnotic orange sweep. If I dared stare at the screen too long, I was shouted at by the second mate, who would send me out on the bridge wing to learn to keep a 'proper' look out.

The other main navigation mode in close waters was 'Decca'. This was a radio-positioning device whereby fixed stations on the shore pulsed out signals that were received and decoded by the decometer. Decca charts were overlaid with parabolic lines of green and red and the signals from the red station would allow us to see which red line we were on, which could then be crossed with signals from the green station. Decca remained the most-used inshore navigation system for five decades, until eventually eclipsed by satellite navigation.

In between the fixing of the ships position, there was plenty of time to stand and stare, which was the main bridge activity. Mostly, the cadet was exiled to the bridge wing in between fixes, to lean on the dodger and watch for other ships, lights, land and anything else of note. In later bridge life, I learned to pace back and forward, back and forward, from one side of the bridge to the other, although as a cadet I was content to lean on the wind dodger and watch the horizon as the ship pitched and rolled according to the state of the sea at the time. To someone who had spent the previous three trips at sea working like a beast, there was a huge satisfaction in watching the sailors and junior cadets labouring away at some cruel task on deck while I lorded it above them all on the bridge in my smart uniform, the ship's binoculars hanging round my neck, working on my tan.

When we were away from land, we took our position from the sun and the stars, using a sextant. All the officers had their own sextants, although I had to use the battered one that belonged to the ship. Buying a sextant and a pair of binoculars was something you did when you became third officer: they were badges that signified you belonged to the officer class. A sextant measures the angle between the heavenly body – the sun or a star – and the horizon. You then calculate the angle that should apply if the ship was where you thought it was: the difference between the two indicates how far out you are from your assumed position. There are several adjustments for height above the horizon and sextant error, after which it is a case of looking up numbers in complicated logarithmic tables until the answer pops out. I found it a near-mystic experience to look at the sun through a shaded lens and translate that into a soft grey positioning line on the chart. It never failed to impress: I was impressed by others who could do this trick and I was impressed with myself.

The midnight-to-four watch was the quietest of all. No one was around – only the watch-keepers. The rest of the ship was asleep. There were three watch-keepers on the bridge: the second mate, the lookout and the cadet. There were also three watch-keepers in the engine room: the third engineer, a fifth engineer and a fireman – and sometimes there would also be an engineer cadet. On occasions, the Old Man would come up to the bridge after midnight, or would be there at the watch changeover, although he never stayed for long. We were groggy with sleep at the start of the watch and didn't speak. I hung over the dodger to catch the upward deflected wind to wake myself up, and the second mate climbed into the tall pilot's chair as soon as he was sure the Old Man was gone. The pilot's chair was strictly taboo: if I had been caught sitting in it I would have found myself back out on deck holding a chipping hammer before I could think of my excuse.

During the four night hours, we would drink coffee every hour – dark and bitter and flavoured with condensed milk. All lights forward of the bridge were off so as not to interfere with our night-vision and I would stand and stare into the dark and lose myself in private dreams. I learnt different things. I learnt to see pin-pricks of light 20 miles distant on a clear night. The light sensors are in the periphery of the eye, so it is best to look 5 degrees above the horizon, which means that any new light is caught early. I learnt to smell approaching fog – it has a seaweed scent. The first time the second mate walked out on the bridge wing, sniffed theatrically, and said: "Fog," I thought he was setting me up to be the butt of some joke. When the fog arrived 15 minutes later, I thought he had supernatural powers.

I spent countless hours on clear nights looking up at the stars. I stood with a torch, holding the star chart from Brown's Almanac, picking out the major and minor constellations – from Ursa Major to Ursa Minor, the Seven Sisters, Cassiopeia's Chair, Hercules, Bootes, Perseus – all the bright stars and the variable stars and the red stars and the ones I could never find. The second mate's jest, feeble in the extreme, concerned the Gemini twins Castor and Pollux – sharp first-magnitude stars. He would arrive to say: "Have you found cast-iron bollocks yet?" Groan. Night after night the same joke. He would always chuckle as he walked away.

Just before the end of the morning watch, at about 3.45 a.m., I would be sent off to do the rounds: walking the deck with a torch; checking any lashings; checking the anchors on the fo'c'sle head; making sure all the doors were secured; making sure nothing was amiss or adrift or out of place. Often I would pause on the fo'c'sle head and switch off the torch, leaning over the bow and listening to the hiss and whoosh of the bow wave in the dark. Sometimes, bioluminescence was tumbling into the wake – green lights flashing and glittering as a million microscopic sea creatures rose and fell.

✶   ✶   ✶

The twelve-to-four was a fine watch for drinking. I usually rose at 09.30 after a few hours dead to the world. The ship could have sunk at 07.00 and I would have stayed asleep. I went up to the bridge to take morning sun sights with the second mate: we stood side-by-side with our sextants, calling out: "Now!" so that the third mate could read the chronometer at the precise second we captured the angle of the sun. We worked out our sun sights before retreating until the start of the noon watch.

I never drank before lunch. But I made up for it after the 4.00 p.m. finish in the afternoon. I would usually be in the bar by 4.30 p.m., cracking open the first Tennants of the day. The other twelve-to-four men would be there by 5.00 p.m.; the day-workers and the eight-to-twelve men usually arrived between 5.30 and 6.00 p.m. By the time we went into dinner at 6.30 p.m., I was in a jolly frame of mind, with seven or eight cans of lager washing around inside me. After dinner, I forced myself to go to bed, although occasionally I found myself being propelled back into the bar, as if someone else's legs were carrying me. However, if that happened, I never stayed long, because the chief mate would be watching me like a hawk. This was almost certainly a good thing. Left to my own devices, I would have stayed until midnight and then arrived for my watch wearing a rictus grin on my freshly splashed face, trying my best to look sober and alert.

Four in the morning was the time for a quiet party for the twelve-to-four watch. Me and the second mate would usually troop down the flying bridge to the aft accommodation and go along to the third engineer's cabin. The third would be sitting on the floor, still in his oily boiler suit, grimy and sweaty, oil ingrained into his hands and under his nails, clutching a cold can of beer in one hand and a cigarette in the other. The fifth engineer would also be there, in similar pose. The two of them always looked fatigued: drained by the intense heat of the engine room. We were clean and would sit on the day-bed or hop onto the third's bunk.

The difference between deck officers and engineer officers in those circumstances was stark: notionally equal in rank though the engineers were as spent and filthy as it was possible to be, while the deck officers were clean and sharp in gold braid and smart uniform. We didn't spend any great amount of time discussing this, although a few jeering insults flew between us from time to time. The engineers called us poofs and softies who didn't know what hard work was all about, whereas we called them grease-monkeys and disgustingly filthy animals who ought to be living down with the crew. They mocked us for having no transferrable skills and said we would be stuck at sea forever, whereas their skills were sort after and they would have no trouble moving ashore into a cushy engineering position. We hooted in derision at the very idea and told them that when they went ashore they were destined to become low-grade car mechanics and general oily labourers, while we would be swanning into pampered positions in port management. The junior and mid-ranking engineers took it all in good sport, though the senior engineers – being more conscious of their dignity – tended to bridle a bit if we were heard demeaning their profession. Some of the old-timers on both sides offered their wisdom, that engineers and deck officers are best kept apart because oil and water don't mix, although I always got along well with most of them.

Of course, when we were in port it was different because we were all dirty and we all huddled together in our oily suits, sitting on the deck, companionable in our equal grubby state. When in port, there were only two smoking cabins – one for the officers and one for the crew – which were respectively the officers' bar and the crew mess. The engineers who did not want to shower and change would go down to the crew mess, although deck officers, and certainly cadets, were not allowed to. This meant that if someone smoked, and I did, there was no choice other than to have a shower to scour out the oil and grease, don uniform and head for the bar. I always thought it was well worth it; the first ice-cold beer and the first draw of a Rothmans cigarette made me close my eyes and hum with the pleasure.

After the twelve-to-four morning watch we would always sit and drink and smoke until at least 5.00 a.m., which was three or four beers. If the mood took us, we might stay up until 6.00 a.m., although rarely longer, otherwise it became too hard to get out of bed. Our signal to go to bed was when we heard the steward sweeping the alleyway outside the cabin, the wooden broom-head clattering gently off the steel bulkheads. The engineers had no morning duties and could lie in bed until 11.30 a.m. if they wanted to, though the second mate was the navigator and always had to be on the bridge for 9.30 a.m., to take sun sights, work out the day's run, prepare the next charts and generally make sure the ship was going in the right direction. Being the twelve-to-four understudy, I had to be there with him.

On some mornings, in the tropics, we would have our post-watch beers on the boat deck and enjoy the warm breeze as we watched the sky slowly lighten from the east, while we listened to the water hissing by below. On those boat-deck occasions, our conversation tended to be muted and we usually drank less.

The sessions when we drank after the afternoon watch were louder, more frenetic, and more competitive. Our early-morning drinking was more reflective, more inclusive, more companionable, as if we were members of a secret club, which I suppose we were.

Whereas drink was one of the strands that held the shipboard day together, drugs were not. Unless the ship was saddled with a druggie crew, as we had been on the *Vexilla*, drugs on board ship were usually quite rare. Not so rare, of course, that someone couldn't find them if they wanted, which I did from time to time. I occasionally smoked weed on the *Vexilla*, which affected me in different ways: sometimes it had little effect, although that was usually when I was already drunk; on other occasions it turned me into a demented person, cackling and talking to myself. People on busy ships sometimes took speed, amphetamines, to keep them going when they were out on their feet and to heighten the journey when they wanted to continue. Tanker personnel tended to be more prone to taking speed than those on cargo vessels, because the tankers were always on the go and turnaround times in port were quick – sometimes a matter of hours. 'Bennies' (benzedrine) and 'dexies' (dexedrine) were the amphetamines more commonly used at the time and were freely available in most of the bigger ports. A number of people took speed on the *Hima*. My attitude towards amphetamines was ambivalent. After all, my father had been issued with benzedrine during the war to ensure he could fly his Wellington Bomber all night without falling asleep and bomb Germans with maximum effect, so while I was wary about drugs in general – particularly hard drugs, which I would never touch – I never acquired a high moral tone towards amphetamines.

Shortly after I joined, I heard that one of the engineer cadets had some dexedrine. I confronted him about this, which frightened him because he thought I was going to tell the Old Man. I had no intention of telling the Old Man and just used the knowledge to slyly bully him out of a few tabs. On the occasions when I had a double-watch and also wanted to go ashore, I would sometimes drop a tab of speed, which would take 20 minutes or so to kick in, after which I would feel a charge of euphoria, become wide-awake, and talk non-stop. I felt as if I could go on forever; I felt unstoppable. I had to judge the time before I took any speed very carefully because when the charge wore off I would fall into the slumber of a dead man for several hours and was nigh impossible to wake up.

During those periods when I reflected on where life was talking me, which I have to say were rare, I wondered whether I was going down a slippery path with drink or drugs or both. From time to time, an older officer would tell me an elaborate story of how drugs had ruined the life of someone they knew, although the story was usually so obviously concocted to scare me onto the right path that it had no influence whatsoever on my behaviour. I never took enough speed or smoked enough weed with enough regularity to make drugs a serious issue and I never dabbled in any of the hard stuff. I was more worried about my drinking and my ever-increasing capacity. Half a case of beer a day was a light load – a limbering up normality whereby I was practicing for the real drinking sessions that took place when I went ashore. Although I didn't have the shakes, I did see spots and lights dancing in front of my eyes on some mornings: nothing that couldn't be cured by a quick drink though.

During my final sea phase, I had to put in engine room time for two weeks, and a week with the sparks in the radio room. This was designed to ensure that I at least had a core understanding as to what everyone else on the ship was doing. I jokingly said to the chief mate that cadets ought to do a turn with the cook in the galley, although instantly regretted it when I saw him mulling over the idea.

The week in the radio shack was strained. David the sparks was a militant Ulsterman with a grating accent that could cut through metal. He wore a Red Hand of Ulster badge and was a rabid supporter of the paramilitary Protestants. In the early 1970s, Northern Ireland was afire with paramilitary outrages from both the Protestant and Catholic sides and the province was on the front pages of the newspapers with depressing frequency. Although any discussion of politics and religion was taboo, David would lose no opportunity to push his argument forward. When someone new arrived on the ship with newspapers from home, he would jab his finger at any Belfast bomb story and work himself into a fury, his voice becoming louder and shriller, his face becoming redder and contorted with outrage and hatred, spittle flying. If someone failed to agree, or had the temerity to disagree, he would freeze, glare, stare threateningly, then check himself and stamp off in a temper. At the time I was *uber*-tolerant of anyone and everyone: people just didn't faze me, whatever their views.

Even then though, I thought: 'David is a nasty and bigoted piece of work.' It clouded our working together and inhibited our conversations.

In those days, virtually all communication beyond close vicinity ship-to-shore radio was in high-speed audio Morse code. I understood Morse from my days at Plymouth and could read and send with a lamp, although listening to high-speed audio was beyond me: my ears just were not attuned and there was little chance of them becoming attuned in a week – particularly at the rates that were used from ship-to-shore stations. Curiously, Morse operators like David could 'read' high-speed Morse coming at them at the rate of 35 to 40 words a minute, although they generally have to reach for a pad and pencil if the speed dropped to below 15. At low speeds, the sound fails to materialise as a word in the operators mind and they have to write down the message as the dots and dashes arrive and then read the whole thing through at the end for it to make any sense. David used the Farnsworth method, which essentially allows that the letters are sent as fast as humanly possible, with a recognisable gap between each word to allow the brain to recognise them. Most operators communicated in Farnsworth.

David tutored me for a couple of hours a day in his hectoring way and by the end of the week I was nudging five words a minute, which to me was so fast as to be on the edge of control, although David thought I was so slow as to be bordering on backward.

Radio Operators at work rarely used plain language; there was a whole world of code available. The basic codes allowed that simple lettering was used to mean the most commonly used phrases. For example, 'QRS' means: 'You are transmitting too fast'; whereas 'QTH' means: 'My position is...' Then there was a raft of abbreviations: 'PLS' means: 'Please'; 'TEMP' means: 'Temperature'; 'RPT' means: 'Repeat'; etc. In addition to this, the messages from head office were in the company code for ease of transmission, with a series of numbers and letters being a whole phrase. There were several large volumes that we used to code and decode all the inward and outward radio traffic. It was fascinating to watch David at work in his world, rattling through complex messages that were incomprehensible to ordinary mortals.

Having a cadet for a week allowed David to get things done he otherwise wouldn't have achieved. We spent many hours tuning the radio directional finder, dismantling bits of the main transmitter and then cleaning and reassembling them, and testing the lifeboat emergency radios. I also acted as general dogsbody, neatly writing out the marconigrams he had scribbled down, filling in the radio log, updating the manuals and doing sundry other drone work.

Leaving aside David's unpleasant manner, I learnt that the sparks' life was a solitary one, stuck in mid-rank with nowhere to be promoted to, totally alone in the job with no colleagues to use as a benchmark: no one to discuss the detail and intricacies of the work, the only company being another person on the other end of the Morse key – someone he never met or spoke to; someone sometimes half a world away. I would probably have enjoyed the week more if I had liked the man.

Engine room time was altogether much more demanding. I could not be a ship's engineer; I am not robust enough. Imagine the blast of heat that hits you in the face when you bend down and open the door of a hot oven: that is the heat in the engine room of a deep-sea ship. The heat wraps around you, it hurts to breathe, it climbs inside and roasts you; you are cooked from the outside in and the inside out. When I first went into a steamship engine room, I could not believe that anyone could survive down there, let alone work down there. Everything was too hot to touch: the rails, the handles, the bulkheads, everything. Then the constant machinery noise was deafening; an assault on the ears.

The engineer officer of the watch stood on the 'plates', which was the metal floor plating directly in front of the furnaces in which the oil was ignited as it was squirted in a pressurised jet out of spray nozzles. The fireman also stood on the plates, where he watched the furnaces, made adjustments to the oil jets and did the behest of the engineer officer. The fiver was generally sent off to carry out some task in an even hotter and more ghastly part of the engine room. There was a direct telephone link to the bridge on a bulkhead to one side of the plates, together with a general telephone to the ship's exchange. The machinery noise was so infernal that the telephone bell was a massive claxon that sent out a banshee shriek to rise above the din. The engineer answering the phone had to scream into the mouthpiece to make himself heard; the person on the other end screamed back and both parties hoped the message was getting through. The brass telegraph – set to 'Full Ahead' while at sea – stood at the front of the plates. The only place of refuge, such as it was, was a chute that came down from above, out of which outside air was blasted. Even in the tropics, the air being powered down felt as if it had come in from the arctic.

On entering the engine room from the aft officers' accommodation, I was perspiring before I had even climbed down the ladder to the first level. By the time I had gone down the two additional levels to reach the plates, I was sweating freely and I was dirty. Oil and grease coats every surface; you get dirty just by walking around.

I loathed my fortnight in the engine room. I built up a respect for those who worked there, although I thought them slightly insane for doing so. I spent my engine room time on the four-to-eight under the second engineer – a three-striper broadly equivalent to the chief mate in engineering terms. The second delighted in making sure that I was kept far away from the only place of sanctuary, the cold air blower, and I was usually farmed out to work with the fiver, squatting in the black bilges or lying under some vile auxiliary engine where we swore and sweated and skinned our knuckles and became ever more filthy.

Entering and leaving port was more interesting. A different sort of steam – live steam – was generated to drive the steam turbines, which resulted in a lively pack of people on the plates. The second engineer was there, together with either the third or fourth engineer. Sometimes the chief engineer would come down, but not often. Then there was a fifth engineer or two, two firemen and a couple more engine room hands. I had little idea of what was going on and kept out of the way as far as I could, skulking near the cold air chute. By the time my fortnight was up, I still didn't know the difference between live steam and ordinary steam. When I walked along the flying bridge to the midships accommodation after my last engine room watch, I was so delighted to have finished, so I threw my head back and shouted "Hooray!" at the top of my voice. A few sailors working on the deck looked up at me curiously and shook their heads.

☆ ☆ ☆

Life as a Phase-4 cadet was much easier. My days were mostly clean and I no longer suffered the patronage of the officers and the mockery of the crew. I had more sea time than the three fifth engineers, the fourth engineer and the junior deckhands; I knew how to act and what to do. The chief mate used me as a tool to make his life easier, rather than a serf to bully. When I moved to the four-to-eight watch, I plotted the ships course and checked the compass and watched the traffic and wrote the log for the chief mate to sign, while he worked on his cargo plans in the chartroom. The sailors all knew I would be given my own watch soon and they became more respectful of me and waited for me to tell them what to do. I was able to tell them with fluency and knowledge because I had done every job, every shipboard task. I knew what needed to be done and how long it would take.

I picked up news of people I knew. Sometimes we would meet another company ship in port and exchange stories. Sparks would have Morse conversations with sister ships across the world; often he would exchange crew lists and pin them up on the noticeboard. New people would join and bring tales of who had been on their last ship. Occasionally, the company would send out full fleet lists so we could see who was serving where. As the weeks went by and it became closer to the end of my time as a cadet, I picked up news that John had been promoted to uncertificated third mate. A couple of weeks later, I learned that Barry had also been promoted, and Jimmy too. I was pleased for them, and a little envious. Next, it was Starling, then Bell, Dick, Des – one after the other, one after the other. I remained at my post as cadet.

With two months to go before my time was up, the third mate received a telegram which said that his father was very ill: he was to be flown home from the next port. Everyone, including me, assumed I would be promoted, but to my dismay, a newly made up uncertificated third mate called Strachan ambled up the gangway. I knew Strachan from Plymouth – he had been in the term ahead of me and I rated him an imbecile. To make matters worse, he knew he was an imbecile; he would tell me how much he didn't know and how unfit he was to do the job. He would continually ask me to help him. Even more painfully, he told me he was the last of his year to be made up and this was because he was known to be the worst of the lot. I fumed at being passed over for an idiot. The chief mate and second mate commiserated with me. They disliked Strachan and bullied him, which made me feel a bit better.

I was supposed to study in that last phase at sea, but I didn't bother. When I paid off the ship, I would have my earned leave plus six months of paid study leave before sitting my exams. I knew I would pass the exams, eventually, and saw no reason to do anything prior to going back to college beyond some token work for the chief mate to sign off in my study record. I had several courses that I was supposed to complete before returning to the Plymouth School of Navigation, but I wasn't intending to return to Plymouth and had already decided to have a change of scene and study at the Navigation College in London. I kept the courses for appearances sake, in case the chief mate or the Old Man asked to look at what I was doing, but I didn't actually work. On the occasional study days the chief mate gave me, I would lie on my bunk and read Joseph Conrad and Jack London, gripped by their tales of going to sea before the Great War, or I would muse over Rudyard Kipling's poetry of the sea. The Old Man caught me idling in this way one afternoon but when he found I was reading *McAndrew's Hymn*, he tossed the slim volume back to me and said: "Very good. That's far better for you than all that college crap."

I knew I was nearing the end of the line when the chief mate put me in charge of cargo temperatures. I would walk the flying bridge and shout at the cadets on the deck below, as they clutched their thermometers and buckets and danced between the shipped waves:

"Don't you break that bloody thermometer or the mate will have your guts for garters!" I would then roar: "Get a move on! It's cold up here! Do you think I haven't got anything better to do than watch you three amble around?"

When all the temperatures were done, I would discuss the results with the chief mate and he would decide if any tanks needed more heating or if any needed cooling down. I would then convey this to the chief engineer, who would either agree or start an argument for me to carry back to the mate.

Boat drills came and went. We mustered in our life jackets at the sound of the 'abandon ship' signal on the ship's horn. We lowered the boats, we raised the boats, we counted ourselves in, we counted ourselves out. I was given command of a muster station: the crew tried to slack and only drop the boat a few feet, but I wouldn't let them. Our boat went right down to the boat deck; we checked the oars, we checked the stores, we checked the water, we tested the radio, I cajoled them, they reluctantly took it from me.

Fire drills came and went. We mustered at the sound of the ship's horn. We checked ourselves in. I was give command of the second fire-fighting team. I checked all my men twice. The cook tried to slope off, complaining that his potatoes would overcook, but I wouldn't let him go: he sulked. We rolled out the hoses. We extinguished a fake fire in the centercastle. I made a junior cadet run around wearing the breathing apparatus to demonstrate how quickly air was used under exertion. We declared one of the other cadets a casualty and carried him up the ladder to the hospital, strapped him into the canvas stretcher, bumping him roughly on each step. We set off two fire extinguishers that had been re-filled more than 12 months ago – one foam type and one water and acid. After we had saved the ship, I supervised the other cadets as they put away all the gear, refilled the extinguishers, replaced the air bottle on the breathing apparatus and rolled up the hoses. I cursed at their ineptitude and showed them how to roll a hose properly so it could be flipped out for use in an instant. They were grateful until I flipped it out and told them to do it again: they glowered; they did it.

In the last month, I started to think: 'What more can I learn?' I wanted to move on. I felt I could do it all: everything that was required of me. The deck officers and the captain knew this. They started to treat me as a junior officer. They no longer had to bully me or trick me or goad me into carrying out some task so I could learn, because I now knew. I could con the ship and chart the course. I could set the tanks to load and discharge. I knew the work that needed to be done to maintain the routine progress of life on a ship, and I knew how to do all the work myself. I knew how to organise and arrange things; I knew how to get things done. I knew how to add value. I had reached the end of the line. I knew. The clocked ticked on towards the end of my time.

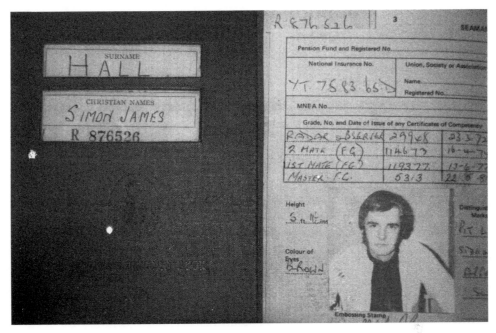

The author's discharge book.

★   ★   ★

And then... it was over.

I leant on the poop deck rails as we slid in to Thames Haven at dawn on a cold March morning. The noise of the telegraph clanged through the engine-room skylights and the wash of foam backed up in the water below us as the engines were put on slow astern. The engines stopped again as the weigh came off the ship and we hung motionless for a moment in the grey, cold water of the Thames, until the tugs nosed into us fore and aft to push the vessel alongside the jetty.

I was hunched with cold and as the steam winches clanked behind me, I blew on my hands. The second mate walked up and clapped me on the shoulder. I looked at him; he said: "It's all yours, Simon." He passed me the walky-talky and climbed the ladder to the boat-deck where he could watch what was going on.

The walky-talky squawked: "Bridge to aft. Are you receiving? Over." I brought it up and pressed the button: "Aft to bridge, receiving loud and clear. Over."

A pause, then the captain's voice: "Is that you running the show there, Hall?"

"Aye, sir."

A pause, longer, then: "Lower a stern line to the boat and let me know when the engine is clear. We'll be mooring three-two-one."

"Aye, sir. Sending out a stern line, mooring three-two-one."

The storekeeper looked at me expectantly. He was looking for orders. A year ago he would have laughed in my face if I told him what to do. "Lower a stern line, Stores." I pointed to the offshore lead.

"Aye, aye."

The line went down to the little mooring boat that had motored up to take the rope. The boat stopped under the stern, directly above the propeller. I spoke into the walky-talky: "Aft to bridge. Propeller not clear."

"Thank you aft. Let us know when it is."

Twenty minutes later we were securely moored: three stern lines, two breast lines and one tight spring line running forward parallel to the hull; the spring was to stop the ship surging. The second mate came down the ladder: "Good show, Simon. You'll do all right."

We walked forward to see to the lowering of the gangway, leaving a couple of sailors to secure the fire-wire.

It was just over three years and four-and-a-half months since I had walked up the gangway of the *Valvata* in Hamburg. I had completed my sea time five weeks early due to short leaves and having served longer on Phase 2 than was necessary. I was the only one of my year who had not been given a sea promotion to uncertified third mate: I had gone on to the bitter end as a cadet, as the lowest form of marine life. I didn't know whether this was down to bad luck, bad timing, no opportunities, poor reports or the fact that someone up in head office thought I wasn't up to the job. I shrugged it off, although a part of me hissed with envy at the promotion of the others. During the last two months I was to all intents and purposes a deck officer: I did the work unsupervised, the officer of the watch merely keeping an eye on me. The crew treated me as an honorary officer and I was effectively the fourth mate. But I wore a cadet's stripe – not an officers gold band – and because of this I felt slightly wounded every time I heard that yet another fellow cadet had been elevated.

When someone joins a British ship, they have to sign the ship's articles, which are a set of regulations that govern the conduct and conditions of the crew. Foreign Going articles govern the conduct of deep-sea crews; Home Trade articles govern ships around the United Kingdom and close continental waters. When a deep-sea ship arrives at a British port, the articles automatically cease: the whole crew is paid off and those staying aboard then sign replacement Home Trade articles. When the ship is ready to go back deep-sea again, the crew sign fresh Foreign Going articles. The crew of the *Horomaya* was being completely replaced in Thames Haven at the article change, although most of the officers were staying. I was leaving, paying off, along with a couple of the engineers. A bus was parked at the foot of the gangway; the replacement crew were getting out and stretching, and someone had started pulling the suitcases and kitbags out of the back of the bus. Onboard, the crew were shouting down to their replacements, excitedly and happily: they were keen to get off – some had been away for over a year. The bosun was swinging the derrick over the side with a cargo net hanging off the hook, to bring up all the cases. I briefly scanned the new arrivals to see if there was anyone I knew; there wasn't.

I walked along the flying bridge to the ship's office. The chief mate was waiting in the doorway. He stepped out towards me as I approached. I thought: 'Damn. He's going to give me one last awful job.'

He said: "I've got one last job for you." I looked at him, waiting. He said: "It's just gone eight o'clock. Your watch is over. I've filled in the log-book, but it's past time you signed it off as officer of the watch. Sign it, then get cleaned up and have breakfast. See the Old Man at ten and you'll be paid off the ship."

He grinned broadly and held out his hand. We shook, firm grips. He said: "You'll make a good third mate: I'll be happy to sail with you any time."

"Thanks, sir," I replied. "It's been an experience."

I thought: 'Now just watch me fly.'

★   ★   ★

My father picked me up from the dock-gate just after lunch. I stood in the rain with my Globetrotter suitcase and kitbag and watched the blue Vauxhall Victor drive towards me. I could see my brother Peter sitting in the front passenger seat. The car pulled to a halt, the rain was glancing off the glass and obscuring the inside. They climbed out.

My father had a wide, wide smile under his RAF officer's moustache. He looked happy and proud and… proud. All his dreams were answered: his son was home from the sea. His son has worked so hard; his son has stuck it out through good and bad and he will now be an officer in his smart uniform. 'My son, my son, my dream fulfilled': I could read it all in his face – I could see into his soul. He was so proud.

I was desperate not to let my father down. I wanted to be the person he believed I was, but I felt such a fraud. The reality to me was so different from the reality to him. To him, the life was of adventure and glamour and order, discipline and respect. To me, the life was of adventure and brutality and dominance, debauchery and borderline anarchy. We shared a common belief in the camaraderie factor, although his was the belief in the camaraderie of the brother officer corps, while mine was the belief in the camaraderie of standing together with my comrades to blunt the forces ranged against us.

My father thirsted for stories. He pumped me. I responded. I spun yarns; I spun out stories like some medieval teller of tales. I entertained them both on the drive home, sitting in the back, leaning over the front to give expression to my tales, me as *quidnunc*. I told tales of ships and tales of the lives of those who go down to the sea in ships. Tales of nights so cold that the water froze on our hands as we hauled in the ropes; of days in the sun so hot we could almost hear the sizzle of our skin as we fried; of seas so high the whole deck disappeared as the waves crashed over the forecastle head and all we could see from the bridge was boiling foam in front of us; of tropical nights so clear the sky was a velvet cushion with pin-pricks of light shining through from an unknown universe behind; of sea so calm it lay like thick gravy, rolling and folding over itself; of wandering albatrosses hanging in the air abaft the poop deck with their 10-foot wingspan, never flapping their wings, just wheeling and dipping and gliding forever; of the yellow morning light over Krakatoa as we steamed through the Sunda Strait, heading east for the Java Sea, dolphins turning over in the water beside us; of keeping the strumming panic in check as we made our way through the Inland Sea of Japan – the most hectic waterway in the world, ships careering close from every direction, throbbing past within a hundred feet, just beyond the hydrostatic suction range that can cause two big vessels to pull themselves together; of sitting on the truck of the mast as the ship swayed, on top of the world, watching the circle of blue to the horizon twenty miles distant and as close to God as you can get; of snapping the sun in the scope of the sextant as it dashed between two clouds, bringing the image down to bounce on the horizon to execute the alchemy of celestial navigation; of stomach-churning panic as we identified the ping-ping orange image on the Raymark 16 radar, just outside the wave clutter on the screen – an unmistakeable image that was not part of the clutter: it was a small boat with no lights and we were nearly upon it; of steaming up the Norwegian coast, inside the arctic circle, the Northern Lights dancing in the sky above us; and of helm hard over to avoid collision in the Channel, the ship heeling and spinning round, the gyro compass clacking with the sound of a *mah-jong* game gone mad, and seeing the ship we missed by a short way slide under our stern, witness an empty bridge and a man charging up the ladder. My father swelled with pride at all these tales.

And as I spoke, in my mind's other eye, I saw the things I couldn't bring myself to tell him: of the captain so drunk on the bridge he couldn't see, riding 18,000 tons of jet fuel into Manila Bay, charging past Corregidor Island, roaring mindless orders, slopping gin down his fat belly, falling over; of the thud of boot on head in Bugis Street as the place exploded at 2.00 a.m., with the rage of all nations; of the 14-year-old whores in Haiti, shouting up to the sailors from their little boats, begging to come onboard, selling themselves for bars of soap; of the spray of glass as a drink-crazed German broke a bottle on the table edge and lunged for my eye; of all the sinners, pimps, perverts, sadists, bullies, liars, thieves, junkies, crooks, rapists, pushers, killers, soldiers of the world – scum of the earth and black-hearted bastards everywhere; of the times I felt so lost and alone in a world with no pity that I just wanted to crawl away into some warm and dark place and pull a curtain around me; and of the times I met people so good they diminished me and made me want to weep – men from fine homes who chose to toil in the slums, mothers who crept away to sell themselves at night so their children could have a better life, missionaries who were spat on yet went back for more, the padre in the seaman's home who every week would give his last dollar to someone, men I sailed with who would come back for me whatever happened. Of people who would never let me down; of all the good men – the saints, the loyal, the brave, the worthy, the committed, the toilers, those who encouraged, those who never mocked, the sharers, the first in, the last out, those with a level gaze, all those who made me feel good about myself.

But I could not speak of those things.

It was all my life – both parts: the life I told my father about and the life I clutched to myself. They were both sides of the same prism; one fit for the telling, one to refract the colours back to me alone. One day I would be my father and then I would only see the sights I wanted to see and hear the things I wanted to hear too.

The Vauxhall sped through the London suburbs on that quiet Sunday afternoon, heading for our English home where my mother waited for her boy to return after all those years, to a tamer place I no longer understood.

Epilogue

Forty years on – John, Barry, Charlie, Dick, Moz, me: sitting in a pub in Plymouth. We were all recognisable, at least to each other: a bit larger, a bit more battered, a bit more lined, less hirsute. Our characteristics and mannerisms are mostly unaltered. We laugh a lot.

John and Barry had bumped into each other in an Indian restaurant, out of the blue. I had been browsing through a Merchant Navy nostalgia web site and had posted my name on a crew list for the *Vexilla*. John looked at the same site, picked up my name and email address and made contact. Contact with Charlie and Moz and Dick had come about in a similar way. We now gathered as a group occasionally, once or twice a year.

To look back nearly 40 years requires a long lens. Most of our talk is of times past, stoking each other's memories; a sudden resurrection of a thought that has lain dormant for half a lifetime. Our rapport is instant, as if it were a Friday night in Phase 3, with all of us in the Unity Pub. Sometimes we just dust off the same conversation we were having all those years ago. We drink too much, or we drink more than we are all used to these days; we laugh and gently mock each other and are too loud. We stay up too late and feel grim the next morning.

We are the same people we were and will always be, but we are also different from each other as well, having taken our separate paths.

John left the sea early and roamed the globe for years. He is mostly at peace with the world now, although a part of him remains slightly unsettled. He tells jokes all the time; he still has the same edginess about him.

Barry hasn't worked in 30 years. He lives alone in a bad part of town. He dabbles in odd work. Life hasn't been rewarding to Barry but he accepts his lot with humour.

Dick makes furniture in Exeter, where he lives with a Russian girl. He keeps a boat in Plymouth Harbour and sails when he can. Dick is a relaxed man; a happy man.

Charlie is now a ship's pilot, guiding ships into south coast ports. He has had a full career with the sea, if not at sea.

Moz has had the full career at sea – the only one of us who did. He is now captain of large deep-sea ships under a foreign flag. Moz is now the Old Man. He tells us how different the life is these days.

The reunion in Plymouth 40 years on (from left to right, Barry, the author and John). The picture is blurred and tired, like the three people in it, but they are all still going strong. Barry is using the same irreverent pose he did for the photograph in Singapore several decades ago.

Jimmy, we never see. He doesn't respond to invitations. He lives with his family in Scotland and we think he is working under some foreign flag. I receive a Christmas card from him.

And all the others? I don't know. I hear occasional stories, but I don't know where they are.

And me? I spent nearly 14 years at sea. I eventually passed my second mate certificate and afterwards transferred to general cargo ships, to do the work I had always longed for. I went on to pass all my examinations and I gained all my licenses including my masters.

Simon Hall, Master Mariner: who would have thought it? Not me.

I paid off a cargo ship in Singapore as chief mate in the mid-1980s and went home to start a new life as a married man. I never went back to sea. I am now chief executive of a financial business. I have earned a lot of money over the years and I have the material success: the big house, the holiday home, the smart car, private schooling for the kids. I work hard and do the best I can, but deep down I have never really liked my job, because it is not what I ever wanted to do. It doesn't compare to my life at sea. It was not hard to climb the greasy pole ashore because what was hard work to others was always a stroll in the park to me. I am still married to the same women I met when I was second officer. Our marriage is strong; we have four kids. All is well with my life – that I cherish more than anything.

And now, when we all stand together in a bar in Plymouth where we had stood together those many years ago, we chink our glasses and say: "Cheers! Here's to us!" The years fall away and I am back in the life I loved: the life that made me what I am, for better or worse; with people I know and trust, with people that understand me, as I understand them all.

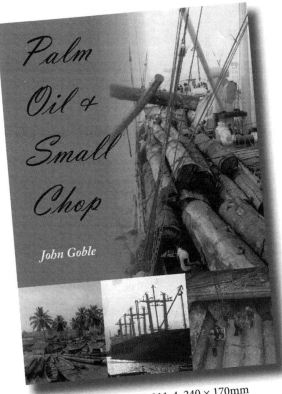

PALM OIL AND SMALL CHOP

John Goble

£16.99 978-184995-011-4 240 × 170mm
224 pages illustrated softback

'The best books by seafarers succeed in combining a personal narrative retaining the reader's interest with a vivid description of a trade and a way of life which have both passed. John Goble's account of his life in three companies trading between the UK and West Africa is certainly one of the best this reviewer has read. ...But it is West Africa, in all its fascinating richness and at times poverty, seen from the bridge and offices of a cargo liner, that is the focus of this book, and one doubts whether it could have been better observed or recorded. ...its content is all but priceless.' *Ships in Focus Record*

'... I would highly recommend the book to our readers.'
Shipping Today and Yesterday

Kirkcudbright's
Prince of Denmark

and her voyages in
the South Seas

David R. Collin

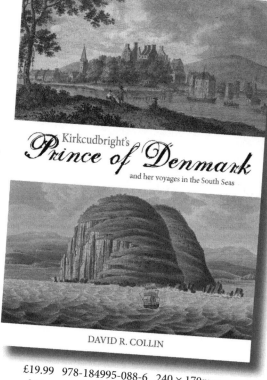

£19.99   978-184995-088-6   240 × 170mm
240 pages   liberally illustrated   softback

...I would recommend the book because, just as soon as you start reading, you will find it hard to put down. ...an excellent example of research resulting in the most intriguing tale of a vessel from yesterday I have ever read'. *Ned Middleton*

∽❦∾

'...is a truly remarkable book. ... If ever a book deserved to be called a labour of love, then this is it. The result is extensive referencing of original material such as personal and business correspondence, press reports and the ship's own logs. ... The author gives as much attention to the many men who owned, captained and crewed the *Prince of Denmark* as he does to the ship herself, and the effect is to bring vividly to life a period in our colonial past which is far less well known than it deserves to be'. *Undiscovered Scotland*

see more at www.whittlespublishing.com